SPITFIRES
OVER BERLIN

SPITFIRES
OVER BERLIN

Desperation and Devastation During WW2's Final Months

DAN SHARP

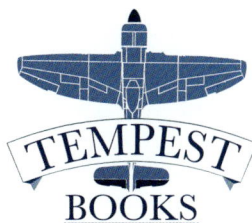

TEMPEST
BOOKS

First published 2015
This edition 2019

ISBN: 978-1-911658-04-7

Tempest Books
Mortons Media Group
Media Centre
Morton Way
Horncastle
Lincolnshire LN9 6JR
Tel. 01507 529529
www.mortonsbooks.co.uk

FRONT COVER:
Spitfire over Berlin by Mark
Postlethwaite. Pilot Officer Des
Watkins flying Spitfire XIV RB155
of 350 Squadron shoots down
a Focke-Wulf Fw 190 over the
outskirts of Berlin on the evening
of April 20, 1945.

To Margaret Neale,
without whom this book
might never have been
written.

Contents

BEGINNING OF THE END

The Supermarine Spitfire was many things but it was never a successful long-range fighter. Therefore, just as the sight of short-range Messerschmitt Bf 109s flying right over London symbolised the terrifying extent of Adolf Hitler's power in 1940, so too did the appearance of Spitfires over Berlin in 1945 herald the hour of his final defeat.

Spitfires Over Berlin tells the story of the last four months of the Second World War through the experiences of airmen on both sides of the conflict. Many myths and half-truths have grown around the events of those final months – like the 'final dogfight' of the war that supposedly took place between an L-4H Grasshopper and a Fi 156 Storch. In fact this was far from the war's last aerial combat.

From a starting point just beyond Germany's borders on January 1, the British and American air forces cut through the Luftwaffe's flagging strength from the west, while the Russians hammered it from the east, until both sides met and Spitfires encountered Yaks over the German capital. Yet even then, Bf 109s, Fw 190s and Me 262s continued to fly sorties until the bitter end on the evening of May 8.

Setting out to write the story of the closing chapter of the air war in Europe, I was surprised to discover that while some tales had been told before individually, and several overviews had been written, no one had brought a collection of stories together to illustrate some of the diverse operations and activities taking place right across the warzone at roughly the same time.

In fact, in some cases, such as the destruction of B-17G 42-31333 'Wee Willie', the operations of 350 Squadron's Spitfires over Berlin in 1945 and the callous murder of P-51 pilot Captain Chester E Coggeshall Jr, very little seemed to have been written before in any detail.

And one fact seems to have been entirely overlooked by history: who did score the very last aerial victory of the war in Europe? Different claims have been reported but can we now say conclusively who did the shooting and who was shot?

This publication is not a full history of the period – rather it seeks to give a flavour of the furious and destructive days of aerial combat that led to the Luftwaffe's, and Germany's, outright defeat on all fronts.

The actions of those who fought with bravery and determination at the end to bring the bloodiest air war the world has ever seen to its final conclusion should never be forgotten.

Dan Sharp

LUFTWAFFE REBORN

❖

The German Air Force at the beginning of 1945

Intensive bombing had crippled the German aircraft
industry by the summer of 1944 as the Third Reich
crumbled on all fronts. But even as disaster threatened,
the genius of Armaments and War Production Minister
Albert Speer was bringing about a near miraculous revival
of the Luftwaffe...

Rome fell to the Allies on June 4, 1944, and two days later the Normandy landings of D-Day heralded the beginning of the Second World War's end game.

Within months, the Western Allies had broken the deadlock around their landing sites on the French coast and were advancing rapidly inland, with the Soviets simultaneously driving in hard from the east.

V-1 flying bombs and then V-2 missiles began hitting targets in Britain, but Germany's air force was struggling to oppose those of the British, Americans and Soviets. In France, airfields held since the Blitzkrieg of 1940 were quickly swallowed up by the Allied advance.

Hundreds of aircraft newly delivered to front line Luftwaffe units had to be abandoned during the summer of 1944 and units suffered casualties as pilots were shot down attempting to switch airfields.

Along the western fringes of Germany, surviving air and ground crew arrived at airstrips in a chaotic jumble of badly under-strength groups and squadrons. Tons of equipment had been destroyed or left behind – not just aircraft but also vehicles, spare parts, tools and a wide variety of other gear.

It was a mess and it was made worse by the fact that the German aircraft manufacturers – concentrated at 27 easily identifiable and well-known production centres such as Messerschmitt's Augsburg plant and Focke-Wulf's Bremen factory – had been repeatedly hit by the bombers of both the USAAF and the RAF.

From the autumn of 1943 onwards those 27 centres had been bombed again and again in a concentrated effort by the Allies to destroy

A huge column of smoke rises from the site of Focke-Wulf's Marienburg aircraft factory during a USAAF raid on October 9, 1943. By this time the Allies were already doing their best to put the German aircraft manufacturers out of business. As 1944 arrived, the raids continued to grow in frequency and intensity.

At the beginning of 1944 the Luftwaffe was beginning to run out of aircraft as the Allied bombing campaign razed all the major German manufacturing facilities. It was Armaments and War Production Minister Albert Speer, formerly Adolf Hitler's architect, who came up with a way to thwart the Allies and dramatically increase production. He is pictured here on the right, walking with Hitler.

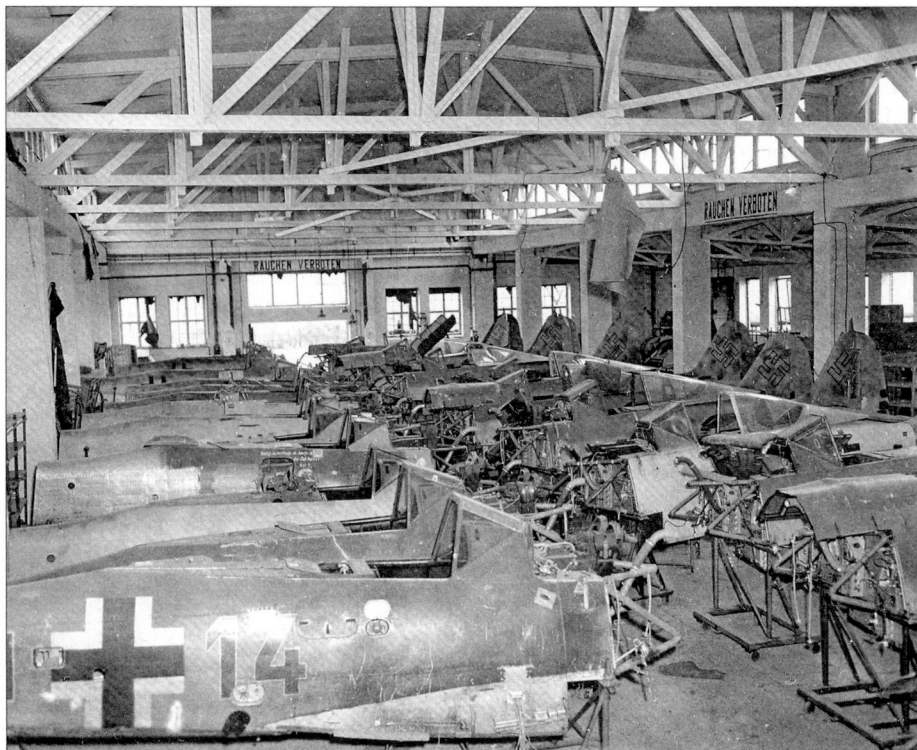

Dispersing aircraft production to small workshops such as this in backwater towns and villages gave the Luftwaffe all the Messerschmitt Bf 109s and Fw 190s it could handle, and then some.

Germany's aircraft manufacturing capability.

American daylight bombing of oil refineries, supply lines and storage facilities was bringing about crippling fuel shortages and steadily inducing a paralysis which afflicted every aspect of German military operations. Although the Luftwaffe had accumulated significant reserves – it had 580,000 tons of fuel in May 1944 – these were quickly depleted by ongoing operations so that by September 1944 it had just 180,000 tons remaining.

Seeing the catastrophic damage they had caused and given the number of German fighters that had been shot down, destroyed on the ground or captured, the British and Americans came to believe that the Luftwaffe was a spent force.

But they had reckoned without Albert Speer, the minister responsible for managing Germany's wartime economy, and his Ministry of War Production. He realised there was a highly

complex but also highly effective way to prevent the Allies from destroying aircraft factories, if not oil refineries – by dispersing them to a large number of much smaller sites.

Most of the 27 centres remained but they were rapidly supplemented by more than 700 additional plants set up in tunnels and caves, forests and on the premises of companies that ostensibly did something else – such as furniture workshops and cigarette machine manufacturers.

By carefully orchestrating this vast web of smaller scale producers, Speer was able to not only restore production to pre-bombing levels but also to actually increase it. A total of 3821 new combat aircraft were delivered in September 1944, the highest monthly figure ever achieved by the German aircraft industry.

Not only had production capacity been increased, it had also been concentrated on the aircraft most urgently needed for Germany's

defence – single-seat fighters. Four out of every five of the new machines were Messerschmitt Bf 109s and Focke-Wulf Fw 190s.

Types such as the Arado Ar 196 maritime reconnaissance aircraft, the DFS 230 and Gotha Go 242 gliders, the troublesome Heinkel He 177 bomber, the reliable Junkers Ju 52 transport and the Ju 290 long-range transport were removed from production schedules. These were followed in September by even front line types such as the Henschel Hs 129 and Junkers Ju 87 ground attack aircraft, the Messerschmitt Me 410 heavy fighter and the venerable Heinkel He 111 bomber.

Narrowing production down to little more than two types had its drawbacks however. With supply lines geared increasingly towards just Bf 109 and Fw 190 components, it was difficult to get advanced types into mass production.

Just 18 examples of the new Arado Ar 234 jet bomber/reconnaissance aircraft were built in September

1944, along with 35 Messerschmitt Me 163 rocket-powered interceptors, 91 Messerschmitt Me 262 jet fighters and 28 Heinkel He 219 Uhu night fighters.

There were other problems that gave cause for concern too. One seemingly minor difficulty becoming a major headache was the weakness of German aircraft tyres. Unable to receive imported rubber, Germany was forced to rely on low grade synthetic and reclaimed rubber tyres which were more prone to burst under the weight of a heavy aircraft. This problem was particularly acute with jet aircraft, which had a higher landing speed.

In spite of all this, however, Germany now had a formidable fighter force at its disposal once again.

With components being moved around Germany in a complex ballet of production, assembly lines for both the Fw 190, as pictured here, and the Bf 109 multiplied exponentially.

The Great Blow

The sudden influx of Bf 109s and Fw 190s in the autumn of 1944 meant all of the Luftwaffe's depleted fighter units from France could be rebuilt with spare aircraft to hold in reserve. But this was just the beginning. By shortening the training courses of new pilots and drawing in pilots from dissolved bomber and heavy

Rows of Messerschmitt Bf 109 G-6 fighters are assembled. The G-6 was mass produced in numbers that dwarfed almost every other aircraft type in Germany.

The sheer space on Germany's production lines occupied by the Bf 109 made it difficult for manufacturers to get new types brought into service – ultimately to the detriment of the Luftwaffe when it faced advanced Allied types. Very few developments were viewed as important enough to risk the disruption of 109 production.

The Heinkel He 177, Germany's only heavy bomber, was axed to make more room on production lines for the Bf 109 and Fw 190.

fighter units, every single-seat fighter group was expanded from three Staffeln to four.

In mid-November 1944, the Luftwaffe's units had 3300 serviceable fighters available, compared to just 1900 two months earlier.

Astonished by this rapid reversal in his fortunes, the Luftwaffe's General of Fighters, Generalmajor Adolf Galland, came up with a daring plan he believed would put a stop to the USAAF's ruinous daylight bombing raids.

With a sufficiently overwhelming force of fighters deployed all at once in ideal conditions, he hoped to inflict devastating damage on the American bomber fleet. If enough bombers could be destroyed all in one go, he reasoned, the Americans might rethink their strategy and would certainly have to call a halt to operations for some time while replacements were brought over from the US.

He called this operation 'The Great Blow' and was somewhat surprised when the Luftwaffe's high command approved its implementation almost without question.

In his autobiography, The First and the Last, Galland wrote: "The Great Blow had been carefully planned and worked out in all details. All commodores and commanders were called together for a rehearsal at Treuenbrietzen, during which four or five different action and approach flights were practised with all variations.

"It was wholly agreed that in the frame of the planned action the following points had to be achieved. First, in the first action at least 2000 fighters in 11 combat formations were to be brought into contact with the approaching bomber formation.

"Second, during the fly-in and the return of the enemy about another 150 fighters of the Luftwaffe Command West were to be sent up. Third, in the second action another

Another of the many types retired as aircraft production was focused on just two main fighters was the Henschel Hs 129 ground-attack aircraft. It had earned a fearsome reputation as a tank-buster but Albert Speer believed it was simply no longer possible for Germany to have dozens of different machines in production at once.

500 fighters were to be brought into contact with the enemy.

"Fourth, about 100 night fighters were to screen the borders toward Sweden and Switzerland to catch damaged or straggling single bombers. Fifth, to shoot down an approximate total of 400-500 four-engined bombers against a loss of about 400 aircraft and about 100-150 pilots.

"This was going to be the largest and most decisive air battle of the war. On November 12, 1944, the entire fighter arm was ready for action: 18 fighter wings with 3700 aircraft and pilots. A fighting force such as the Luftwaffe had never possessed before. More than 3000 of these were expecting The Great Blow.

"Now it was a question of awaiting favourable weather. Good weather was one of the essentials for this mass action. It was a difficult decision to hold back the defensive fighters, which were standing by in the face of the air armadas dropping gigantic bomb loads daily. But contrary to my previous experience the leaders kept calm and did not insist on vain and costly forced action."

Galland believed that by this stage the Allies had an inkling of

what The Great Blow entailed, particularly since large numbers of Luftwaffe fighters were now being sent up on a daily basis for training flights, but he held his nerve in readiness for the ideal moment to strike.

The Luftwaffe's general of fighters, Generalmajor Adolf Galland, pictured right, was amazed by the huge numbers of aircraft suddenly being delivered to his units during the autumn of 1944 and quickly came up with a plan he believed would see his rebuilt forces strike a crippling blow against the USAAF Eighth Air Force bomber fleet. This would give German industry a chance to recover and might even force the Americans to stop daylight bomber raids.

Two Waffen-SS soldiers cross the road near the Belgian village of Poteau after ambushing an American armoured column. An M8 Greyhound armoured car is still burning in the background. This was early in the morning on December 18, 1944 – the third day of Operation Watch on the Rhine, also known as the Battle of the Bulge.

Another photo from the ambush at Poteau. Soldiers on both sides were hampered by bitterly cold weather during the first week of the battle.

Generalmajor Adolf Galland was a skilled and flamboyant fighter pilot who was also a huge fan of Mickey Mouse and cultivated an image of cigar-chomping bravado which made him popular with his men. His Great Blow plan to destroy a large portion of the American bomber force resulted in huge reserves of fighters being built up – only for Hitler to find a different use for them.

The events of November 2, 1944, proved to be his undoing however. That day 1174 bombers and 968 fighters from the USAAF's Eighth Air Force, split into five groups, attacked a selection of oil industry and rail targets across Germany. It was a fairly typical mission for the Americans.

The Luftwaffe put up a large fighter force to oppose them – 490 fighters from 10 Gruppen. The Germans initially had some success; armoured bomber-killer Fw 190 Sturmbocks of IV.(Sturm)/JG 3 shot down 11 bombers from the 91st Bomb Group and destroyed another two by ramming them. II./JG 4 downed another nine bombers, this time from the 457th Bomb Group.

In both instances, American escort fighters then showed up and inflicted heavy casualties on the unwieldy attackers. There had been 61 Sturmbock aircraft taking part in the defensive mission and 31 of them were shot down by P-51 Mustangs. In total, the Luftwaffe destroyed 40 of the 1174 bombers and 16 of the 968 fighters, for a loss of 120 of its own fighters.

The Führer himself reviewed these figures at length four days later, on November 6, and concluded that the outcome of the defensive action had been "thoroughly unsatisfactory". It seemed clear to him that repeating the exercise on a much greater scale by allowing Galland's Great Blow to proceed was likely to see much greater losses for a similarly ineffectual result.

Instead, he approved another plan drawn up by his generals which involved using Germany's similarly rebuilt army to strike a decisive blow on the ground against the British and Americans in the west, with the fighter force providing aerial cover and support. Operation Wacht am Rhein or 'Watch on the Rhine' would involve seven Panzer divisions – some 200,000 men.

Its objectives were primarily to capture the strategically important harbour of Antwerp and to drive a wedge between the British and American ground forces.

When the tanks began to roll, the Luftwaffe's fighters would simultaneously launch an attack on the Allies' forward air bases to put them out of action. This was Operation Bodenplatte or 'Baseplate'. Next they would provide what amounted to an air exclusion zone over the battlefield to prevent Allied aircraft from harassing the advancing ground forces and give close air support when necessary during the operation.

When Galland was informed that The Great Blow had been cancelled in favour of Watch on the Rhine, he was horrified. What seemed, on paper, to be a sensible and reasonable use of his rebuilt fighter force was, he knew, a recipe for disaster.

He wrote: "In the middle of November I received an alarming order, the whole impact of which I could not foresee. The fighter reserves were to be prepared for action on the front where a great land battle was expected in the west. This was incredible!

"The whole training had been aimed at action in the defence of the Reich. All new pilots should have had some training in the totally different conditions at the front, but petrol shortage prevented this. The experience and standard of the unit leaders and pilots could be regarded as just passable for the defence of the Reich, but for action at the front they were absolutely out of the question.

"Besides, the squadrons had now without exception a strength of 70 aircraft and were therefore much too large for the airfields at the front. On November 20 the transfer to the west was ordered regardless of my scruples and objections."

The beginning of the attack had been slated for November 27 but was delayed for more than two weeks while sufficient fuel reserves were gathered.

A column of prisoners from the US Army's 99th Division are marched along the street in Merlscheid, Belgium, in December 1944. The Americans were captured by the German 3rd Parachute Division on the first day of the Battle of the Bulge – when the Luftwaffe was to have launched an opening attack on Allied advanced landing grounds.

A German Tiger II heavy tank passes a column of captured American soldiers in Belgium in December 1944. By December 20, the German advance had ground to a halt and fierce fighting ensued. In attempting to support and cover ground units, the Luftwaffe's carefully husbanded reserves of pilots, aircraft and fuel were steadily depleted. Yet on the last day of 1944, the order was given to launch Operation Baseplate – what ought to be a decisive and devastating attack on the Allied fighter and fighter-bomber force.

Watch on the Rhine

In readiness for Operation Baseplate, the Luftwaffe units due to participate flew to their forward airfields at low altitude, under the Allies' radar, and maintained radio silence. The element of surprise was vital. Everything was ready by December 14 and on that day the unit commanders were gathered together at the headquarters of Jagdkorps II near Altenkirchen, western Germany, by Generalmajor Dietrich Peltz, the mission commander.

He outlined the plan in detail – to attack 16 airfields in Belgium, France and Holland at the same time with 1000 fighters, causing maximum damage before turning around and heading for home, hopefully with minimal casualties.

Watch on the Rhine was launched at 5.30am on December 16 with a thunderous 90-minute artillery bombardment from around 1600 guns across a front that stretched for some 80 miles. Then thousands of 6th Panzer Army troops moved forwards.

The code words that would have launched Operation Baseplate were not broadcast, however, and the Luftwaffe's simultaneous attack on 16 airfields did not take place. The airmen were stood down due to heavy banks of low cloud and thick fog over the battlefield. Neither the Germans nor the Allies were able to mount any significant airborne operations.

An attempt by the Germans to mount an airborne assault using paratroopers dropping from Junkers Ju 52s was a disaster and the poor visibility extended into December 17 too. The Luftwaffe flew 600 sorties on the 17th but lost 55 pilots in various air combats. For the next six days, while battle raged on the ground, aircraft on both sides sat idle and every airfield was covered with snow.

The Watch on the Rhine assault ground to a halt on December 20, with the German advance having created a 40-mile deep 'bulge' in the front line, but the weather did not let up until December 24, Christmas Eve 1944, when it finally relented and a series of furious air battles began.

Again, the Luftwaffe suffered severe casualties – 85 pilots killed in a single day. The clear weather presented the Allied bomber forces with a golden opportunity too, and 11 of the Luftwaffe's forward fighter bases were badly hit.

The Battle of the Bulge was now well under way and after two weeks of appalling weather and appalling casualties, the Luftwaffe's commanders had all but forgotten about the plan to attack Allied forward airfields. The huge fighter force assembled for Adolf Galland's Great Blow was being steadily worn away and the remainder was engaged in a fight to the death with a numerically far superior foe.

So it came as something of a surprise when the codes triggering the commencement of Operation Baseplate were broadcast on December 31, 1944.

ALL-OUT ATTACK

❖

January 1, 1945: Operation Baseplate

It was nearly two weeks since the beginning of Operation
Watch on the Rhine – the Battle of the Bulge – and the plan
to begin it with a large-scale assault on the Allies' forward
air bases had been almost forgotten. Then the code words
activating Operation Baseplate were transmitted at last...

Luftwaffe units on the front line in the west received two code words in the early afternoon of December 31, 1944: Varus and Teutonicus.

Varus was the signal indicating that Operation Baseplate would be called into effect within the next 24 hours and Teutonicus gave authority for senior officers to brief their pilots on the mission objectives and get all their fighters armed and ready for takeoff.

At 6.30pm the final code word was given: Hermann. This was accompanied by confirmation of the date of the attack, January 1, and the time that the aircraft would be expected to reach their targets: 9.20am.

The line-up of Luftwaffe units was formidable, despite losses already sustained while supporting the initial phase of Watch on the Rhine. It included most of JG 1, JG 2, JG 3, JG 4, JG 6, JG 11, JG 26, JG 27, JG 53, JG 54, JG 77 and SG 4 – 12 Geschwader with 36 Gruppen in total, operating around 850 fighters and fighter-bombers between them.

ABOVE and BELOW: North American B-25 Mitchell IIs from 98 Squadron RAF burn on the ground at Melsbroek in the aftermath of the dawn attack on the airfield by JG 27 and IV./JG 54.

Messerschmitt Bf 109 K-4s of 11./JG 77 at Neuruppin in November 1944. JG 77 would suffer heavy losses during December, leaving it badly depleted for the Operation Baseplate attack. Closest to the camera is W.Nr.330 176 'Yellow 8'.

Among these were around 110 Focke-Wulf Fw 190 D-9 'long noses' and 50 Fw 190 F-8s, the latter being flown exclusively by SG 4. The remainder were a mixture of Fw 190 A-8s and A-9s, and Messerschmitt Bf 109 G-10s, G-14s and K-4s, plus at least one G-6.

In addition, 24 Me 262 A-2 jet fighter-bombers of I./KG 51 and six Arado Ar 234 B-2 jet bombers of E.Staffel III./KG 76 were due to take part.

Rather than allow the fighter formations to make their own way to their targets, it was decided that Junkers Ju 88s seconded from night fighter units should be allocated to help the fighters form up and then guide them in. A total of 72 Ju 88s were used for this purpose, with two each per Gruppe.

The formations were to attack 17 airfields. Five were in Holland: Eindhoven (Advanced Landing Ground B-78), Gilze-Rijen (B-77), Heesch (B-88), Woensdrecht (B-79) and Volkel (B-80), and one was in France, Metz-Frescaty (Y-34).

The remainder were in Belgium: Gent-St Denis-Westrem (B-61), Grimbergen (mostly abandoned, although the Germans did not realise this at the time), Maldegem (B-65), Melsbroek (B-58), Ophoven (Y-32), Ursel (B-67), Asch (Y-29), Deurne (B-70), Evere (B-56), Le Culot (A-89/Y-10) and St Trond (A-92).

Based at these airfields were 58 RAF squadrons from 2, 83 and 84 Groups of the 2nd Tactical Air Force, variously operating Hawker Typhoons and Tempests, Spitfire IXs, XIVs and XVIs, Mustang IAs and IIs, Mitchell IIs, Wellington XIIIs and Mosquito XVJs. In addition, there were 31 squadrons from the USAAF's Ninth Air

Force – 24 of them operating P-47 Thunderbolts, six P-51 Mustangs and a single photo recon squadron flying F-5 Lightnings.

The 2nd Tactical Air Force had been moved on to the Continent during the autumn of 1944 to provide ground forces with constant aerial support as they advanced through territories formerly occupied by the Germans. The USAAF units were under the operational control of the RAF.

First thing in the morning on January 1, 1945, most of these aircraft were likely to be on the ground and it was hoped that they would present easy targets for the attacking forces.

At 8.12am, 23 Fw 190s of I./JG 1 took off from Twenthe in Holland on a course that would take them over Ursel and Maldegem. Their Ju 88 guides were already airborne, waiting for them. Three minutes later, the dozen or so Bf 109s of III./JG 1 also took off, and followed their Ju 88s along roughly the same course.

At first, as the two Gruppen flew along just 330ft above the snow-covered Dutch countryside, nothing stirred. Then the German flak batteries along the route, which had not been pre-warned about the attack due to the strict secrecy with which it had been organised, opened fire on them.

The first casualty was Feldwebel Heinz-Jürgen Kilian of 3./JG 1. He

Messerschmitt Bf 109 G-14s of 9./JG 1 in late 1944. During Operation Baseplate, 9./JG 1's target was Maldegem in western Belgium. While I./JG 1 and II./JG 1 flew Fw 190s by January 1945, III./JG 1, including 9./JG 1, continued to fly Bf 109s.

The Fw 190 A-8 flown by Wilhelm Ade on January 1, 1945, W.Nr. 960553 'Black 3'.

RIGHT: Oberfähnrich Wilhelm Ade of 2./JG 1 battled with Spitfires close to B-65 Maldegem airfield.

succeeded in bailing out as his flak-damaged aircraft plunged towards the ground, but at 330ft there was no way his parachute could have opened in time to save him.

Unteroffizier Egon Comtesse died after his aircraft was hit and crashed into the sea, and Oberstleutnant Herbert Ihlefeld managed to belly land his Fw 190 after it took serious but not immediately fatal flak damage. Unteroffizier Heinz Böhmer was killed when his 'Yellow 15' was also shot down by flak.

Following on behind, III./JG 1 was also hit by the flak gunners but this time it was the leading Ju 88 that went down first. The pilot, Leutnant Josef Hettlich, was killed when the aircraft crash-landed on an area of flooded land. The other two crew members were seriously injured but survived. III./JG 1's second Ju 88 was then also destroyed by flak, this time with all three crew members killed.

There was another problem when the Ju 88 the fighters had been following peeled off and disappeared. Fw 190 pilot Oberfähnrich Wilhelm Ade later recalled: "We flew from the Zuiderzee to the coast where the coastal batteries had not been

informed and they opened fire. We lost more aircraft at that stage than we did later. The Ju 88 was still leading us so we did not watch where we were as we usually did.

"Suddenly this Ju 88 turned away and we had to find the target for ourselves."

At the last turning point of I./JG 1's route, the four Fw 190s of 4. Staffel broke off and headed for

Burned out remains of a Spitfire IX – one of 12 destroyed during the JG 1 attack on Maldegem. Most of them belonged to 485 Squadron, which lost nearly all of its aircraft.

More ruined Spitfires litter the airfield at Maldegem after the Baseplate attack.

B-24s burn on the airfield at St Denis-Westrem. Most of the casualties at the airfield were Spitfire IXs, however.

This Short Stirling V, serial LJ986, 8Z-Y, was another St Denis casualty.

Boeing B-17G-40-BO Flying Fortress 42-97059 'Marsha Sue' of the 533rd Bomb Squadron, 381st Bomb Group, was another four-engine aircraft destroyed at St Denis-Westrem. It had made a forced landing at the airfield on December 12 and was still there when the January 1 attack commenced.

Luftwaffe pilots taking part in Operation Baseplate were ordered to destroy enemy aircraft on the ground but also any stores of ammunition or fuel they could identify. This fuel dump at St Denis made an ideal target.

Ursel while the remainder – down to around 12 fighters – flew directly towards Maldegem. The airfield was rather closer than expected, however, and the aircraft initially overshot it.

Ade remembered: "I was already over the airfield with my Staffel before I could react. We banked and went in. I remember seeing about three four-engine bombers at Maldegem. Together with my Staffel, I followed the others. Now we flew no longer next to each other, but behind each other.

"Stupidly enough, we still had to maintain radio silence and therefore could not give any instructions. We simply had to assume that the others did the same as we did. I do not understand why we had to maintain radio silence over the target.

"They knew we were there so what was the point? No one dared to break radio silence fearing repercussions. Later I discovered that my radio hadn't worked at all. At this stage we were still with about 10 aircraft. Everything was covered in smoke now and it was difficult to orientate.

"Strafing the airfield, I fired at the parked aircraft, achieved hits at some of them and pulled up again. There was a considerable mix-up over the airfield and aircraft of 1. Staffel and even of II. Gruppe mixed with my Schwarm. It seems that we also flew over St Denis-Westrem. Suddenly somebody broke the radio silence and shouted: 'Spitfires!' and I thought 'This one is for me'.

"I got hits on the Spitfire but could not follow him as my fuel indicator already showed that I had to return. Later a 4. Staffel pilot confirmed my victory. I banked to the right and suddenly I was alone. I looked around for other pilots of my Staffel but looking at my fuel indicator I had to fly back to base if I did not want to end up a POW."

Although I./JG 1 seemingly had little success at Maldegem, the Bf 109s of III./JG 1 fared much better. They spotted rows of Spitfires belonging to 349 and 485 Squadrons and methodically destroyed them on the ground. They got 14 in total before running out of ammunition and having to depart. The Gruppe's only loss was when the Bf 109 flown by Lt Anton Guha suffered engine failure and he was forced to make a belly landing before being captured by the British.

There had been no anti-aircraft batteries at Maldegem and although the RAF pilots – many still wearing their pyjamas, or sweaters and underpants – opened fire with revolvers and rifles, none of the attackers were hit.

When 4. Staffel got to Ursel, having lost one of their number to anti-aircraft fire, they shot up a B-17, two Lancasters and a Mosquito – seriously damaging all four.

After the confusion of the attack, the survivors of I. and III./JG 1 tried to make their way home. Most had become separated and were flying alone. Four were shot down by anti-aircraft fire and a fifth crash-landed after running out of fuel. In total, the two Gruppen lost 16 aircraft and 12 pilots. They had managed to destroy around 20 Allied aircraft and no pilots – a poor exchange rate.

Unwelcome guests

While their JG 1 comrades were being hit by 'friendly' flak, something worse still awaited the pilots of II./JG 1 at their target airfield, St Denis-Westrem. The unit's 36 Fw 190s took off from Drope airfield at 8.10am and headed for their first turning point near Spakenburg behind their Ju 88 guides.

The journey passed without incident and they turned towards Rotterdam. They followed the coast down to Zeebrugge before heading inland directly towards St Denis-Westrem. Arriving at 9.30am, they found the airfield undefended and set about shooting up the many Spitfires and other aircraft parked around it. Soon a pall of dense smoke hung in the air but still the Fw 190s circled the base, strafing every target that presented itself.

This was the scene that greeted the 12 Spitfire IXs of 308 Squadron when they returned to the airfield, their home base, after having set off at 8.15am to bomb a ferry. First to come back was Flight Lieutenant Waclaw Chojnacki in MJ281 ZF-P. He had encountered problems with the aircraft's bomb release mechanism and resolved to come back early and get it sorted out.

As he was coming in to land he saw Fw 190s coming the other way and immediately shot one of them

ABOVE and LEFT: The P-47 flown by 1st Lieutenant John W Ginder, 'Hershey Hellion No. 2', when he shot down a Ju 88 that had been acting as a guide for JG 2.

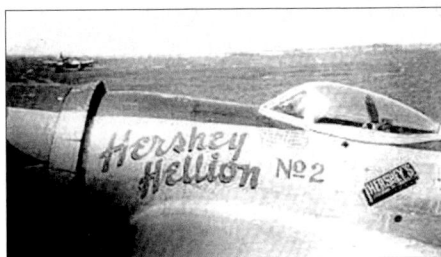

down. Flight Sergeant Bogdan Strobel saw what happened from the ground: "Approximately seven minutes after the attack had begun, I noticed a single Spitfire arriving over base at 2000ft height in a port turn. Three Fw 190s were just coming in to strafe.

"Flt Lt Chojnacki noticed these enemy aircraft and while still in the turn fired at the rearmost from

Fw 190 D-9 pilot Feldwebel Werner Hohenberg of I./JG 2 was shot down on his way home after attacking St Trond.

about 800 yards range. The enemy aircraft was hit in the tail and a large part of the tail flew off. The enemy pilot lost control over the aircraft and being low, below 200ft, and diving for the attack hit a tree with its starboard wing, then hit the top of a small building on the airfield perimeter, finally coming to rest inside a B-17 Flying Fortress standing on the ground.

"I lost the Spitfire behind the smoke from the burning Fortress but saw him a moment later chasing another Fw 190 with three other Fw 190s on his tail. The Spitfire broke off his attack with a starboard turn and I last saw him, in that turn, with three Fw 190s on his tail."

The Fw 190 shot down was that of Feldwebel Karl Hahn and he is presumed to have been killed on impact and his body thrown clear, because although his personal possessions were found in the wreck, his body was not. He was never seen alive again.

Despite his courageous lone attack, Flt Lt Chojnacki could not hope to win against such overwhelming odds. The trio of Fw 190s shot him down and he was killed.

Then another solitary Spitfire showed up – this time it was Flight Sergeant Jozef Stanowski who had run short of fuel. He saw the Fw 190s still at it and flew in to attack.

He got two before his tank ran completely dry and he was forced to make a belly landing near Ghent. By now the other 10 Spitfires had returned and laid in to the attacking Focke-Wulfs.

Flight Lieutenant Ignacy Olszewski, who had earlier spotted a formation of Fw 190s from JG 26 and JG 54 en route to their targets, engaged them, and saw three of them accidentally crash into the ground because they were flying too low. He reported: "I quickly neared the airfield and I saw the glitter of lights which soothed my nerves after all the previous events of the day. I turned left and headed through the smoke on the lookout for any enemy fighters.

"Everything seemed quiet but suddenly I saw a plane on the other side coming out of a cloud of smoke. My first reaction was that it was one of ours getting ready to land but then I noticed that it was a Fw 190. I dived and followed the plane, sending a spurt of machine gun fire into its tail, and saw smoke getting thicker and darker."

The Fw 190 then rolled and crashed into the ground.

Flying Officer Tadeusz Szlenkier, Flight Lieutenant Bronislaw Mach, Warrant Officer Stanislaw Bednarczyk and Flight Sergeant Jerzy Glowczewski each claimed an Fw 190 each. The last victory was by Pilot Officer Andrzej Dromlewicz. He reported: "I turned towards base and saw one Fw 190 attacking one of our Spitfires.

"I closed in and opened fire with cannon and machine guns from dead astern, range 600-700 yards and at 2000ft height. The enemy aircraft broke off his attack and made a starboard turn. I followed, closing in to approximately 300 yards. I continued to fire in short bursts with all armament and saw hits on the fuselage and wings of the enemy aircraft.

"Then my cannon gave out. The enemy aircraft straightened out and started to climb. I fired another long burst from machine guns only and saw pieces flying off the enemy's starboard wing. The Fw 190 then turned on to its back and the pilot baled out."

This last pilot was Feldwebel Fritz Hofmann of I./JG 1, who had suffered engine problems earlier in the morning, delaying his takeoff by 10 minutes. Before long, without the rest of his unit and the Ju 88 guide, he became lost and when he spotted II./JG 1's aircraft he had decided to tag along.

B-78 Eindhoven received the most severe punishment of any Allied airfield during Operation Baseplate. This 400 Squadron photo recon Spitfire PR.XI survived but was damaged.

Most of the aircraft destroyed at Eindhoven were Hawker Typhoons – including this 137 Squadron example.

Smouldering remains of Typhoons litter the airfield at Eindhoven as a ground crewman poses for a photo.

He successfully parachuted from his doomed Fw 190, which exploded when it hit the ground, only to be captured by angry Belgian civilians who, along with police officers, gave him a severe beating. He was then locked up in a Belgian jail cell for two hours before finally being handed over to the British.

This was not the end of II./JG 2's problems however. Shortly after 308 Squadron's return in force from their early morning mission, another squadron came back – No. 317.

Sergeant Kazimierz Hubert of 317 Squadron reported: "On my way back from the operation I heard over the R/T that B-65 was being attacked by enemy aircraft. The squadron patrolled the area for approximately 10 minutes before another message came through that it was B-61 which was attacked.

"We flew immediately over, arriving over the base at 2000ft. I attacked a red-nosed Fw 190 which was flying at 300ft from astern and opened fire with all armament at a range of about 400 yards. I fired one long burst and the Fw 190 caught fire, turned over on its back and crashed in a street in Ghent."

After a series of rapid dogfights, the two squadrons' pilots claimed a total of 14 Fw 190s destroyed. Two Spitfires had been shot down, killing both pilots. Another seven Spitfires either crash-landed or made emergency landings across the area due to damage sustained or through running out of fuel.

Another 18 Spitfires had been destroyed on the ground at St Denis-Westrem and five damaged. The B-17 was burned out, alongside a Short Stirling, a quartet of Avro Ansons, a Mosquito and an Auster which had belonged to 85 Group Communications Squadron.

On the flight back to Drope, II./JG 1 suffered still more casualties from Allied flak and battle damage. Seventeen of the 36 Fw 190s that had set out failed to make it back – nearly half.

After making a single pass over St Trond, the engine of 19-year-old Gefreiter Walter Wagner's Fw 190 A-8/R2 'White 11' cut out and he was forced to belly-land it just beyond the perimeter of the airfield. The damage caused to the aircraft was minimal, however, and it was quickly repaired by mechanics of the 404th Fighter Group. It is pictured here under 'new ownership'.

A huge explosion rocks St Trond as P-47s attempt to take off. Ten Thunderbolts were destroyed on the ground during the attack, with another 31 suffering varying degrees of damage.

Another shot from St Trond shows the airfield strewn with damaged P-47s after the Luftwaffe's attack.

In total, JG 1 lost 33 aircraft and 24 pilots, only seven of whom had been taken prisoner. The remainder were killed. This compares to around 60 Allied aircraft destroyed and two pilots killed.

A simple error

During the last two weeks of December, I./JG 2 took delivery of 54 Focke-Wulf Fw 190 D-9s to its base at Merzhausen on the south-western tip of Germany. With one being destroyed during a bombing raid and others out of action due to mechanical unserviceability, I./JG 2 had 29 available on December 31, plus six Fw 190 A-8/R6s.

II./JG 2 had 20 Messerschmitt Bf 109s: 13 G-14s and seven K-4s. III./ JG 2 had been even more fortunate with its supply of D-9s and had 34 available, in addition to a single A-9 and five A-8s. It only had enough pilots to fly 28 of the D-9s however. Stab JG 2 had one A-8/R6 and three D-9s.

On January 1, the target of all three Gruppen was St Trond – thought to be home to about 130 Republic P-47 Thunderbolts. Also to be involved in the attack was a specialist ground attack Geschwader, Schlachtgeschwader 4 (SG 4).

This had 152 Fw 190 F-8s on its books but only around 60 were serviceable due to the constant attrition of operations throughout December. The entire assault would be led by Hauptmann Franz Hrdlicka.

On the morning of January 1, I./JG 2's 35 aircraft took off just after 8am and headed for their initial assembly point at Koblenz in western central Germany. III./ JG 2 set off at 8.19am, one of its D-9s crashing on takeoff, and II./ JG 2 set off a little later, forming up over their airfield at 8.30am. Each formation of fighters was led by a Ju 88 or 188.

Arriving over Koblenz, II./JG 2 aircraft were fired on by German AA gunners but no casualties were taken. En route to Koblenz, another of III./JG 2's D-9s went down. The engine of Unteroffizier Fritz Altpeter's 'Yellow 4' caught fire and he peeled away from the formation but was too low to bail out and died when his aircraft hit the ground.

II./JG 2 was swiftly joined over Koblenz by the other two Gruppen before all three set off, flying separately from one another, for their next waypoint – the Eifel mountain range on the Belgian border.

When they got there at about 9am, their Ju 88s turned for home. One of them, however, was shot down 15 minutes later by 1st Lt John W Ginder of the 10th Fighter Squadron, flying his P-47 'Hershey Hellion No. 2' – which had a Hershey chocolate bar painted on its side.

At 9.05am, all JG 2 aircraft were nearing the front line close to Malmedy in Belgium. The plan was for them to cross over into enemy territory at right angles to the line, heading straight for St Trond, so that as little time as possible would be spent lingering over the warzone.

Seconds after the 84 aircraft crossed the line flying at about 1000ft, they were abruptly subjected to the most intense anti-aircraft fire any of the pilots had ever seen. Attack leader Hauptmann Hrdlicka was apparently unaware that the area around Malmedy and Aachen had been filled with AAA guns by the US Ninth Army in an attempt to protect the city of Liège, to the west, from the V-1 flying bombs German artillery units had been regularly launching at it.

As soon as the gunners spotted the huge formation of fighters flying their way, they opened fire with devastating consequences. Dozens of fighters were hit and their altitude was so low that few of the pilots could even bail out.

Some of the survivors, now flying individually or in small groups, still attempted to reach St Trond and carry out their mission. However, it is believed not a single one actually reached the correct target. It is believed they mistakenly attacked Asch and Ophoven instead. Further casualties were then inflicted by Mustang fighters already in the air and the AAA guns of those airfields.

Making their way home after this unmitigated disaster, still more JG 2 aircraft were shot down or succumbed to damage sustained during the outward flight and crashed. In total, I./JG 2 lost 18 Fw 190s with another six heavily damaged. II./JG 2 lost five Bf 109s and had three damaged, and III./JG 2 lost a staggering 19 Fw 190s with three more damaged – which meant only six came back unscathed out of

A rear-side view of Walter Wagner's 'White 11', WNr. 681497.

Walter Wagner's Fw 190 A-8/R2 in profile. The R2 variant of the A-8 was equipped with a pair of MK 108 30mm cannon in the outer wing positions and had a windscreen and quarter panes made of armoured glass fitted. Art by Bjorn Huber

28. JG 2 had paid a heavy price for a simple error of planning.

SG 4 did no better. Its mechanics had trouble with the BMW 801 engines of its battle-weary Fw 190 F-8s first thing in the morning, attempting to start them in temperatures as low as minus 10 degrees. Some would not start at all. Twelve of III./SG 4's Fw 190 F-8s took off at 8.53am but almost immediately two had to turn back due to mechanical failure.

Then without warning the formation crossed the flight path of another large group of Fw 190s heading west and was forced to dive into cloud to avoid a collision. During this manoeuvre, five III./SG 4 pilots got lost and some actually joined the passing formation, which was JG 11 heading for Asch. All this happened in strict radio silence, so no one could check what was happening.

Now just five of III./SG 4's Fw 190 F-8s reached the SG 4 rendezvous point at Zülpich at 9.05am. Waiting for them were about 25 other F-8s circling above the town, but no one turned towards the target. Ten minutes later they were still circling. After another five minutes, a small number of Fw 190s were seen to peel off and head west but none of the others followed. They assumed the mission was cancelled and returned to base.

Of the five pilots who got lost, two were shot down and killed, one was shot down and taken prisoner, and two managed to return home.

Attack on Eindhoven
The objective of JG 3, led by the famous ace Major Heinz Bär, was Eindhoven – home to the 2nd Tactical Air Force's 124 and 143 Wings, comprising 137, 181, 182 and 247, and 168, 438, 439 and 440 Squadrons respectively. All eight were equipped with Hawker Typhoon fighter-bombers. Being a substantial ex-Luftwaffe airfield, it also accommodated 39 (Recce) Wing's 400, 414 and 430 Squadrons, flying Spitfires and Mustangs.

Having managed to find a replacement BMW 801 D-2 engine, the Americans got 'White 11' running again – though they never flew it. After press photographers and a film crew arrived, it became one of the most photographed Fw 190s then in existence.

First thing in the morning on January 1, 1945, around 300 aircraft were parked out on the airfield, covered with frost. Most of them were in lines and around them were ammo dumps, fuel tanks, vehicles and assorted equipment.

At 8.20am, four Typhoons of 439 Squadron set off for a reconnaissance mission over German-held St Vith.

The first Luftwaffe pilots to begin attacking their large and inviting home base, at 8.22am, were the 19 heavily armed Fw 190 A-8/R2s of IV./JG 3, led by Leutnant Siegfried Müller. Once all were airborne, they flew south to meet up with rest of the Geschwader. Shortly thereafter, the 15 Bf 109s of III./JG 3 and the 22 Bf 109s of I./JG 3 took off and headed for the rally point over Lippstadt in western central Germany.

Meeting up on schedule at 8.45am, the three Gruppen merged into a single large formation of nearly 60

'White 11' was repainted in garish red after the 404th's commanding officer Colonel Leo Moon was heard to remark that he had always wanted a red aircraft. The 'L' on the fuselage was for 'Leo'.

ABOVE, LEFT and BELOW: The remains of Leutnant Theo Nibel's Fw 190 D-9 'Black 12' during inspection by Allied technicians. The 10./JG 54 aircraft was brought down near Grimbergen by a partridge hitting its radiator – rather than by enemy fire.

aircraft, including the Fw 190 A-9s of the JG 3 Stabsschwarm. Major Bär himself had taken off separately in a Fw 190 D-9 – the only one his Geschwader possessed – and began making his own way to Eindhoven.

At 8.50am, six more Typhoons took off from Eindhoven, this time from 137 Squadron en route for an armed reconnaissance of the Minden area. Five minutes later, six Spitfire IXs of 414 Squadron took off. Another two embarked on tactical reconnaissance at 8.59am.

A minute later, as the JG 3 formation was passing Dorsten and heading for Helmond, six 168 Squadron Typhoons took off bound for targets in Prüm. Another six minutes passed before a single Typhoon, MN486 QC-D, piloted by Flight Lieutenant Howard Plaistowe 'Gibby' Gibbons, took off for a flight test. It was now 9.06am and other aircraft were taxiing up in readiness for takeoff.

At 9.15am, JG 3 had just passed Helmond when Leutnant Hans-Ulrich Jung's Bf 109 suddenly burst into flames and fell apart before its remains fell to the ground. As he passed low over a power line, it caught on his drop tank, tearing it away and engulfing the rest of the aircraft in fire.

The formation was now approaching Eindhoven and suddenly Major Bär appeared, overtaking the formation on its right hand side in his D-9. The Stabsschwarm pilots opened the throttles of their A-9s and caught Bär just as he arrived over the Allied airfield.

Making a sharp left-hand turn, Bär targeted a pair of Typhoons in the process of taking off and shot them up. One of the pilots, Flight Lieutenant Pete Wilson, powered down his stricken aircraft and rolled it off the runway before dragging himself from the cockpit with a severe bullet wound through his torso which claimed his life just minutes later.

The other Typhoon pilot, Flying Officer Ross Keller, throttled up and took off but either he or the aircraft took a fatal hit and his body was later found in its burned-out shell where it had crashed shortly afterwards.

Wilson and Keller's six 438 Squadron colleagues, who had been behind them in the queue to take off, leapt from their Typhoons and took shelter as the full force of IV./JG 3 arrived and opened fire with their MK 108 cannon, shooting up four of the aircraft.

Panic immediately set in. Several Typhoon pilots attempted to take off while others tried to escape their stationary aircraft. As the Bf 109s and Fw 190s passed over, Pilot Officer R A Watson opened fire with his Typhoon's cannon and damaged one of them before his own aircraft was hit and set on fire.

Two 430 Squadron Spitfire XIVs were hit and damaged on the perimeter, injuring both pilots. The Spitfires of 83 Group Communications Squadron, also on the airfield, were strafed. Pilot Officer Lance Burrows of 137 Squadron was killed as bullets

A pair of Hawker Tempests from 3 Squadron undergo servicing at B-80 Volkel in Holland. Though JG 6 was sent to destroy the aircraft at Volkel, they simply never got there. A few lost aircraft from other units destroyed a single Typhoon on the ground but the airfield was otherwise unscathed.

entered the cockpit of his Typhoon, JR260 SF-Z, on the perimeter track.

At this moment, Flight Lieutenant Gibbons returned in MN486 QC-D. Seeing the airfield under attack, he picked out the closest Fw 190, probably 'Black 16' piloted by Feldwebel Gerhard Leipholz,

and fired into it from above and behind. He was at 100ft, his target at 50ft and they were so close that Gibbons' four 20mm cannon blew the German fighter's tail off before the two halves span into the ground.

Within seconds, a trio of Bf 109s were on Gibbons' own tail and there

A pair of Fw 190 D-9s belonging to 3./JG 26 during the winter of 1944-45. The unit attacked Grimbergen on January 1 – an airfield that had largely been abandoned. It achieved very little but lost 21 D-9s and 11 of its pilots were killed.

Leutnant Theo Nibel, who attempted to destroy his Fw 190 D-9 after crash-landing but failed. His aircraft was subsequently captured and thoroughly examined by the Allies.

Emerging from their dispersed positions are Fw 190 D-9s of 7./JG 26. The unit attacked Brussels-Evere on January 1, 1945.

could be no escape – his Typhoon going in close to Leipholz's aircraft.

The four anti-aircraft units around the field opened up, along with ground personnel who grabbed Bren guns and joined in, and over the next 23-25 minutes, the duration of the attack, shot down three Bf 109s and two Fw 190s.

In the midst of this chaos of strafing aircraft and hammering AAA guns, a lone Spitfire IX appeared overhead. It was flown by Flight Lieutenant Robert C Smith of 442 Squadron, who had taken off from Heesch airfield at 8.57am but was forced to turn back due to a problem with a drop tank. He had heard that one of his colleagues had gone down near Eindhoven and went looking for him.

Within seconds he was caught up in the maelstrom of combat. He later reported: "I identified Fw 190s and Me 109s flying in a circle at about 200ft. I went down to 400ft and circled over the top of them. When I could pick one out that wasn't followed too closely by another, I would nip in and fire a quick burst, then break and climb up again.

"In this way I attacked three Me 109s, however I could not observe strikes all the time being on the lookout for other enemy aircraft. I had not yet seen any other Allied aircraft. After firing at the third Me 109, I noticed a Fw 190 closing in on me from the port side. He had already opened fire as I broke port.

"He stayed with me so I climbed steeply and he fell off to port. I came down on his tail and gave him a short burst from about 200 yards, no strikes observed. I then broke port again into a Me 109 which I chased down to the deck. My windscreen had oiled up so I broke off the attack and climbed to about 800ft.

"I then noticed a Fw 190 coming up from the deck at the port side. I dove and made a head-on attack. We both opened fire at about 300 yards, no strikes observed. He broke to port at the last second and passed over the top of me going away. I sighted another Fw 190 on the deck going away. I chased him and we had a bit of a do.

"He was a very good pilot and I couldn't get in a shot. He finally straightened out. I closed in, but my ammo had run out. I broke off the attack and headed for base, as my fuel was low. My engine cut at 7000ft and I glided to base making a successful wheels-down landing."

Smith later claimed one Bf 109 destroyed and another damaged, after witnesses on the ground said they saw rounds from his Spitfire fatally damage a Messerschmitt, its pilot bailing out, but neither claim was acknowledged.

With Smith gone, another single Spitfire IX arrived over the airfield – one of the 414 Squadron machines that had taken off at 8.55am, flown by Squadron Leader Gordon Wonnacott. He had become separated from his wingman and was coming home when he was confronted by an incredible scene of carnage.

His report stated: "I immediately went into attack with cannon only from about 5000ft. I opened fire at about 450 yards using 20-30° deflection on the first enemy aircraft I saw – either a Fw 190 or a

Me 109. I saw no strikes and broke off the attack as my aircraft seemed to be skidding and I was unable to hold my line of fire correctly (one cannon had stopped firing).

"I pulled up and saw a Me 109 which I attacked using machine guns only. I opened fire at 100 yards, seeing strikes, and the enemy aircraft took evasive action. I again closed, firing from below and using 10° deflection. Strikes were again seen and after more evasive action the pilot jettisoned his coupe top and then bailed out.

"I then attacked another Me 109, opening fire at 300 yards and using some deflection. I saw strikes, the enemy aircraft took violent evasive action, doing a loop and pulling out very close to the ground. I dove after this enemy aircraft, closing from 250 to 100 yards, taking short bursts and seeing many strikes, black smoke and flames issuing from the enemy aircraft.

"I did not see this aircraft hit the ground as I had to take evasive action to avoid three Fw 190s which were attacking me from astern. I turned into these aircraft, attacking No. 1 from 200 yards, saw strikes, broke hard left to avoid the two

A 16 Squadron Spitfire PR.XI at Melsbroek beside another that has become completely engulfed in flames.

A burning Spitfire PR.XI slowly disintegrates after the attack on Melsbroek.

A Vickers Wellington XIII of 69 Squadron burns at Brussels-Melsbroek. After Eindhoven, Melsbroek was next hardest hit.

behind me which had opened fire and attacked the last of the section.

"My machine gun ammunition gave out after 10 rounds were fired and I tried to get my cannon to fire, but it ceased after about three or four rounds. No strikes were seen. I saw a large column of smoke about 1½ miles distance and on the track of the last Me 109 which I had attacked. I claim two Me 109s destroyed and one Fw 190 damaged."

Wonnacott's victims are likely to have been Feldwebel Walter Rutowski of 4./JG 3, who bailed out and was taken prisoner, and Oberfeldwebel Freidrich Hameister, acting Staffelkapitän of the same unit, who crash-landed 15 miles from Eindhoven and was eventually captured and taken prisoner.

There were further furious skirmishes away from Eindhoven as JG 3's remaining aircraft attempted to return home, and more losses were incurred on both sides. The overall damage caused at the airfield was significant – with 44 aircraft destroyed and at least another 60 damaged. Fifteen men were killed and another 40 wounded. The airfield itself was barely touched, however, and once the debris was bulldozed off the runway it was ready for use again that afternoon.

JG 3 lost 15 fighters, with three more damaged. Nine pilots were killed and six taken prisoner.

All clear at Le Culot

The two airfields of Le Culot, 30 miles northeast of Charleroi, were being used by the Ninth Air Force. The 36th and 373rd Fighter Groups, comprising the 22nd, 23rd and 53rd, and the 410th, 411th and 412th Fighter Squadrons respectively, were on the first airfield, A-89. All six operated P-47 Thunderbolts.

The second, smaller auxiliary airfield, Y-10, was occupied by the 363rd Tactical Reconnaissance Group's 33rd and 155th Photo Recon Squadrons, operating the F-5 version of the Lockheed P-38 Lightning.

Assigned to attack these targets was JG 4. Rather than meet up and attack as a single formation, it was decided that the Geschwader's four Gruppen would attack individually.

Beginning at 8.08am, 17 Fw 190 A-8/R2s of II.(Sturm)/JG 4 took off from Babenhausen airfield and began to follow their assigned Ju 88s. Shortly after takeoff, one Fw 190 returned with radio problems. After these were fixed the pilot, Unteroffizier Walter Hübner, crashed on takeoff, suffering injuries from which he died nearly two weeks later. Two more aircraft took off 10 minutes after the others and were then unable to find them.

Near Malmedy, the 16 remaining Fw 190s entered the same heavy AAA barrage that devastated JG 2. Their leading Ju 88 was the first aircraft hit, then one after another, a dozen others went down – leaving just four Fw 190s still flying, all of them damaged. They found an Allied airfield, probably Asch, and

The body of 24-year-old Unteroffizier Herbert Maxis, a pilot of 13./JG 53, lies face down, partially on the wing of his Bf 109 G-14. He was forced to make a belly landing near an American AAA position and was shot as he climbed from the cockpit. No identification was found on his body and he was buried in an unmarked grave, the location of which is unknown today.

The wreckage of a P-47 lies on the temporary airstrip mesh at Metz following the attack by JG 53.

Me 262 A-2a fighter-bombers from KG 51 were involved in the fighting on January 1 but their effect was minimal and none were destroyed during the attacks.

made a brief strafing run, shot up two trains and then dispersed to find somewhere to land. None of them made it back to Babenhausen.

IV./JG 4, led by Major Gerhard Michalski, had six serviceable Bf 109 G-10s, 11 G-14s and two K-4s. In the event, at 8.20am on January 1, only 16 Bf 109s were ready. These, and another from Stab/JG 4, set off from Rheim-Main and followed a Ju 88 in the direction of Bingen. A few minutes later, Michalski suffered mechanical problems and had to turn back.

His command was taken up by Oberleutnant Lothar Wolff, Staffelkapitän of 15./JG 4. Another 15 miles further on and the Messerschmitts were joined by the two Fw 190 A-8/R2s from II.(Sturm)/JG 4 that had been delayed taking off and were now lost.

Close to the front line, the 18 aircraft began to draw heavy AAA fire and the large cumbersome Ju 88 was forced to leave. Two of the Bf 109s were shot down and as the remainder flew into clouds to escape, some got lost. Unteroffizier Werner Anetzhuber of 13./JG 4 completely

lost touch with his unit and ended up near Eindhoven, where he was shot down and killed by a pair of Tempests from 56 Squadron.

The survivors travelled on and on. Just when Wolff had all but given up hope of finding Le Culot, an airfield suddenly appeared below. It wasn't Le Culot, however, it was St Trond – which JG 2 had failed to find.

Believing they were in the right place, Wolff led the attack. Rows of P-47s belonging to the 48th and 492nd Fighter Groups were strafed, including several aircraft that had been taxiing into position for takeoff.

Numerous American aircraft took hits but the airfield's AAA gunners' concentrated fire exacted a heavy toll on IV./JG 4. Both of the Fw 190s accompanying the unit were shot down. Obergefreiter Hans Peschel made three strafing runs before taking a critical hit, climbing as high as he dared and bailing out. He landed safely and was quickly apprehended by the Americans.

Gefreiter Walter Wagner, 19, belly landed his Fw 190 A-8/R2 'White 11' in a beet field after his engine cut

out. Gefreiter Karl Noppeney's Bf 109 K-4 was hit in the cockpit by AAA, probably killing him outright before his aircraft crashed near Wilderen. Oberfähnrich Arnolf Russow's 'Yellow 13' Bf 109 G-14/AS suffered severe damage from an AAA hit and although he was able to leave St Trond, his aircraft went down a few miles further on. He survived and was taken prisoner.

Only Wolff and another pilot, Leutnant Josef Kunz, managed to return to German-held territory after the attack, the latter despite being intercepted by P-51 Mustangs on the way home and suffering damage to his oil tank which caused him to make a forced landing near Idar-Oberstein.

Wolff alone landed back at Rhein-Main. An American report on the attack stated: "It is believed from the tactics employed that the squadron was led by an experienced pilot and that the remainder were young and inexperienced.

"The leader got away and his flying was reported as being far superior to the others. After completing a strafing run, he would

The jet-powered Arado Ar 234 B-2 bombers of III./KG 76 pictured in December 1944. Like the Me 262s of KG 51, they had little effect during the January 1 mission.

make a tight low-level turn while the others did not turn as tightly or at as low an altitude. All AAA claims were made on hits inflicted on the turns. Some of the enemy aircraft were carrying belly tanks but no bombs were dropped or observed. At no time during the attack did the altitude exceed 500ft."

The aircraft of I./JG 4 and III./JG 4, both based at Darmstadt-Griesheim, also began taking off at 8.20am. III.'s nine Bf 109 K-4s went first, followed by the 26 Bf 109s of I. Gruppe, a mixed group of G-10s, G-14s and K-4s.

Following their Ju 88s, the formation of 35 aircraft headed for Bingen, just as the other JG 4 Gruppen had. Within moments, they had run into intense AAA fire – from their own side. This caused the leader, Hauptmann Friedrich Eberle, kommodore III./JG 4, to give the order to cancel the mission.

His own III./JG 4 aircraft turned for home and the bewildered pilots of I./JG 4 were unsure of what to do. Two were shot down. Some tried to continue the mission but it is unlikely that any of them reached Le Culot. In fact, no German aircraft attacked Le Culot on January 1, 1945. Eberle was hauled before a military court and stripped of his rank before being sent to an infantry unit.

The unnoticed airfield

Volkel, aka B-80, was another former Luftwaffe station now crammed with Allied aircraft – 121 and 122 Wings of the RAF. The former was composed of three Typhoon squadrons while the latter boasted five squadrons all flying Tempests.

Ordered to destroy as many of them as possible was JG 6. The Geschwader's III. Gruppe began

taking off at 8.19am on January 1 and by 8.31am its three Bf 109 G-10s and 18 Bf 109 G-14/As types were all airborne and following their assigned Ju 88s. Four minutes later they were over Quackenbrück, where they collected the 25 Fw 190 A-8s of II./JG 6.

At around the same time, the last of I./JG 6's 20 Fw 190 A-8s was taking off. One of the unit's aircraft suffered engine failure on takeoff and crashed, killing its pilot, but the rest flew on to join up with the other JG 6 aircraft. Once all three Gruppen were together, the huge formation of some 70 aircraft set off in the direction of Volkel.

What they did not know was that between them and their target, the Allies had actually built another airfield, B-88, also known as Heesch. Construction had taken place from October to November

1944 and it seems likely that German intelligence had simply failed to notice it.

The pilots flew right over it at low level at 9.15am. Only the back markers realised they were over an Allied airfield and fired on to it as they passed.

Heesch, however, had already been busy that morning. Eleven 411 Squadron Spitfires took off for a fighter sweep at 8.50am, followed at 8.57am by 13 442 Squadron Spitfires on an armed recce mission.

When JG 6 appeared suddenly overhead, 10 Spitfires from 401 Squadron were already on the runway about to take off. It was the ideal opportunity for the RAF pilots. They took off as quickly as they could and gave chase.

One of them, Flying Officer Doug Cameron in MJ448, a Spitfire IX, later reported: "I took off and turned slightly starboard and sighted two Me 109s on my port side on the deck at 100ft.

"I attacked the starboard one from astern, about 10° starboard and 300 yards with a very short burst. I saw an explosion on the fuselage near the cockpit and the aircraft dove straight down towards the deck at less than 50ft. I immediately turned on the other about 15° starboard, about 200 yards and fired a short burst. I saw a large explosion on the fuselage behind the cockpit followed by flames.

"This aircraft also dove down to port, with flames, at less than 50ft. I then sighted another Me 109 to starboard. I at once chased him and opened fire at about 400-500 yards, from about 30-40° port. I saw a small flash on the rear fuselage. I continued to fire short bursts with no results seen.

"I then chased to about 200 yards astern and after a fairly long burst (2-3 seconds) saw glycol streaming out. I was out of ammunition and flew very close on his starboard until he crash-landed in a large field approximately two miles north of the aerodrome. This aircraft smoked but was not burning. After two orbits of the crash I took a short cine camera shot of this aircraft. I claim three Me 109s destroyed."

Ground control had by now recalled 442 Squadron's 13 Spitfires from their mission and arrived in time to shoot down at least one Fw 190 of JG 6.

Confusion now reigned in the JG 6 formation. So much so that all three Gruppen missed Volkel. I./JG 6 ended up joining the Eindhoven attack, II./JG 6 stumbled across an unfinished and unoccupied, but AAA defended, airfield B-86 at Helmond, and attacked it instead, and III./JG 6 flew into heavy AAA fire elsewhere. All three also suffered further losses from Spitfires and Tempests already airborne when they had arrived in the area.

Overall, Stab JG 6 lost one of its three Fw 190 A-9s, I./JG 6 lost seven Fw 190s, II./JG lost eight Fw 190s and III./JG 6 lost 12 of its 21 Bf 109s. Not long after its utter failure against Volkel, JG 6 was withdrawn from front line operations in readiness for a transfer to the Eastern Front.

The disaster unfolds

It was a similar story for JG 11 attacking Asch (Y-29). Through a combination of AAA fire and P-51 Mustangs already being ready to fight, it lost 24 Fw 190s and Bf 109s out of 60. Twenty of their pilots were killed and only four taken prisoner. Among the dead were Major Günther Specht – who had led JG 11 since May 1944 – and his wingman, Unteroffizier Sophus Schmidt. Their aircraft, and indeed their bodies, have never been found.

There was more success for the highly experienced JG 26 and III./JG 54, who attacked Brussels-Evere and Grimbergen. II. and III./JG 26 hit Evere as planned and managed to destroy 31 single-engine aircraft, 21 twin-engine types and nine four-engine aircraft, for a loss of 13 Fw 190 D-9s and six Bf 109s.

I./JG 26 and III./JG 54 did rather less well in their attack on Grimbergen – which had been home to the Spitfires of 132 Wing but which was now largely abandoned. They destroyed a single Mustang, one twin-engine aircraft and four B-17s. To achieve this, they lost 21 Fw 190 D-9s plus another 10 damaged. Eleven pilots were dead.

There was more success for JG 27 and IV./JG 54 at Melsbroek. Seventeen of the former's Bf 109s were destroyed along with three Fw 190s of the latter. In exchange, they managed to destroy more than 50 Allied aircraft, including 12 Mitchells, 13 Wellingtons, five Spitfires, four Mosquitos, four B-17s, two B-24s and an assortment of other types.

Attacking Metz-Frescaty and Etain, JG 53 suffered heavy casualties. Out of 80 Bf 109s taking part in the mission, 30 were shot down and another eight were damaged. The aircraft heading for Etain never reached it, having been intercepted and badly disrupted by American P-47s beforehand.

Those that made it to Metz-Frescaty managed to destroy 22 P-47s and damaged another 11 – losses that were made good within a week. JG 53 itself also received a full complement of replacement aircraft but the pilots it received were raw recruits unfit for front line duties, diminishing its effectiveness despite its apparent renewed strength on paper.

Antwerp-Deurne was the target of JG 77 and its attack also proved to be a failure. It managed to destroy 14 aircraft, most of them Typhoons, and lost 11 Bf 109s along with their pilots – six of whom were killed and the remainder taken prisoner.

Finally, the jet aircraft of KG 51 and KG 76 also participated in Operation Baseplate. Four of KG 76's Arado Ar 234 B-2s flew a weather reconnaissance mission in darkness at 4am on January 1, 1945 – the first night-time operation by jet aircraft in history – followed by a bombing mission.

This should have involved 10 Ar 234s but four suffered mechanical failures so only six participated in the attack, on Gilze-Rijen, in the end. They reached their target and each opened its AB 500 container, dropping 24 SD 15 bombs per aircraft. These did little damage, however, destroying just one Typhoon, but at least all six jets made it back to base.

KG 51's Me 262 A-2s were to carry out bombing and reconnaissance missions to Eindhoven, Gilze-Rijen and Volkel, so each of the 22 available machines was fitted with two 250kg bombs on its nose racks and a robot camera. Certainly, individual Me 262s were spotted by observers at all three airfields

but damage caused by their bombs – those that dropped them – was again minimal. All 22 of KG 51's jets also returned safely home.

Counting the cost

When the dust settled and every German fighter that was going to fly home had done so, the mammoth task of assessing what damage had been inflicted on the Allies began. Overall, based on reports of pilots and aerial reconnaissance, the Luftwaffe believed it had destroyed 479 aircraft and damaged another 114. Its own casualties amounted to 271 fighters and nine Ju 88s destroyed and 69 more aircraft damaged, with 213 fighter pilots killed or missing, including those captured, plus 21 wounded.

In reality, Allied losses were closer to 305 aircraft destroyed and 190 damaged. Just 15 Allied fighters

were shot down, with only a handful of pilots being killed, including those who died on the ground.

While both the Germans and the Allies were able to replace their material losses – the Germans with considerably more difficulty – the loss of 213 pilots, including more than 60 highly experienced fighter pilots, was a grievous blow indeed.

The greatest single cause of Operation Baseplate's failure was Allied anti-aircraft fire. Some 47% of the German aircraft lost were shot down by it. The second largest contributing factor was attacks by Allied fighter aircraft, accounting for 23% of the Luftwaffe machines lost. In another 5% of cases either AAA fire or Allied fighters – it is uncertain which – was responsible. Some 11% of German losses were due to unknown causes and 5% were due to German flak.

Harsh winter conditions and delicate near-prototype jet engines do not mix well. Here technicians of KG 51 prepare to get to work on their charges.

Why were the Allies' defences
so effective? Poor route planning
meant several formations flew
directly over some of the heaviest
flak coverage to be found anywhere
on the Western Front. A lack of
night and instrument flying training
meant the attack had to be carried
out in daylight – when numerous
Allied units were already in the air
or ready for takeoff.

Having the fighters follow Ju 88s
which were unable to proceed all
the way to the targets was also a
recipe for disaster. The pilots failed
to check their own maps and trusted
their guide, who then departed
some miles away from their
ultimate destination.

An insistence on radio silence
may have helped maintain secrecy
but it also resulted in total confusion
in several instances where proper
coordination by experienced leaders
might have saved the day.

Instead, the operation was a
failure that the Jagdwaffe would
spend the next four months living
to regret.

3

DICING WITH PIGGYBACKS

❖

February 3, 1945: The Double Nickel's Mistel encounter

After escorting B-17 bombers to Berlin, four P-51 Mustang pilots of the 55th Fighter Group, Eighth Air Force, went hunting for targets of their own. Diving down to strafe a pair of locomotives, none of them expected what happened next...

Gun camera footage from the P-51 Mustang of Lt Bernard H Howes, taken on February 3, 1945, shows a crewman leaping from the Junkers Ju 88 section of a Mistel combination at extremely low altitude. Note the water spraying from bullet impacts to the left of the image. The cockpit of the Messerschmitt Bf 109 on top is burning and the whole combination is stalling, with the tail dipping towards the ground.

The USAAF went all-out to destroy the Tempelhof rail marshalling yards in the centre of Berlin on February 3, 1945 – it was believed that the German Sixth Panzer Army was passing through them on its way to the Eastern Front.

A total of 937 B-17s were sent to destroy the target with an escort of 575 North American P-51 Mustangs. Arriving in waves throughout the late morning and into the early afternoon, the bombers did their work well, shattering a large area and starting a fire that lasted four days.

Among the P-51s which escorted the B-17s were squadrons of the 55th Fighter Group, the 'Double Nickel', led by the unit's flamboyant executive officer Lieutenant Colonel Elwyn C Righetti.

With fuel still in their tanks and the bombers well protected by others, Righetti decided his men could conduct a ground sweep on the way home to Station 159 – the 55th's base at Wormingford in Essex. Strafing was his speciality and he organised two flights before setting out to look for targets.

His men were all members of the 343rd Fighter Squadron: 1st Lieutenant Bernard H Howes, 22, from Brockton, Massachusetts, was flying P-51K CY-C 44-63745 'My Li'l Honey', 2nd Lt Patrick L Moore from Griffin, Indiana, flew P-51D CY-Y 44-14235 'Lil Jan' and 2nd Lt Richard G Gibbs, from Nantucket, also in Massachusetts, flew P-51D CY-Q 44-14175 'Cherry'.

'Eager El' Righetti himself, from San Luis Obispo, California, flew P-51D CL-M 44-72227 'Katydid'.

At about 12.30pm, near Boizenburg, Germany, the Americans spotted two locomotives and dropped down through a low layer of cloud to attack. What happened next was a remarkable free-for-all as the Mustangs vied with one another over a fresh set of targets that suddenly presented themselves.

A formation of Mistel combinations, each a fighter fixed atop a Junkers Ju 88, appeared flying at low level beneath the clouds.

Howes reported: "I was flying White 3 on the mission of February 3. At about 1230 we dropped to the deck to strafe. On pulling up from the first pass on a locomotive I sighted a formation of three pick-a-backs, Fw 190s on Ju 88s, in string formation at about 400ft.

"I turned into the second combo with my wingman Lt Moore behind me. I fired a short burst from 90° at about 350 yards, observing a few strikes on the 190. As I fired on this, the 190 on the third unit was released.

"The prop was windmilling, and on release the 190 seemed to nose up for a minute and then, apparently out of control, the nose went down and it headed for the ground. I claim this Fw 190 as destroyed. As soon as the 190 was released, the 88 turned sharply left. I followed, firing a short burst but observed no strikes. I fell outside the turn and lost sight of the 88 momentarily.

"My wingman behind me was in position and shot the 88 down. When I looked back I saw it crash

Two of the three Mistel combinations encountered by four P-51 Mustangs from the Eighth Air Force's 55th Fighter Group on February 3, 1945. They are still flying in formation with both aircraft attached to one another, suggesting that this gun camera image was taken at the beginning of the Americans' attack.

Lieutenant Colonel Elwyn G Righetti sits on his P-51 Mustang 'Katydid'. He flew as Tudor White Leader on February 3, 1945. Note the unusual victory markings on the nose of his aircraft – a smaller version of his 'Katydid' logo with wings spread over a stylised swastika.

The Ju 88 section of a 6./KG 200 Mistel banks to the left to avoid the P-51 Mustang firing on it from behind. The Bf 109 that had been attached to its back has already detached. None of the three Bf 109s involved in this encounter survived.

P-51 pilot 2nd Lieutenant Richard G Gibbs was Lt Col Righetti's wingman on February 3 and was Tudor White 2.

A close-up of 1st Lieutenant Bernard H Howes who flew as Tudor White 3 on February 3.

into the ground. On pulling up I saw the first unit I had fired at about 300 yards in front of me. There were flames coming out of the 190, so I went after it again. I started firing and the combo turned into me, dropping to the deck.

"As I fired, another large burst of flame came from the 190. On making a second pass, the right engine of the 88 burst into flames, and I saw them both crash into the ground. From this entire encounter I claim two Fw 190s and one Ju 88 destroyed. Ammunition expended: 1440 rounds."

The aircraft attacked by Howes are clearly visible on his gun camera footage.

Righetti reported: "Near Boizenburg on the Elbe River I located a small hole in the unbroken overcast. Through the hole I could see two locomotives and called them in and started down.

"Visibility was about two miles and scattered fuzz on the overcast ran down in some places to 500 to 600ft. I rolled out of my turn and started my final approach to the locos about four miles off. I had already assigned the locos and

parts of the train to the flight. We were echeloned to the right with my position on the extreme left.

"At a distance of two miles from the train I spotted three piggy-back aircraft at 10.30 to me, at our same altitude of about 600ft, heading almost directly at us, and half a mile off. I mistakenly identified them as buzz bomb equipped He 111s and broke off rapidly, left and up, in a 200° chandelle, positioning myself on the tail of the middle one.

"I started firing two short bursts at 600 yards and missed. I swung into trail and closed to point blank range, firing a long burst, I saw many excellent strikes on the fuselage and empennage of the large aircraft and scattered strikes and a small fire on the fighter.

"Both aircraft, still fastened together, went into a steep dive straight ahead. I was about to overrun them and did not see them crash, but a few seconds later I saw a large explosion and spotted considerable burning wreckage.

"I still did not know what we were attacking; I turned slightly to port for another look. As I closed, and before I could open fire, I discovered that the buzz bomb was actually a Focke-Wulf 190 fastened atop the heavy twin-engined aircraft. As I was closing to fire, the heavy aircraft seemed to be jettisoned, went into a shallow diving turn to the left, and crashed and burned in a small hamlet.

"Apparently it carried no bombs, for the gasoline thrown from its tanks burned for some time, and I did not observe any unusually large explosion. The Fw 190, relieved of its load, snapped to the right and

then began a wild evasive action, I drove up to 200 yards directly in trail, firing intermittently, and secured excellent strikes along the fuselage, wing roots, canopy, and induced good fire.

"Jerry went out of control and crashed straight ahead. At this time I noticed a few tracers too close and coming behind. I broke sharply left and up into a low cloud. I don't know who or what was firing at me, but it might have been the third Fw 190, having jettisoned its bomber."

Gibbs was also attacking the Mistel combinations. He reported: "I was flying Tudor White 2 on the mission of February 3, 1945. We were on the deck and about to strafe a loco in the vicinity of Boizenburg, when Tudor Leader Lt Col Righetti called in a gaggle of three Fw 190-bomber combos, flying a sloppy 'V' formation at about 600ft. We attacked from a level turn port stern.

"Lt Col Righetti took the middle combo of the three, and I took the third and last one of this gaggle. I started firing on the Ju 88 at about 45° from about 800 yards, closing to about 300 yards with a two-second burst. I observed many strikes on the left wing root of the Ju 88, where it began to burn.

"After a short dive the Fw 190 was released. The 190 appeared rather unstable in the air, but managed to conduct violent evasive action during the ensuing combat. I fired a short burst from astern, beginning at about 200 yards and closing to zero yards. I saw strikes all over the aircraft and observed parts of the cowling and canopy fly off.

"There was also a fire in or around the cockpit. I then overran the enemy aircraft and skidded out to the right. As I looked back I saw where the 190 had crashed into the ground."

The original P-51D 'Katydid' of Lt Col Righetti, 44-14223 CL-M.

Lt Col Righetti's second and longest serving P-51D, the second 'Katydid', 44-72227 CL-M.

Lt Gibbs's P-51D, 44-14175 CY-Q 'Cherry'.

RIGHT: Tudor White 4, 2nd Lt Patrick L Moore, gives the photographer a cocky grin.

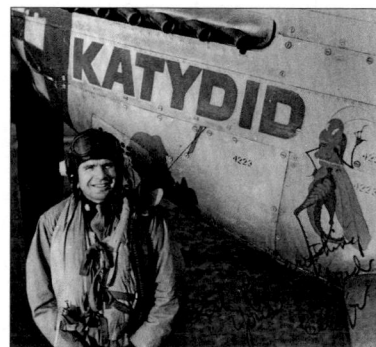

The 'female' grasshopper logo on the nose of Righetti's first P-51D 'Katydid'. The pilot, who became the 55th Fighter Group's commanding officer in 1945, is pictured standing beside his machine.

As stated by Howes, Moore also claimed a Ju 88.

There had been three Ju 88s and three fighters but the four US pilots claimed one Ju 88 each and a total of five Fw 190s – two for Howes, two for Righetti and one for Gibbs. In the confusion of combat, it was difficult to decide who had destroyed what.

In fact, German records show that at least two of the combinations were Mistel 1s, with Messerschmitt Bf 109s mounted atop Ju 88s rather than Fw 190s. The Ju 88 pilots were Feldwebel Willi Kollhoff, Oberfähnrich Franz Pietschmann and Feldwebel Fritz Lorbach of 6./KG 200, based at Kolberg but on their way to Tirstrup in Denmark.

Lorbach managed to put his Ju 88 down safely in the woods, albeit with the left engine on fire. Pietschmann was killed when his Ju 88 dived into the ground and Kollhoff was injured after he made a forced landing and was strafed by a P-51. His gunner, who also survived the landing, was killed. All three of the fighter pilots were shot down and killed.

Where the Mistel came from

The three combinations shot down on February 3 had been on their way to participate in Unternehmen Drachenhöhle, or Operation Dragon's Lair, a plan devised by Hermann Göring with the goal of attacking the Royal Navy's home fleet at Scapa Flow and inflicting a high-profile Pearl Harbor-style blow against the British.

The genesis of the Mistel, however, came about three years earlier in 1942, when work was carried out in Germany to enable a glider to carry a full military load by launching it into the air using a smaller powered aircraft mounted on its back.

This combination was eventually to become known as the Mistel (mistletoe), since the powered aircraft could be given an extended range using fuel drawn from the glider below – like mistletoe drawing sap from its host tree.

The upper portion was to be a Bf 109 E fighter, the lower a DFS 230 glider. Both were piloted.

In June 1943, it was decided that this technology could be used for launching a 'grossbombe', or large bomb, at a ground target. The Bf 109 would still be the upper portion, now a 109 F, but the lower would be a 'war weary' unmanned Junkers Ju 88 A-4 filled with 3.5 tons of explosives.

The Bf 109 pilot would control the whole Mistel up to its arrival over the target, whereupon the Ju 88 would be aimed and an autopilot unit within it activated. The Bf 109 would separate from the Ju 88 by firing explosive bolts and then peel away as the bomb flew down to its target.

P-51D 44-14243 CY-Y 'Lil' Jan' was flown by Lt Patrick L Moore.

A closer study of the nose art on Lt Moore's P-51.

LEFT: Lt Moore at the controls of his P-51D. His name is emblazoned on the side of his canopy in large letters.

Operation Dragon's Lair

Fifteen Mistels from 6./KG 200 were intended to form the strike force for Göring's ambitious 'British Pearl Harbor', supported by 12 flare-dropping Ju 88s and 188s from 5./KG 200 to illuminate the target. They were to set off from Tirstrup on a date after January 20, 1945.

Everything initially went to plan and Mistels from II./KG 200 arrived at the Danish base without any problems in mid-January 1945, along with the Ju 88s and 188s.

One of the pilots due to take part, Feldwebel Rudi Riedl of 6./KG 200, recalled: "As far as the Scapa Flow attack plan was concerned, we only received one proper briefing which took place in a large room of the country house near the airfield, in which was a large map of the Scapa Flow area.

"Each pilot was assigned an individual target since we received regular reconnaissance updates on British shipping movements – I knew exactly where my target ship was anchored. To help us further, at

The Ju 88's high-explosive warhead was a huge hollow charge with a plunder detonator at its tip which was fitted in place of the aircraft's cockpit. They were to be used against high-value targets such as capital ships, power stations and bridges.

When a Ju 88 was converted for Mistel use, its crew compartment was removed at the aft bulkhead. Four quick-release bolts were then fitted which allowed the compartment to be re-attached

for training or for ferrying the combination around. The warheads were moved separately by road or rail for safety.

Once the aircraft and the warhead were both at the operational airfield, the crew compartment could be easily removed using the quick-release bolts and the warhead attached.

The Mistels being flown on February 3, 1945, therefore, had their crew compartments in place complete with working controls, rather than warheads.

These images show first a Ju 88 with its entire cockpit section removed in readiness for conversion to the lower component of a Mistel combination. The removal work could be done relatively quickly. Next the huge hollow charge 'Elefantenrüssel', or Elephant's Trunk warhead, is shown being moved into position, and finally a Ju 88 with its warhead in place and ready for pairing with a single engine fighter.

Eleven Mistel 1s of 6./KG 200 on the runway at Burg in readiness for an operation in late 1944 or early 1945.

our base at Tirstrup, we had a large, specially built model of the harbour on which were laid scale models of all the ships known to be there.

"The real prize was to be assigned an aircraft carrier. It was felt among the pilots of 6./KG 200 that if the Mistel had been introduced earlier and in greater numbers, its effect against certain pinpoint targets – such as ships – could have been far more decisive. Any ship – no matter what size – if hit by a Mistel would have gone under.

"There were to be 12 aircraft – no reserves – and the idea was to fly to the target in cloud so as to minimise the risk of being spotted by British patrols or flak. Fuel for the outward flight would be drawn from the Ju 88 lower components and the amounts required had been calculated down to the last drop.

"Marker buoys had been laid out to guide us in. We were to adopt a line astern formation. We all wanted the mission to work, because we knew we would be decorated when we got back – there was even talk of the Ritterkreutz.

"Once the attack had been made, the plan was for our Fw 190s to climb as fast as possible to 7000m and make for Stavanger which was

closest point for a safe landing. Both our forces in Norway and the navy had been warned to expect us, and the navy had been briefed to watch out for any pilot unable to make it as far as Stavanger who might have to bail out due to lack of fuel."

Bad weather prevented the attack from going ahead however and it was decided that more Mistels would be needed.

Four fresh combinations were sent from 6./KG 200's Kolberg

station, one flying separately from the other three. The Mustang attack by Righetti and his men was only the first disaster to befall the mission.

Eleven days later, a pair of de Havilland Mosquito Mk.VIs from the RAF's Fighter Experimental Flight attacked the airfield at Tirstrup. Two of the Mistel combinations were destroyed and on the same day Operation Dragon's Lair was cancelled.

The first operational Mistel combinations utilised a Bf 109 F, in this case W.Nr. 10130, paired with a Ju 88 A-4, W.Nr. 10096.

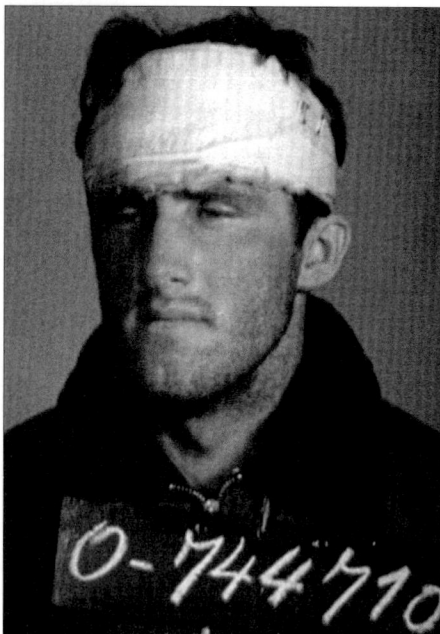

A mugshot of Lt Bernard H Howes taken by the Germans who captured him after his failed attempt to rescue his downed friend Lt Brooks J Liles. *National Archives via Kurt Spence*

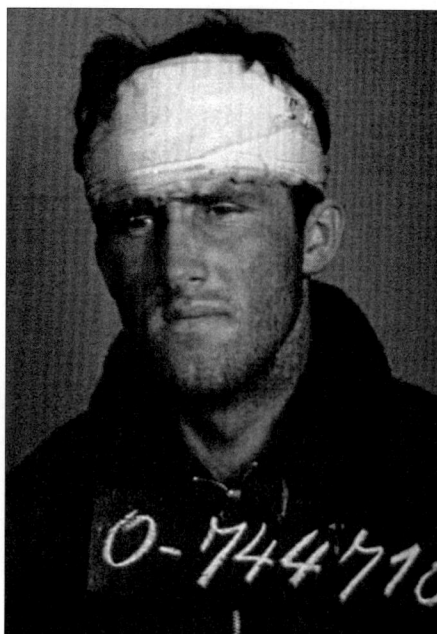

Lt Howes was blinded for two days by the head injury he sustained during the crash of his P-51D. *National Archives via Kurt Spence*

Lt Brooks J Liles, who was captured by the Germans alongside his friend Lt Howes on March 3, 1945. *National Archives via Kurt Spence*

Howes's rescue mission

The pilots of the 55th who shot down the three Mistel combos on February 3 continued to fly front line missions.

Exactly a month after the attack, on March 3, 1st Lt Howes was flying one of seven P-51s taking part in another hunt for targets of opportunity on the ground, this time in the vicinity of Prague, Czechoslovakia. One of the other aircraft was flown by his friend Lt Brooks J Liles. They had trained together, gone overseas together and then ended up in the same unit.

It was about 1pm and the Mustang pilots, organised into Red and Yellow flights, were cruising at 2000ft when they spotted rows of enemy aircraft parked out in the open at Prague-Letnany airport.

Another 343rd pilot, 1st Lt Marvin Satenstein, later reported: "My flight, Red flight, and the remainder of Yellow flight decided to attack it. We did so, making our passes individually.

"On Lt Liles' pass from north to south he was hit on the right side of his engine by light flak from the guns at the southwest end of the field. I observed flames coming from the engine. Lt Liles said that he had been hit.

"I was directly above and behind him and could see that he had the aircraft under control but could not get much power. He flew the aircraft for about three or four miles south of the airdrome where he bellied it in successfully on an open field. I saw Lt Liles get out of the aircraft, just after that it caught fire.

"The remaining six aircraft circled the spot and Lt Howes, Tudor Yellow 3, called over the R/T that he was going to land to try to pick up Lt Liles. After one try, Lt Howes made a successful landing in the same field.

"After discarding their parachutes both Howes and Liles were able to get into the aircraft. It appeared as if it was hard to get the plane started rolling from its parked position. As they started to roll, Howes called, 'Gang, keep your fingers crossed and we'll make it.' The aircraft rose into the air once,

but apparently didn't have enough flying speed because it settled to the ground again.

"Then it bounced into the air, dropped off on its left wing in a stalled attitude and cartwheeled to the left, eventually flattening out. The aircraft caught fire but when I buzzed the wreck I saw both Howes and Liles walking away in an easterly direction towards a large highway. Both pilots looked all right and they waved to me as I passed over them."

Interviewed after the war, Howes said what his colleagues did not see were bursts of small arms fire being directed at his aircraft from the direction of the airport as he tried to take off.

The aircraft hesitated just before take-off and its undercarriage hit a ditch, causing it to crash. Liles had a broken nose and Howes took a blow to the head that rendered him blind for two days. Examining the wreck, Liles saw it had taken a bullet in the throttle quadrant, probably causing a reduction in power during take-off.

A few hours later, both men were taken prisoner by the Luftwaffe and transported to Prague for medical treatment and interrogation. From there, they were moved to Oberursel in Frankfurt, Germany, for further interrogation, then to the nearby Dulag Luft transit PoW camp at Wetzlar and then to Stalag Luft III at Sagan, 100 miles south-east of Berlin.

Finally, they saw out the remainder of the war at Stalag VIIA at Moosburg. With the German war situation worsening dramatically by now, there was no fuel to drive the prisoners to Moosburg so they were forced to walk – a 19-day march. During their two months of imprisonment, the pair subsisted on bread and barley soup. Howes weighed nearly 11.5 stone when he was captured but was only nine stone when he was freed.

Moore, Righetti and Gibbs

Patrick L Moore was promoted to 1st Lieutenant after the Mistel attack and awarded the 1st Oak Leaf Cluster to his Air Medal.

At 2.30pm on April 16, 1945, he was flying P-51D CY-Y 44-14235 'Lil Jan' with Tudor Yellow flight on a bomber escort mission to Salzburg, Austria, with fellow 343rd pilots 1st Lt Lloyd D Boring and 2nd Lt Raymond G Allen. The weather was clear and visibility was unrestricted.

The pilots had completed their main duties and were once again flying at low level looking for targets of opportunity in the area south-east of Munich.

Moore then crashed and was killed. A Missing Air Crew Report was filed on his crash and in a section of the report marked "aircraft was lost, or is believed to have been lost, as a result of: (check only one) enemy aircraft, enemy anti-aircraft, other circumstances as follows", the first two boxes are unchecked and the 'circumstances' are given as "unknown".

Boring reported: "I was flying Tudor Yellow Three, April 16, on a bomber escort and strafing mission. We were driving along over an autobahn south east of Munich at approximately 3500ft when suddenly I noticed a plane in a steep dive ahead of me.

"It went out of view under my wing; about this time someone called over the R/T and reported a plane from White Flight had spun. Coming to the scene of the incident, I dipped my left wing and investigated. It appeared that he had set a large portion of the woods on fire where he went in. I saw no chute."

Another pilot, 1st Lt Walter Strauch, also saw Moore go down. He reported: "I was flying Tudor Red Three on April 16, 1945, on an escort and strafing mission. We were flying along over an autobahn south and east of Munich at 3000ft when suddenly Tudor White Four flipped up a wing to see below, and the plane snapped upside down and started a split-S. Lt Moore tried to roll out and pull up at the same time, and succeeded in doing both, but as he levelled out he hit the ground and exploded. I called Tudor Leader about the accident. I saw no chute."

It is believed Moore crashed while strafing at an extremely low level and was killed. Not long afterwards, two of his colleagues were still in the area, now over Chiemsee, a large lake.

Tudor Yellow Leader had been forced to return to base but Boring and Allen, the remainder of the four-man Tudor Yellow fight, attacked what they later reported as a pair of Blohm & Voss Ha 140 seaplanes, of which only three were ever built,

Lt Patrick L Moore, right, was killed during a strafing mission in April 16, 1945.

nearly eight years earlier in 1937-8. They reported destroying an Ha 140 apiece before returning home.

During the same mission, Tudor Red also lost a pilot. Captain Chester E Coggeshall Jr, 25, had also been flying with Strauch, who was Tudor Red 3, strafing an airfield at Ainring west of Salzburg, when his aircraft suffered flak damage and he was forced to make a belly landing. His fate is recorded in Chapter 13.

The following day it was Lt Col Elwyn Righetti's 30th birthday. He had been promoted to commanding officer of the 55th Fighter Group on February 22, 19 days after the Mistel attack, but still flew missions with the callsign 'Windsor'. This time he was flying P-51D CL-M 44-72227 'Katydid' looking for an aerodrome to attack near Dresden with his wingman, 1st Lt Carroll D Henry.

Henry later reported: "I was flying Acorn White 2 position off Lt Col Righetti's wing. We broke and started looking for aerodromes. One was called out at 10 o'clock. We let down under about 5/10 clouds with base at 5000ft and made one 360° port turn at 3000ft. Windsor called in and told the rest of White flight to orbit while he went down and checked for flak. I then called and asked if I could come down with him and he said 'yes'.

"We were going across the northern edge of the aerodrome at about 500ft from east to west. One Fw 190 was landing at the time from north-east to south-west, and he told me to go in after it since I was between him and the aerodrome.

"I made the pass and drove past the field on the deck for about three miles avoiding flak. I then came back around and made a pass on a large field, which was a large dispersal area about one half mile north-west of the aerodrome. I pulled up and was orbiting the aerodrome again when I saw a P-51 streaming coolant as he was making a pass on the field from west to east.

"I called him and told him. He called in saying, 'This is Windsor and I am hit bad, oil pressure dropping. I can't make it back. I have enough ammo for one more pass.'

"He then made one more pass from west to east, destroying a Fw 190. I called him telling him that I was tacking on. He acknowledged saying that he was heading out on 270°. I was about 3000ft and overran him due to excess speed gained while letting down. He was at six o'clock to me and I rolled out on 270°. I chopped my throttle and when I looked back I couldn't locate him.

"About 30 seconds later he called in saying 'I broke my nose but I am okay, I got nine today, tell my family I am okay, and it has been swell working with you.' I made

Lt Richard G Gibbs, left, was the only one of the four Mustang pilots of February 3's Tudor White flight who saw out the war alive and free.

E. G. RIGHETTI

Lt Col Righetti was shot down the day after Moore, April 17, 1945, and survived the crash, radioing his wingman to tell him he was all right. He was never heard from again and it is speculated that he was lynched by German civilians.

one orbit and couldn't locate him on the ground. Being by myself I then headed out."

Righetti is believed to have been hit by flak before being forced to make a belly landing. He survived the crash and radioed Lt Henry to say he was all right. After that, he was never heard from again and his body was never found. It is speculated, based on anecdotal evidence, that as he climbed from his wrecked aircraft he was surrounded by a crowd of angry civilians who lynched him.

The only one of the four men who engaged 6./KG 200's Mistels on February 3, 1945, to survive the war without being captured or killed was Lt Richard G Gibbs. He was promoted to 1st lieutenant in March/April 1945 and destroyed a pair of Fw 190s on the day Righetti was killed.

Three weeks after the war's end however, on May 29, 1945, he had a close shave in his P-51 when, according to an East Suffolk Police report, he was "stunting in mid-air and collided with another plane". He bailed out and came down safely near Chediston Hall. The report notes he did suffer a sprained ankle, however. His aircraft was completely destroyed.

4

THE FATAL MISTAKE OF LOTHAR SIEBER

❖

March 1, 1945: Bachem-Werk M23 test flight

The career of talented Luftwaffe pilot Lothar Sieber was on
the rise when charges of drinking on duty saw him arrested
and stripped of rank. To redeem himself, he undertook one
hazardous mission after the next until on March 1, 1945,
he took on the most dangerous of them all...

Having been interested in flying from a young age, 14-year-old Lothar Sieber attended a rally in his home city of Dresden in 1936 and found himself shaking hands with First World War flying ace and recently appointed Reich Aviation Minister Hermann Göring.

It was an inspirational moment, and afterwards Sieber was determined to become a pilot in the newly formed Luftwaffe. Four years later, as soon as he was old enough, he signed up and before long he not only qualified as a pilot but also specialised in large bombers, mastering a wide variety of aircraft including captured Allied examples such as Boeing B-17s and Soviet Tupolev TB-3s.

He was promoted to Leutnant and given his first command in 1942 – a meteoric rise. His world fell apart in February 1943, however, when he was caught drinking on duty. He was demoted to ordinary pilot and sentenced to four months in prison. His father wrote to Göring himself, explaining the circumstances and pleading for clemency, and the sentence was reduced to six weeks' close arrest – but the demotion stuck.

Back on duty, Sieber threw himself into his work as never before. In April 1944, he was involved in trials of the Arado Ar 232 A, which was designed for short-distance take-off on rough terrain using its centreline row of 10 smaller wheels mounted beneath the fuselage. He also carried out rocket-assisted take-off trials

using the aircraft and was so confident of his skills that at one point he looped the loop in a Junkers Ju 52. In August 1944 he was posted to I./KG 200.

While Sieber's quest to regain his original rank continued, work was going on elsewhere which would ultimately ensure that he never succeeded.

Rise of the snake

It was during Sieber's period of close arrest that the Allied bomber fleets began causing disastrous damage to German cities and industry. The Luftwaffe seemed unable to stop them by conventional means, so a number of unconventional ideas were examined by the Reichsluftfahrtministerium (RLM) – the German Air Ministry.

Test pilot Lothar Sieber speaks with a man identified in most sources as Erich Bachem shortly before his first and only flight in BP-20 M23. The fully prepared rocket-powered vertical take-off aircraft awaits him in the distance.

The first manned test of the Bachem BP-20 was carried out using the M1 glider towed by a Heinkel He 111. It took off from a trolley with Flugzeugführer Erich Klöckner at the controls but was destroyed on landing, Klöckner having already bailed out.

Lothar Sieber was an outstanding pilot but had his career ruined by a charge of drinking on duty. He was looking for any opportunity to redeem himself and regain his original rank.

An aircraft was needed which could climb at high speed to intercept the bombers as they appeared, inflict maximum damage, and then return quickly and safely to earth.

The idea of a vertical take-off rocket-powered interceptor had originated with a 27-year-old Dr Wernher von Braun in 1939. Already working on a number of rocket projects for the German military, he had submitted a proposal to the RLM outlining a fighter that could be launched vertically from the back of a lorry, up to an altitude of 26,250ft in 53 seconds before switching to horizontal flight.

The aircraft's main engine would then cut out and a smaller secondary unit would take over. When the mission was over, the aircraft would land on a skid. The RLM turned

Erich Bachem and famous test pilot Hanna Reitsch on July 17, 1938, at an air show in Kassel-Waldau. Bachem, then the technical director of Fieseler, oversaw the day's events. Six years later he would be responsible for building one of the most dangerous aircraft ever flown.

Natter airframes under construction within the cramped confines of the Bachem-Werk factory.

von Braun's report over to Heinkel, the company already responsible for building the world's first liquid rocket powered aircraft, the He 176, for assessment.

The firm's development team was sceptical about the idea, suggesting that the engine envisioned by von Braun would not be powerful enough, its fuel would run out too quickly, and there was no tactical benefit to having a very short range high-altitude fighter.

The proposal was not rejected however, and was next handed to Gerhard Fieseler Works, which carried out some preliminary work on a vertical take-off aircraft under the designation Fi 166. Fieseler's engineers, under the leadership of the firm's technical director Erich Bachem, developed the idea in two directions – a pure vertical-launch rocket fighter design referred to as 'Höhenjäger I', and a 'rider and horse' design, where a rocket would be used to boost a jet-powered aircraft to high altitude, 'Höhenjäger II'.

This was purely a paper exercise, however, as Fieseler was busy with other projects such as expanding production of the highly successful Fi 156 Storch. Von Braun resubmitted his idea in 1941, only to have it finally rejected outright by the RLM a few months later.

By now, the RLM was already backing a different team, led by Alexander Lippisch, building a different rocket interceptor – the Messerschmitt Me 163 Komet.

Work on the Me 163 was slow and disagreements between Lippisch and Willy Messerschmitt led to the former leaving the company in 1943. When the bombs started to fall on Germany in earnest, the Komet was woefully behind schedule and beset with teething problems.

It was also complex and at best offered only four minutes and 11 seconds of powered flight at full throttle.

A requirement was therefore issued in 1944 for an even smaller fighter that could be built from basic materials such as wood and

powered by a Walter 109-509 liquid rocket unit – the same power plant as that fitted to the Me 163. It would also have to be capable of being flown by a pilot who had received only minimal training, since all qualified fighter pilots were urgently needed by the front line units.

Meanwhile, Bachem had left Fieseler in 1941 with the intention of setting up his own business. Bachem-Werk GmbH was formally established on February 10, 1942, at Waldsee, Upper Swabia, by Bachem and his business partner, former Fieseler test pilot Willy Fiedler. The new company specialised in wooden aircraft parts and was initially kept busy with contract jobs – eventually designing and making parts for the Dornier Do 335 Pfeil and Heinkel He 162. It may also have manufactured parts for Fieseler's Fi 103 V-1 flying bomb.

The only uniquely Bachem aircraft at this time was an ultralight known as the Lerche or 'Lark'.

The unmanned M17 test vehicle was brightly painted for visibility, with asymmetrical stripes painted on its wings so that its orientation could be better discerned from photographs of the launch.

Fired off on December 29, M17 flew vertically as planned but its parachute detached on the way down and it was destroyed when it hit the ground.

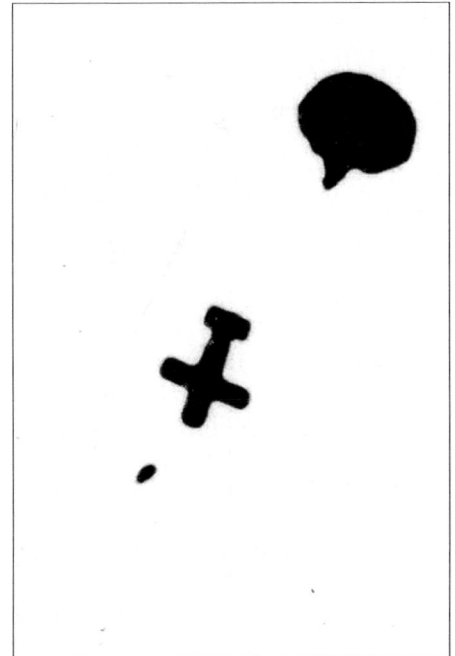

The Natter was designed with a disposable nose but it was intended that the rest of the fuselage would float safely back down on a parachute once its mission had been completed.

Camouflage netting clings to the tail of the M23 vehicle on the morning of March 1, 1945, as the aircraft is prepared for Lothar Sieber's test flight.

Netting still in place, ground crew work to fill M23's tank with C-Stoff – the chemical which, when combined with a second chemical, T-Stoff, produced the violent reaction which provided the rocket engine's thrust.

When the RLM requirement was issued for a small wooden rocket fighter, Bachem found himself in an excellent position to draw up a proposal that could successfully fulfil it. He said later that he vaguely remembered seeing von Braun's proposal during his days at Fieseler and resolved to design something similar, which he named 'Natter' or 'Snake'.

He began with a rough sketch of something resembling a manned missile on July 16, 1944. The parachute-wearing pilot lay prone within a cigar-shaped fuselage, a rocket projectile weapon ahead of him in the 'aircraft's' nose.

Further design drawings fleshed out this concept and it was given the factory designation BP-20-01. Bachem wrote up a terse outline of his design's purpose in a document headed 'Projekt Natter': "Annihilation of enemy aircraft especially bombers by bringing up a gunner within the immediate vicinity of the enemy and discharging rocket projectiles at him with the smallest possible amount of manoeuvring and propellant.

"No self-destruction of the pilot, on the contrary, armoured protection of him. Smallest possible production cost, maximum use of wooden parts, reduction of iron. No burden on standard aircraft industry. Exploitation of the large, partly free, timber resource. Repeated use of the most critical airframe and propulsion unit parts by parachute recovery.

"Little requirement of the pilot, due to the omission of a normal landing. Little ground input. Little transport cost. Easy transferability. Good camouflage potential."

With Bachem providing the outline, the project's chief designer was Dutchman Henri Frans Bethbeder. At an early stage, it was envisioned that the Natter's nose would house nineteen 55mm R4M rocket projectiles but no firm decision was made on armament. As for the rest of the aircraft, several design variations were worked on simultaneously.

The overall cost of the Natter was expected to be about 1/50th of that for a normal fighter aircraft and it was further anticipated that full production could begin within six

months. By September the favoured design had shifted to that of a manned rocket aircraft, BP-20-09, rather than a manned missile – the pilot now seated rather than prone. The single rocket engine in the rear of the fuselage was augmented by a pair of disposable Schmidding SG 34 solid fuel boosters attached on to each side of the aircraft.

The launch sequence was to involve the pilot bracing himself against padded head and back rests and gripping handles on either side of the rear nose frame. On the left handle was the button to fire the boosters.

Once this was pressed, the Natter would rise under the control of a basic autopilot and after 10 seconds it would be at an altitude of 4000ft and a speed of 550mph. The exhausted boosters would then automatically detach and the Walter engine would take over.

Within another 50 seconds, the Natter would reach the same altitude as the bomber formations. The pilot would then turn off the autopilot, grab the control column and bring the aircraft around in a shallow curve to line up a target.

At a distance of 300m he would fire the Natter's weapons at the bomber. The Walter engine would then run out of fuel and the pilot would put it into a dive. Pulling out at low level, the pilot would activate a mechanism to detach the aircraft's nose, which would fall away, and he would then be catapulted out by the sudden deceleration – activating his parachute.

The Natter's fuselage, minus the nose, would descend to earth on its own parachute, ready to be refurbished and reused.

Tendering for the RLM requirement had, however, ended in August and Bachem's early design was the one submitted for consideration. It was up against advanced designs from three much larger firms – Messerschmitt, Junkers and Heinkel.

Friends in high places
In early September, the RLM awarded Heinkel a contract for 20 prototypes of its P 1077 vertical take-off rocket aircraft design – later known as the 'Julia'. Messerschmitt and Junkers, which had both tendered horizontal take-off designs, and the Natter were seemingly out of the race.

Bachem refused to accept this rejection. He took his idea to SS-Obergruppenführer Hans Jüttner and Sturmbannführer Otto Skorzeny who, excited by it, took it

Fully fuelled and ready to fly. M23 hangs from its launch ramp awaiting only its pilot. Sieber's padded head rest, attached to the cockpit hatch lid, can clearly be seen.

Lothar Sieber, having scrambled up a precarious wooden gangplank, grips a handle on the nose of M23 as he struggles to manoeuvre himself into the cockpit.

With nothing between him and a plunge to the ground, Sieber clambers into the Natter's cockpit legs first, assisted by ground crew.

directly to the leader of the Waffen-SS, Heinrich Himmler. Himmler granted Bachem an audience and offered him the full support of the SS for his "war deciding device".

Now under pressure from the SS, in mid-September the RLM was forced to give Bachem a contract for 15 BP-20 aircraft. Himmler sent some of his own people to oversee the project too – SS-Obersturmführer Heinz Flessner, who led a team of 120 Waffen-SS construction workers seconded to Bachem-Werk, and SS-Obersturmführer Gerhard Schaller.

The Natter launch procedure called for its Walter rocket engine to be ignited first. The thrust produced was insufficient, on its own, to lift the aircraft so it produced a dense cloud of smoke instead, completely enveloping the machine.

Solid-fuel boosters ignited, M23 roars skywards with Lothar Sieber attempting to hold the control column in the neutral position, despite a 3G load on his arms. The production Natter was intended to have an autopilot for this stage of the flight but this was not yet ready on March 1.

The first Natter V1 prototype was finished on October 4, 1944, and on October 28 it was given the official RLM designation 8-349, later Ba 349, though this name was seldom used at the time; the aircraft being commonly referred to as the BP-20. Construction was well under way on the 15 aircraft 'ordered' by the RLM. The Natter's basic dimensions now featured a stubby wingspan of 11ft 9in, a short fuselage of 19ft 2in and a fuselage width of 2ft 11in.

Various different armaments were discussed including a pair of MK 108 30mm cannon, a battery of 28 R4M rockets and a cluster of 32 single-shot 30mm cannon barrels, but again no satisfactory conclusion was reached.

On November 3, a manned gliding trial took place with an engineless Natter airframe designated M1. It was towed along the runway behind a Heinkel He 111 on a take-off trolley with Flugzeugführer Erich Klöckner at the controls.

A Junkers Ju 87 was used as an observation platform. All three aircraft became airborne at around 4pm but Klöckner struggled to control the M1 until he moved a trim weight inside it, altering the centre of gravity. Even so, he was forced to bail out when he realised that the aircraft could not be brought into a normal towed position and therefore its parachutes could not be deployed.

The M1 landed behind the He 111, twisted, detached and then span away, coming apart in the process.

A second glider, the M3, was fitted with an undercarriage so it could be properly landed and reused. It was completed on November 20 and test-flown by Klöckner on December 14. Again, he was forced to bail out but this time the Natter glider landed safely without its pilot.

The first attempted vertical take-off test of the Natter was on December 18 at Heuberg – a military training area about 40 miles west and slightly north of Waldsee – using prototype M21. While the boosters went off as planned, the release clamps failed and the aircraft was engulfed in flames and burned out on the ground.

On December 22, 1944, the first successful launch took place with prototype M16. It flew to about 230ft before tipping over onto its side. It crashed 5250ft away. That same day, a new test pilot arrived at Bachem-Werk – Lothar Sieber.

Last will and testament

Sieber was recommended for the job by Sturmbannführer Skorzeny who had met the 22-year-old after he had gone behind enemy lines in an Ar 232 to rescue 23 of his KG 200 comrades encircled by the Soviets in Ukraine. It was a close-run thing. Despite being under heavy fire, Sieber managed to get the transport aircraft off the ground and flew it at low level all the way back to base.

This feat earned him a personal letter of commendation from KG 200 commander Oberst Werner Baumbach and the Iron Cross 1st Class. After further heroics on the front line, Skorzeny recommended him for another bravery decoration, the German Cross in gold. He also offered him the opportunity of promotion to oberleutnant if he would undertake a mission for the SS – fly Bachem's new SS-sponsored rocket-powered interceptor.

After arriving at Waldsee, Sieber watched several vertical take-off trials of Natter prototypes, including the successful test of version M22 on February 25, 1945, where a dummy pilot was fired into the sky and then floated safely down on a parachute after the nose separation was activated automatically. The fuselage parachute also activated but traces of fuel left in the Walter engine's tanks ignited and M22 burned out.

The first manned test, Sieber's first flight in the Natter, was scheduled for March 1. Asked how he felt about the prospect, he apparently replied: "In the course of this war I have already done riskier things, let me worry about this. I look upon the testing of the device as a self-imposed task that I would like to accomplish and I firmly believe in a successful outcome."

Despite this bullish attitude, he still prepared a last will and testament on February 28 leaving all his worldly goods to his fiancée Gertrud Nauditt, four years his senior.

The day of the launch saw grey skies over the Heuberg launch site and mist on the ground which began to clear as the morning wore

With Lothar Sieber dead, the Natter test programme reverted to unmanned testing. Here, vehicle M52 is winched into position on a newly designed single-rail tower.

on. M23 was the Natter prepared for the launch and its design had been significantly altered from M22.

It had a safety chute to decelerate the fuselage as the pilot bailed out – in place of a parachute to 'rescue' the fuselage, which was to be sacrificed on this occasion – rudders were installed in the tail and the elevons were increased in size by 20%.

There was a pitot tube on the right wing for monitoring air speed and other sensors were fitted to monitor the aircraft's performance. There was no autopilot – the control column was fitted with a slight depression of 2° but otherwise Sieber was required to simply hold it in the neutral position during take-off.

Take-off was scheduled for 11am and while final checks were being carried out on M23, Sieber stood on a low hill overlooking the launch site. He wore his full bulky flight suit and helmet. At some point he received final words of advice or encouragement from both Erich Bachem and Willy Fiedler.

Close to 11am, he walked over to the launch tower and climbed vertically to a steeply angled wooden gangplank which took him up to the leading edge of M23's left wing. A trio of ground crew helped him awkwardly scramble around the outside of the machine and into the cockpit. Going in legs first, he lay on his back in the seat and buckled on his parachute before fastening his seat belts. He put on his oxygen mask and the canopy hatch was closed by the crew.

They climbed down from the tower and retreated to a safe distance before signal rockets were launched to tell Sieber that it was time to start the Walter engine. This was allowed to build up to full thrust – a cloud of smoke enveloping the Natter in the process – before Sieber ignited the four boosters with a bright flash visible through the haze.

The Natter's locking mechanism released flawlessly and Sieber's machine shot upwards. After climbing to about 330ft, the aircraft began to curve onto its back at an angle of about 30° – then the canopy hatch flew off. Something had gone badly wrong but the aircraft continued its ascent to about 5000ft, whereupon it disappeared into a bank of low-lying cloud.

Just 15 seconds into its climb, the Natter's engine stopped and

Another view of M52 attached to its pole launcher – essentially a straight tree trunk shorn of branches.

Americans examine one of four damaged production Ba 349 A-1 Natter aircraft captured in Austria.

it rolled right over on to its back before entering a nose dive. Several kilometres from the launch site, Lothar Sieber's first and last flight in the Natter ended when it crashed vertically into the ground. It had been in the air for less than a minute.

The final moments

After waiting an hour in the hope that Sieber had parachuted to safety and would come walking back, the Bachem team went in search of the crash site. Writing several years later, Bachem himself described the scene: "We found the machine completely destroyed. The pilot had made no attempt to escape. Of our comrade we found only the left hand with a piece of forearm and a left leg that was ripped off below the knee."

The crater left by the impact was 5m deep and when it was excavated a small shard of Sieber's skull was found. What little remained of him was buried with full military honours in the cemetery at Nusplingen.

The investigation carried out by Bachem-Werk afterwards had little hard evidence to go on but attention was concentrated on the canopy hatch that had broken away from the aircraft during its ascent. It was recovered intact not far from the launch site and the latch meant to fasten it in place appeared to be bent.

Over the next few days a sequence of events was pieced together. It was suggested that for the first few seconds after take-off, Sieber's body would have been subjected to forces of about 3G – pinning him back in

his seat and applying backwards force to his arms.

Since he was holding the control column, this would account for the aircraft curving steadily on to its back. As the aircraft became increasingly upside down, Sieber's body would have been pushed up against the hatch – his seatbelt having enough 'give' to allow this to happen. The latch might well have then given way, causing the hatch to be caught by the slipstream and spin away.

The pilot's headrest was a part of the hatch so when the hatch suddenly parted company with the aircraft, Sieber's head would have been violently flung back 25cm, against the wooden rear wall of the cockpit. This was likely to have concussed him, rendered

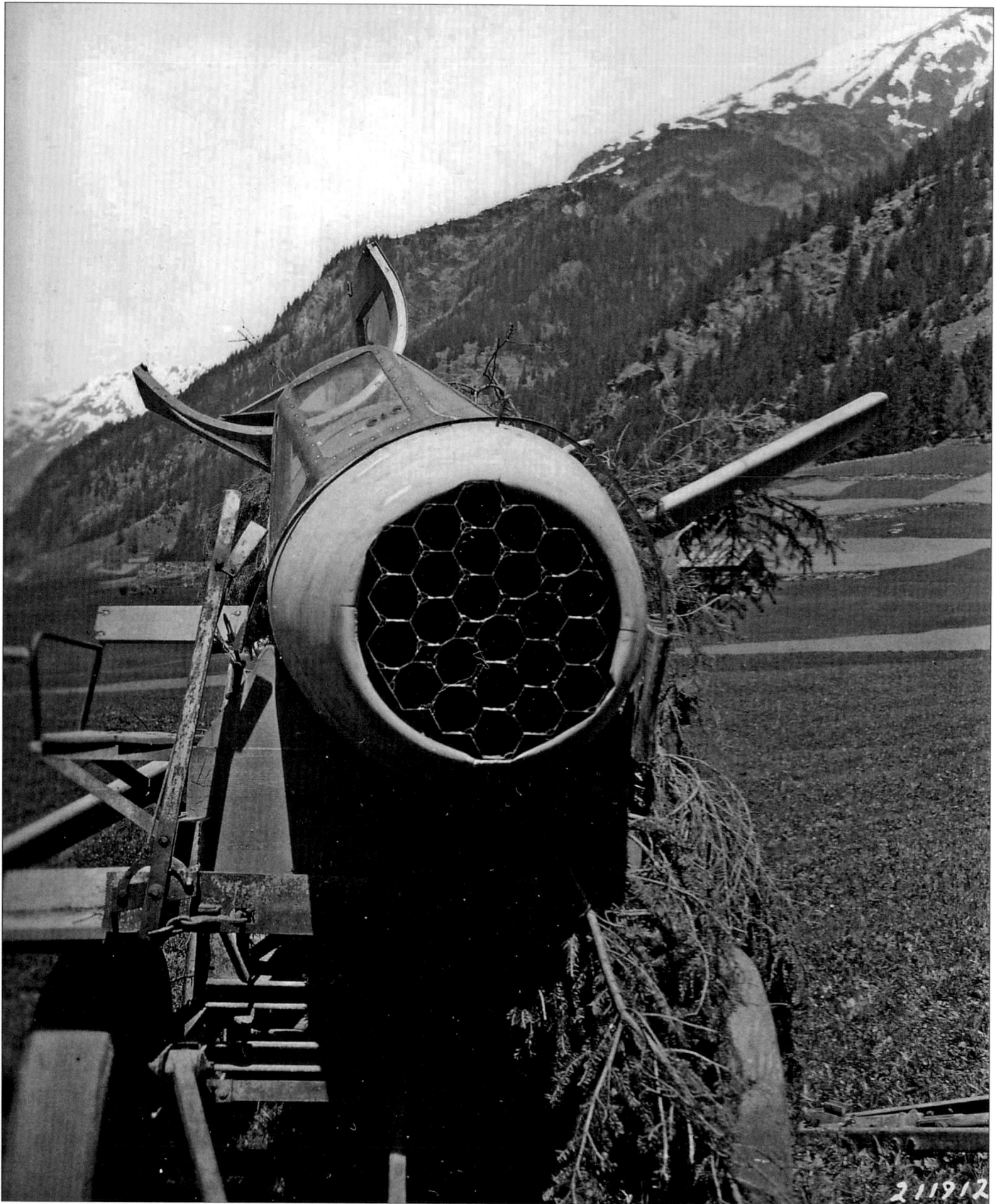

A frontal view of a Natter captured by the Americans, showing the honeycomb Föhn rocket launcher finally chosen as the aircraft's armament.

him unconscious or even broken his neck.

It was considered possible that a dazed Sieber might have shut down the rocket engine himself after 15 seconds but it was equally possible that the odd angle of ascent might have caused air bubbles in the Walter engine's fuel, causing it to cut out.

Either way, the Bachem team felt they had been pressured into conducting a manned launch too early. It seemed as though Sieber's accident might have been avoided if an autopilot had been available to prevent the control column from moving.

This was small consolation to his family and fiancée.

The infamous Natter

The first Natter flown with automatic guidance, M14, flew on March 16. After a successful take-off, it went into a spiral and was destroyed after its safety chute failed to prevent a hard landing.

Seven more vertical launches were carried out from the tower after Sieber's death and plans were advanced to bring the Natter into service under the code name Krokus. This was chosen because the crocus blooms in March, when the attacks on bombers had very optimistically been expected to begin.

A mobile pole launcher was designed for use with the Ba 349 A-1 and a test machine, M52, was successfully fired from it some time after April 5. Ten production Natters, still regularly referred to as BP-20s, were under construction during late March and into early April. The final armament of a nose-mounted honeycomb type launcher for 24 Henschel Hs 297 Föhn rockets was fitted.

A handful were completed by mid-April when French ground forces entered the vicinity of the Bachem-Werk factory. Attempts were made to put the Natters into operation but in reality the personnel involved were only just able to keep the aircraft away from the advancing Allies by driving them around on the back of trucks.

Four lightly damaged Natters and the personnel accompanying them were captured at St Leonhard in Austria on or around May 6, 1945.

After the war, Bachem's factory was closed by the French and the firm was dissolved, its holdings being sold to the Wolf Hirth company. Bachem tried various subsequent business ventures but died in 1960 after a long illness. Willy Fiedler got a job working for the American military and after some initial involvement with Northrop, ended up working for Lockheed. He helped to design submarine-launched missiles such as Polaris, and died in California in 1998.

5

YAKS OVER KÖNIGSBERG

❖

March 31, 1945: Normandie-Niemen joins the last battle for East Prussia's capital

Général Charles de Gaulle sent a Free French Air Force
group to serve alongside the Soviet Air Force on the
Eastern Front in November 1942. This was Groupe
Normandie. By 1945 the Frenchmen were battle-hardened
Yak-flying veterans about to face their sternest test – the
advance on Königsberg.

Königsberg was a fortified city that marked the furthest eastern extent of the old German Empire. It was the capital of East Prussia and an important port on the Baltic Sea. Since 1941 it had been on the front line of the war against the Soviet Union – being repeatedly bombed by the Soviet Air Force.

Being close to the departure point for Germany's invasion of first Poland and then the Soviet Union, the city was a centre for slavery and a collection point for looted treasures from the east.

Within and around the city were about 85,000 Polish and Soviet slaves as well as Allied prisoners of war, working in labour camps.

The summer of 1944 had also seen two devastating night raids on the city by the RAF, which destroyed the historic old city, gutted the cathedral and severely damaged the castle and other large civic buildings.

Nevertheless, Königsberg kept huge fortified positions on its landward side that remained untouched by aerial attack. These included three defensive rings – the outermost consisting of 12 fortresses linked by subterranean tunnels and concrete structures, a secondary ring around the outskirts of the city itself and the main city fortress in the centre.

All three were protected by an impressive array of anti-tank positions and structures, barricades and minefields. In addition, there were a number of other heavily fortified positions both within and immediately outside the city.

Manning all these positions were five full divisions of German infantry – 130,000 men all together.

There was also strong support for Königsberg in the air. As of January 11, 1945, Luftflotte 6, based in East Prussia and western Poland, was the strongest Luftwaffe formation to be found anywhere on the Eastern Front.

Luftflotte 6 boasted JG 51 with 108 Bf 109s (78 serviceable), and 86 (70) Bf 109s of JG 52. It also had two night fighter units, NJG 5 and NJG 100, with 94 (76) aircraft between them, a mixture of Bf 109s and Ju 88s.

KG 55 was still equipped with 14 (10) He 111 bombers, and perhaps most importantly Luftflotte 6 had three large ground-attack units – SG 1, SG 3 and SG 77. Between them they had 294 (262) Fw 190 fighter-bombers which could also serve as pure fighters if need be, although in doing so they were handicapped by the weight of their extra armour. In addition, 10./SG 77 still had 19 (16) Ju 87s.

There was also the night ground-attack unit NSGr. 4 with 60 (47) Ju 87s and Si 104s, the maritime reconnaissance unit SAGr. 126 with 21 (11) Ar 196 floatplanes and nine (six) Bv 138 flying boats, strategic reconnaissance units FAGr. 1, FAGr. 3, AGr. 22, AGr. Nacht and AGr. 122 with 124 (88) Ju 188s, Me 410s, Ju 88s and Do 217s, and tactical reconnaissance units NAGr. 2, 3, 4, 8 and 15 with 159 (126) Bf 109s and Fw 189s.

Finally, Luftflotte 6 could also call on a single depleted transport unit – I./TG 3 with 36 (27) Ju 52s. Overall this amounted to 1024 (817) aircraft, 582 (486) of them fighters.

A Yakovlev Yak-3M painted in the colours of the Normandie-Niemen regiment. Deliveries of the original Yak-3 began in late 1944 but Normandie pilots were still flying the Yak-9 until the beginning of 1945. *Sebastian Tenguy*

Groupe de Chasse 3

At the beginning of 1945, the front line was less than 50 miles to the east of Königsberg. Ranged against the German forces in East Prussia were more than 1.6 million Soviet troops commanded by Ivan Chernyakhovsky – at 38, he was the youngest commander of an entire front during the Second World War.

His forces included large tank armies and four air armies – the 1st, 3rd, 4th and 15th. Each of these comprised of more than a thousand aircraft.

Within the 1st Air Army was a highly unusual unit. The Free French Air Force's Groupe de Chasse 3 (GC3) had been sent to Russia in November 1942 at the behest of Général Charles de Gaulle. The Free French leader set up the National Committee in 1941 as a sort of war cabinet and was determined that the Soviet Union should give official recognition to Free France.

Part of this was offering military assistance. Soviet leader Joseph Stalin was cautious at first but with the formation of the National Committee opted to encourage mutual military assistance between the two nations.

De Gaulle signed the order forming Groupe de Chasse 3 on September 1, 1942. Shortly afterwards it was agreed that the unit should also use the title 'Normandie' so its members would always remember that region of France and the fact it was under German occupation.

By early December the unit's pilots and equipment had been incorporated into the Soviet Air Force and on January 19, 1943, its first fighters, six Yak-1Ms, were delivered.

The unit's first operational mission, involving 13 of the new Yak-1Ms, took place on March 22, 1943, and its first aerial victory was on April 5; Lieutenants Albert Préziosi and Albert Durand shot down a Fw 190 each in the Smolenski area. Both were killed in action later that year.

Having started out as a single escadrille or squadron, Normandie expanded to two in August 1943 – named Rouen and Le Havre.

After eight months of incredibly fierce fighting on the front line, nine of the groupe's original 15 pilots had been killed in combat, including its commandant Jean Tulasne. And of the 23 replacement pilots received between May 10 and the end of November 1943, 12 had been killed.

The 38 pilots had accumulated 72 claimed victories between them, however. Up to March 1944, this total increased to 84.

Now the groupe was expanded to a regiment, with third and fourth squadrons being added – Caen and Cherbourg. The Yak-1Ms were

German soldiers man a Pak 40 75mm anti-tank gun as part of Königsberg's outer defences in early 1945. The sign reads 'We will defend Königsberg'. When the air war recommenced on the Eastern Front on January 13, 1945, many of Normandie-Niemen's missions were flown in defence of bombers heading for targets in and around the city.

Another defensive position beside the Tower of the Don in Königsberg. The city's many historic fortifications and strongpoints were stormed and captured or destroyed during the final battle which saw the city attacked from all sides, including from the air, in April 1945.

The commandant of Normandie-Niemen from December 12, 1944 to the end of the war was Lieutenant-Colonel Louis Delfino. He was a highly experienced pilot who had joined the Armée de l'Air in 1931 and by the beginning of 1945 had racked up 12 aerial victories, though 10 of them were shared with other pilots.

Sous-Lieutenant Jacques André was one of Normandie's most successful pilots. During the third day of the Soviet push along the 3rd Belorussian Front he shot down four Focke-Wulf Fw 190s single handed and claimed another 'probable' in the Gumbinnen/Kussen area.

Captain Gabriel Mertzisen was among the first Normandie pilots to score a victory during the opening stages of the Soviet East Prussian Offensive, shooting down a Messerschmitt Bf 109 on January 14 east of Insterburg.

replaced by Yak-9Ds and more front line combat quickly followed during what became known as the regiment's second campaign.

It was during this campaign that Stalin ordered the regiment, which was operated under Soviet control and frequently made appearances in Soviet propaganda publications such as Pravda, to call itself Normandie-Niemen. This was to commemorate its role in the fighting to liberate the Niemen river – traditionally regarded by Germany as the marker of its true eastern border.

Deliveries of a remarkable new lightweight fighter, the Yak-3, began on August 17, 1944, gradually replacing the Yak-9Ds which continued to be used in combat until the end of the year.

By the beginning of 1945, the regiment had amassed 201 claimed 'kills' but had been reduced to just three squadrons as a result of personnel shortages. It had been stationed at Gross-Kalweitchen on the southern fringes of Lithuania and close to East Prussia since the end of November 1944.

Little flying was done during the first 12 days of 1945 but Normandie was moved to Dopenen, closer to the front. January 13 saw the beginning of Chernyakhovsky's East Prussian Offensive. His vast armies, including Normandie-Niemen, were unleashed against Germany's battered forces along the northern sector of the Eastern Front – and drove towards Königsberg.

First five days

Dense fog shrouded the region on the first day of the offensive, and those Normandie-Niemen patrols that were sent up had to turn back within minutes of takeoff.

The fog cleared by the following day, and at 1pm on January 14, a patrol from the 1st Escadrille encountered a pair of Bf 109s near Gumbinnen, about 80 miles directly east of Königsberg.

The Germans attempted to turn away but the Frenchmen followed in hot pursuit. Sous-Lieutenant René Martin hit one with his 20mm cannon and it began to burn before abruptly breaking up in mid-air. The second dived to extreme low altitude as Martin turned to fire on it too – attempting to lose him by hedge hopping. Instead, the pilot brought himself into range for both Sous-Lieutenant Pierre Dechanet and Aspirant Lionel Menut, who each scored several hits on his machine and watched as he ploughed into the ground.

Three more Bf 109s were then engaged over a nearby railway line but although Martin and Sous-Lieutenant Roger Versini both claimed hits, the result was inconclusive.

A squad from the 3rd Escadrille found four Bf 109s near Insterburg but lost them. Captaine Gabriel Mertzisen found them again but became separated from the rest of the squad. In spite of this, he doggedly followed them unnoticed until he got close enough to take the rearmost Messerschmitt by surprise and fired into it from point blank range, rapidly destroying it.

While this was going on, the rest of his squad encountered 15 Fw 190s north of Gumbinnen and shot two of them down before disengaging. Late in the afternoon,

The Yak-3 of French ace Sous-Lieutenant Roger Sauvage, photographed shortly after the war's end. His aircraft shows his 16 'kills' in three rows of five with one more to the right just behind the cockpit canopy.

An ace with only two victories. Sous-Lieutenant Francois 'The Baron' de Geoffre also contributed to five more, giving him a tally of seven under the French scoring system. De Geoffre gained a reputation for getting into scrapes during the war and survived several near-death experiences – particularly when he was shot down and landed in the Friesches Haff.

Sharing two 'kills' with Jacques André, Aspirant Roger Penverne was promoted to Sous-Lieutenant shortly before his death on February 4, 1945, aged 27. He had been engaged in a battle with 12 Fw 190s and his aircraft was last seen going down in the Pillau region. His body was never recovered.

as darkness was falling, yet another Bf 109 was downed, this time by Aspirant Charles Miquel. Returning to base, Miquel forgot to put his undercarriage down and landed his aircraft on its belly instead.

Snow fell on January 15, which reduced patrols to a minimum, but on the 16th Sous-Lieutenants Jacques André, Francois de Geoffre and Pierre Lorillon, and Aspirant Roger Penverne, happened upon 12 Fw 190 fighter-bombers and attacked immediately. They got one each in the ensuing battle.

Another dozen Fw 190s were encountered by the pilots of the 1st Escadrille. Aspirant Léon Ougloff fired into one which seemed to release a shower of small metal fragments. Sous-Lieutenant Roger Sauvage hit and fatally damaged another at close range which then dived into the ground. Then he did the same to a second, and Ougloff claimed another blown up in mid-air.

On the way back to base, one of the 1st's pilots, Captaine Marc Charras, spotted some Pe-2s being attacked by Bf 109s. Also engaged in the battle were some P-39 Airacobras. Charras paired up with one of these to jointly claim a Bf 109.

The 2nd fought still more Fw 190s, with Sous-Lieutenant Georges Lemare opening fire on one – only to see the pilot immediately eject his canopy and take to his parachute. The German's wingman was shot down by Aspirant Georges Henry. At this point, Miquel was seen going down, his engine struggling and billowing white smoke.

The leader of Normandie-Niemen himself, Commandant Louis Delfino, and four other pilots then caught a large formation of Fw 190s flying at low level by surprise. Delfino dived into them and used his cannon on one at very close range, causing pieces of the aircraft to fly off and hit his left wing. What was left of the Fw 190 fell to earth.

André, attacking close by, had a similarly frightening experience when the Fw 190 he was firing into suddenly erupted into a ball of fire right in front of him. Quick reflexes narrowly prevented the resulting large chunks of debris from crashing through his aircraft's canopy.

On a second patrol towards the end of the day, André and three comrades engaged another group of around 20 Fw 190 fighter-bombers. Again, André poured fire into one at close range but this time it simply dropped its bombs, peeled off and crashed into the ground.

Aspirant Pierre Bléton, André's wingman, shot down two more.

Normandie's Sous-Lieutenant Roger Sauvage was a fighter pilot during the Battle of France. In April 1940 his twin-engined Potez 631 was shot down by a British pilot flying a Hawker Hurricane who mistook it for a Bf 110. He bailed out but landed badly and suffered total amnesia for four days. The following month, however, he scored his victory – shooting down a Dornier Do 17. A Heinkel He 111 followed in June.

Whenever Normandie was called upon to display its aerial prowess, its commanders turned to Sous-Lieutenant Roger Marchi. A lieutenant from March 1945, Marchi is pictured here in the cockpit of his Yak-3. One of Normandie's highest scoring aces with 13 victories, seven of them shared, he had a reputation for being able to perform incredible aerobatics that wowed even his fellow pilots.

André's own total for the day was four Fw 190s destroyed and one 'probable'.

There was no let-up the next day, January 17, 1945, as the battle raged on the ground below – the depleted German forces fighting a desperate delaying action against overwhelming odds. The Soviets were taking heavy casualties and making only painfully slow progress.

During a morning patrol, a squad of four from the 1st Escadrille found 12 Fw 190s strafing Soviet positions and ploughed into them. Captaine René Challe severely damaged one fighter and saw it go down before a second caught him in its crosshairs and blew a hole in his Yak, wounding him in the left arm. Sous-Lieutenants Robert Marchi and Robert Iribarne destroyed another Fw 190 each.

Russian by birth, Léon Ougloff's parents settled in France when he was a one-year-old and he became a naturalised French citizen in 1933. He is pictured at the controls of another pilot's Yak-3 in this rare air-to-air photo taken by fellow Normandie pilot Roger Sauvage. The aircraft in question was the regular machine of Captaine René Challe. When the photo was taken, some time in March 1945, Ougloff and Sauvage were flying over Königsberg.

As part of a second patrol that caught up with some Fw 190s just as they were beginning their bombing run, Sauvage shot yet another down in flames – its pilot successfully bailing out.

This time though, it was Normandie's turn to be surprised.

A formation of 20 Bf 109s appeared and attacked – sending Sauvage's comrade Aspirant Jean Piquenot crashing to his death. Captaine Charras was also lost, missing in action.

Flying was curtailed in the afternoon as a powerful snowstorm blew in and made further missions impossible.

After three days of intense combat, January 18 began relatively peacefully – the morning being written off due to heavy fog. Flying commenced early in the afternoon. Not far from Kussen, Captaine Pierre Matras and de Geoffre caught up with a formation of four Fw 190s and managed to down two of them.

On a separate patrol, Sous-Lieutenant Gaël Taburet got a third. As part of another patrol from the 1st Escadrille, Sous-Lieutenant Marcel Perrin destroyed one Fw 190 and damaged a second before the remaining eight Fw 190s from the formation closed in and forced him to withdraw. His comrade Aspirant Pierre Genès was killed when the Luftwaffe pilots shot his Yak to pieces.

Delfino led a squad comprising of Sous-Lieutenant Pierre Douarre, Mertzisen, Penverne and Bléton against 20 Fw 190 fighter-bombers, only to be bounced by another 20 that were flying escort. The French swiftly withdrew as the fighter-bombers dived away but Douarre managed to catch up with a straggler and shot him down about three miles northwest of Insterburg.

Later in the day, Charras made a surprise appearance at Normandie's base. He had evaded the Bf 109s of the previous day and then spotted a single one flying on its own.

He surprised the German pilot, who saw him at the last second and dived to the deck, attempting to flee at treetop height. Charras told his fellow pilots he had been just about to open fire when the Bf 109's wingtip struck a branch and span the aircraft into the ground.

In the afternoon, Lieutenant Robert Castin, André, Bléton and Sous-Lieutenant Maurice Challe flew another patrol. Again, they happened upon a large group of bomb-laden Fw 190s heading for the front. Challe damaged one but

Ahead of the final battle for Königsberg, Normandie pilots watch one of their number making a pass over their airfield.

Three of Normandie's highest scoring pilots together, from left, Sous-Lieutenants Georges Lemare (13 victories), Jacques André (15) and Roger Sauvage (16). The photo was taken during a parade for Soviet generals on March 20, 1945.

Normandie's Yaks lined up shortly after the end of the war. The one nearest the camera is the aircraft of Lieutenant-Colonel Louis Delfino, the regiment's commandant. When he was a child his father was killed in the First World War and he was brought up by his mother. On August 12, 1942, under the Vichy government, his unit was ordered to prevent British incursions into French West Africa and he ended up shooting down an RAF Vickers Wellington bomber with his Curtiss H-75A Hawk for his eighth shared victory.

Captaine Marc Charras served with the French Air Force both before and after the Battle of France until his unit was dissolved by the Germans in 1943. He escaped to Spain but was imprisoned by fascists. After being liberated by the British, he volunteered to serve with Normandie. He survived the war, only to be killed in combat during the First Indochina War in 1949 – the French Vietnam War.

then part of his fairing came away, forcing him to return to base – a common problem with the lightly built Yaks.

Bléton chased two, shooting one down and damaging the other, while André saw something very strange. He was pursuing a pair of Fw 190s and was about to open fire when his quarry suddenly opened fire on his comrade. The second Fw 190 burst into flames and crashed.

Hardly able to believe his eyes, André double-checked the aircraft he was following was, in fact, a Luftwaffe liveried Fw 190 and when he saw that it was, he opened fire. The apparently treacherous German fighter began to belch out smoke but André had to break off before he could finish the job. Castin, meanwhile, spotted an Il-2 being set upon by an Fw 190. He flew in, guns blazing, and forced the German to break off the attack – only for a second Fw 190 he hadn't seen to shoot his Yak's engine dead. He was forced to make a belly landing near Naumiestis in Lithuania.

On January 19, a squad from the 1st Escadrille found another 20 Fw 190 fighter-bombers being escorted by 20 more Fw 190s and while Charras claimed one, Sauvage claimed two.

A short while later, André,

Challe and Bléton spotted a trio of Henschel Hs 129s tankbusters flying in formation at low level. Attacking together, they put two of them down but the other escaped.

Sauvage was in action again during his second patrol of the day – attacking nine Fw 190s with Iribarne, Marchi, Perrin and Taburet. He got one to begin with, then took another with the aid of Iribarne. Marchi destroyed a third, and a fourth was claimed by Perrin and Taburet together. Finally Perrin shot down one that appeared to have already suffered damage elsewhere.

That evening, the regiment heard that Stalin had mentioned them in his order of the day.

Breakthrough

Bad weather again hampered operations on January 20 and 21 but the Normandie pilots heard that Soviet forces had finally broken through into Silesia and were closing on Breslau. At midnight, they heard that, far to the south, the Red Army had also entered Tannenberg, Saxony, inside the German border.

Ground crew prepare to refuel one of Normandie-Niemen's Yak-3s.

Chaotic scenes as viewed from the Tower of the Don in Königsberg during the last stages of the siege. Königsberg was an important port but few could escape the city by water as the Soviets closed in during early 1945.

Snow continued to fall on January 22 and 23, fog taking its place on the 24th and 25th. The following day, Normandie relocated to another small airstrip, this time at Gross-Skajsgiren. The move was completed by the end of January 27 and operations resumed at last on January 28.

During the first patrol of the day – in the Königsberg region – Matras and de Geoffre spotted a pair of Fw 190s and went after them. The Germans fled but the Frenchmen caught one and shot it down. Rather than exploding, spinning or otherwise coming apart, the Fw 190 reportedly skidded 650ft on its belly before coming to rest.

A second patrol tangled with three Fw 190s but without success and a third found just a single Fw 190.

Three Normandie pilots claimed hits on it but later acknowledged that the aircraft was being flown so skilfully it was difficult to get near it. With a last burst of gunfire from Henry, the fighter began to give off black smoke and then vanished into cloud under 1000ft off the ground.

Patrols resumed on January 29 but without encountering any enemies. January 30 was another write-off due to appalling weather but the snow cleared enough on January 31 to allow a strafing mission against the German airfield at Gross Kubuiken – resulting in a Junkers Ju 52 being destroyed on the ground. Activity in the air was now reduced because the Germans had suffered a catastrophic series of reversals on the ground.

The German 4th Army had been pushed back to the Baltic, where Soviet forces encircled it, trapping it against the shores of the Vistula Lagoon in East Prussia in what became known as the Heiligenbeil Pocket. With these battered divisions now contained, the Red Army continued its relentless drive westwards into northern Germany.

There were several Luftwaffe airfields around Königsberg at the start of 1945 but all were destroyed by heavy and relentless Soviet bombing.

The final battle for Königsberg saw vicious street fighting. The German defenders threw up barricades across streets and dug trenches in the city's marketplaces when the outer defences failed.

ABOVE, RIGHT and BELOW: Sustained bombing by the Soviets after several heavy raids by the RAF left much of Königsberg in ruins at best, or at worst as an endless carpet of rubble.

At the same time, what was left of the 3rd Panzer Army had been pushed into Königsberg and Samland – the peninsula to the northwest of the city.

Normandie's efforts now became focused on helping to crack this tough but isolated defensive bastion.

A thaw arrived on February 1, bringing with it mud and heavy rain. Despite these conditions, Normandie flew several reconnaissance missions over Königsberg. Two days later, strafing missions were undertaken on the airfield at Gross Kubuiken and on February 4, Penverne was shot down and killed during an encounter with 12 Fw 190s. Normandie was moved to Powunden, about 12 miles directly north of Königsberg, on February 5.

The rain intensified until the clouds finally relented on February 10. The first patrol saw Matras, de Geoffre and Lorillon all firing into a Fw 190, one of a group of six, which soaked up their bullets and caught fire but did not go down.

On the second patrol, Perrin, Henri and Lieutenant Maurice Guido ganged up on a Bf 109 which had been attempting to escape with a comrade and saw it crash into the ground. Another four Bf 109s were spotted north of Bladiau, to the southwest of Königsberg. Sauvage and Taburet hit one, only to see it disappear into the clouds, while Charras hit another on its left wing. Sauvage and Marchi then chased the damaged machine towards Pillau before Marchi finished it off and watched it crash.

On February 11, Iribane was shot down and killed by a Fw 190. Guido shot down a Bf 109 after interrupting a huge turning dogfight between a large force of Messerschmitts and Yaks of a different unit. Martin finished off another and Perrin got a third. Aspirant Maurice Monge failed to return and no one was sure what had become of him.

Two more days of bad weather followed and on February 14 Normandie transferred to Wittenberg – a former fully-fledged Luftwaffe airfield almost directly south from Königsberg, rather than a muddy airstrip. Although it could boast concrete buildings, hangars and properly built runways, much of this infrastructure was in ruins and booby-trapped. Soviet sappers took more than 12 hours to destroy all the German devices, blowing several up where they had been laid because they were in such a dangerous state.

Operations recommenced on February 15 and although the first three patrols encountered no enemy activity, the fourth found a dozen Fw 190s preparing to attack some Il-2s. They were caught napping and Lemare got one straight away, then damaged a second.

Sauvage and Aspirant Joseph Schoendorff worked together to turn another into a ball of fire, crashing with its left wing shot to pieces.

Despite the earlier thaw, a snowstorm blew up and only a handful of further missions took place before February 20. That day there were a number of uneventful patrols but during one, 12 Bf 109s appeared and immediately shot down Bleton, who managed to bail out.

By now, with just 24 pilots to call on, Delfino decided to reduce Normandie to two escadrille – the 1st being dissolved and its pilots redistributed to the other two. The next day, Monge reappeared and told everyone how he ran out of fuel before he could return to Normandie's airstrip and how, having crash landed, he was forced to travel on foot to rejoin the unit – which had taken all of 10 days.

The big freeze continued from February 22 to February 25, when it was announced that Normandie would be relocated again, this time to an airstrip at Friedland. This occurred that same day without incident, despite the icy conditions.

Normandie was temporarily stood down the following day due to the ongoing manpower shortage and the terrible weather. This lasted until March 7.

At 11am, the Soviet General Staff announced abruptly that Normandie would resume operations that day and ground crew immediately set to work clearing snow from the runway. This took until 3.30pm, leaving barely enough time for four patrols to provide a few minutes' coverage over the front line some

The central castle in Königsberg was destroyed during the fighting. In the foreground on the right can be seen a monument to Bismarck which, by accident or design, has been shot in the head.

190 miles away to the west in the Elbing region of West Prussia.

The next day Normandie provided cover for Pe-2s bombing the Braunsberg area inside the Heiligenbeil Pocket. During the third patrol, a group of 12 Fw 190s intercepted the Pe-2s and began attacking them. Pierrot raked one with fire and it dived slowly away trailing smoke, the pilot making no effort to control it – leading André, who saw it, to later report that he believed the pilot had been shot dead.

He also saw a Fw 190 on its own, being pursued by the Yaks of Challe, Ougloff and Lorillon.

Challe fired a burst but then realised he had an oil leak and peeled off. Lorillon took a shot and

saw that he too had an oil leak. Ougloff could not target the Fw 190 and it sped for home at extremely low altitude out onto the waters of the Frisches Haff.

March 9th to the 24th passed without contact with the enemy; for much of that time the Friedland runway was in a poor state and all but unusable. At last, on March 25, the day dawned to clear blue skies and the runway was clear of ice and mud. Several patrols were flown, with André and Challe taking on three Fw 190s close to Königsberg at Pillau. The former managed to down one of them, which crashed into the sea.

On March 26, the second patrol of the day was set upon by half dozen Fw 190s. During the lengthy dogfight that followed, Marchi damaged one of the enemy machines but suffered a mechanical failure and was forced to crash-land his aircraft in a field near Normandie's airstrip. Monge was shot down and killed during the encounter.

During the fourth patrol, Perrin and Guido saw a pair of Bf 109s harassing an Il-2 before setting it on fire and speeding away when it crashed. They gave chase but their Yaks were initially outpaced by the Messerschmitts. They eventually caught up and Guido destroyed one of them.

Late in the day, a commissar ordered Normandie to escort a group of Pe-2s that had turned up too late for its expected fighter escort. Four of the unit's pilots went up but on arriving at the rendezvous point were attacked by a lone Fw 190. It dived on them at high speed but failed to fire and banked away.

Two more Fw 190s then appeared and one was shot down by Sauvage and de Geoffre.

It was decided on March 27 that sorties should only be made in force – with the first mission of the day comprised of 16 Yaks. This was meant to be an escort run but the Pe-2s never showed up so it became a patrol over the Pillau region.

A number of Bf 109s and Fw 190s were encountered and sporadic dogfights broke out. Dechanet crippled a Fw 190 which fell into the Frisches Haff but in return de Geoffre went down. He had been flying parallel to the coast when his aircraft began to shudder violently and his engine caught fire. When it finally stalled he had no option but to bail out. As he tried to leave the cockpit of his stricken machine, he discovered his right leg was caught up in his harness. Freeing himself with only seconds to spare he jumped, opened his

parachute and smacked into the freezing cold water.

His aircraft hit the water an instant later and sank immediately. Despite pains from his leg, he swam to the shore and was picked up by Soviet soldiers, who gave him a swig of vodka and basic medical care.

The second patrol of the day comprised of 10 Yaks and was again flown over Pillau. Contact was made at 13,000ft – high altitude for aerial combat on the Eastern Front – and Delfino opened fire as he climbed into a formation of eight Fw 190s, hitting one.

This aircraft then dived directly into the guns of Perrin, who destroyed it and saw the wreckage crash into the sea far below. Lemare and Schoendorff spotted a Bf 109 and Lemare shot it down.

As daylight waned, Guido took part in a five-strong aircraft patrol but failed to return. Marchi fired into

In honour of Normandie's achievements, Stalin himself presented the new French government with 40 Yak-3s. They are pictured here at Le Bourget in Paris.

a Fw 190 which was then finished by Henri after a lengthy chase. Sauvage and Ougloff destroyed another by working together, Lorillon downing yet another which then crashed on to the shore.

When the pilots finally returned to base it was realised that Challe was no longer with them.

The following day, Guido showed up at Normandie's airstrip. There were celebrations because everyone thought he was dead. It turned out he had simply suffered engine problems and had been forced to land elsewhere; the area was not short of Soviet-controlled airfields.

The final battle
March 31 saw Normandie ordered to occupy the airfield at Bladiau to the southwest of Königsberg, but bad weather closed in and made a move impossible. It was not until April 7 that the weather improved sufficiently for the unit to make the transfer.

Bladiau was close to the southern shore of the Frisches Haff, the lagoon directly to the west of Königsberg. Across the water was Pillau – a seaport on a narrow spit to the north – southwest of which was Pillau-Neutief airfield where the Bf 109 G-6 and G-14 fighters of III./JG 51 were based.

To the north-east, a vast column of black smoke was rising from Königsberg – a clear indication that the ground assault was well under way.

Having arrived, the Normandie pilots began patrols immediately. A four-strong squad, André, Sauvage and Ougloff, with Capitaine Charles de La Salle bring up the rear, were flying over the sector towards the city at 11,500ft during the afternoon when André spotted four fighter-bomber Fw 190s flying east towards the battlefront at 5000ft.

Diving to attack, the three aspirants flew into a wall of heavy flak and were forced to break

off. The Fw 190s got away in the confusion that followed.

Moments later, André spotted them again and this time dived down, accompanied by de La Salle. The French pilots noticed that the German aircraft, flying in a straight line, were still carrying bombs under their fuselages – which meant they had not detected the threat.

This situation lasted only a few seconds, as de La Salle flew in too fast and caught the Fw 190 pilots' attention. Seeing the threat, all four dumped their bombs and attempted to flee. André closed in, chasing one of them towards the north-west of Königsberg. He put four bursts of gunfire into it but once again extremely heavy flak forced him to disengage and he never saw what became of his intended victim.

Then the weather closed in again. Schoendorff, who had been flying with another patrol, got lost and was forced to land some 10 miles away from Bladiau at Normandie's old base of Wittenberg.

Meanwhile, Normandie's DC-3 had been busily moving the regiment's staff and supplies from Friedland to Bladiau. At 7pm, Normandie personnel went to their quarters in the three remaining houses that had not been gutted by bombing, only to have their dinner interrupted by a massive bombardment taking place over the Frisches Haff at Pillau.

Wave after wave of Petlyakov Pe-2s and Il-2s bombed the seaport and nearby airfield, and several Normandie pilots went outside to watch.

The following day, three patrols were sent up but found no targets – probably unsurprising given the heavy bombing of the night before. Towards the end of his patrol however, André spotted another four Fw 190s flying towards a group of Il-2s on a bombing mission. His squad engaged the Focke-Wulfs and

he again chased one that attempted to get away.

It headed south then west towards the now distant German front line. André fired on it five times before it sank to the ground and landed on its belly in a marshy area near Königsberg.

At around 1pm, two squads of six Yaks each were sent up by Normandie to protect bombers making an all-out assault on the city's already shattered defences. Nearly every available Soviet Air Force aircraft capable of carrying bombs was sent on this attack.

Aspirant Lorillon was among those sent to protect the bombers. While flying cover for Il-2s, Pe-2s and Douglas Boston IIIs, he noticed a DC-3 among them. As he stared in amazement, the crew opened the side door and began tossing bombs out by hand.

Peering down, Lorillon found it impossible to see what effect the bombs were having. The whole city was invisible beneath a blanket of smoke and flames.

For the rest of the day, Normandie pilots strafed ground positions and hunted for targets of opportunity. One spotted an E-boat attempting to escape the city's port and make a run for the Baltic. He flew down and attacked, watching his 20mm cannon shells cutting into it. He then made a second pass before leaving the wreckage of the vessel sinking into the icy waters.

The end of Königsberg
During the final assault on Königsberg, including the devastating bombing raids, some 40,000 German troops were killed and another 92,000 taken prisoner afterwards. Just 30,000 civilians remained within the city's ruined walls and an uncounted number of slaves.

Three Soviet armies were involved in the attack – the 11th, 43rd and 50th Guards Armies comprising some 106,600 soldiers.

About 24,500 of these were specially trained and equipped assault troops. Casualties on the Soviet side were comparatively light, at 3700 killed.

Assessing the battle in its aftermath, the Soviets counted 193 tanks or SPGs on the German side compared to 538 of the Red Army, 120 aircraft to 2174 and 3216 field guns to 2567 – plus another 2358 heavy artillery pieces.

Normandie-Niemen saw out the war in the east and in June 1945 was allowed to return to France with a gift of 40 Yak-3s from Stalin himself. These modern fighters formed the basis for the fledgling post-war French Air Force.

6

KING OF
FIGHTERS

❖

The best single-seaters of 1945

**Technology was advancing rapidly towards the end of the
war, with the most powerful piston-engined types the world
had ever seen fighting alongside or against the first jet
aircraft. But how did they compare?**

There were around 20 high performance fighter types at least nominally in service in Europe when the war there came to an end.

Each had its strengths and weaknesses – a higher top speed, a better rate of climb or simply being quicker in a turn, but it is worth bearing in mind that even the best aircraft in the hands of a novice was usually a poor match for a lesser machine in the hands of an experienced ace.

The 'official' statistics available for each machine have been endlessly scrutinised in the decades since the war's end and some of the figures, for example for top speed, were achieved only under special conditions – with particular equipment fitted and at a particular altitude.

The fastest Messerschmitt Bf 109, the K-4, for example, has an 'official' top speed of 440mph, but this could only be managed with methanol-water injection (MW-50) to allow increased boost pressure in its DB 605 DB or DC engine, and then only for a maximum of 10 minutes. It also required a broad-bladed 3m diameter VDM 9-12159A propeller and even then the 440mph was only achievable at 24,600ft.

Without MW-50, the Bf 109 K-4's best performance was 416mph, at 26,528ft. These figures also relate to well-built aircraft running high octane fuel in engines allowed to run at full power. De-rating engines was a common practice in the Luftwaffe, to reduce maintenance time, since the beginning of 1944. Fuel shortages meant there was no opportunity to thoroughly test engines and aircraft before they were accepted into service either. And by the end of the war, many, if not all of Germany's aircraft manufacturers were relying on slave labour to produce components and assemble the finished product.

Sabotage and shoddy workmanship were routine – a situation that worsened as the end of the war approached. Hans Knickrehm, of I./JG 3, wrote about the new Bf 109 G-14/AS aircraft received by his group from the manufacturer in October 1944: "The engines proved prone to trouble after much too short a time because the factories had had to sharply curtail test runs for lack of fuel.

"The surface finish of the outer skin also left much to be desired. The sprayed-on camouflage finish was rough and uneven. The result was a further reduction in speed. We often discovered clear cases of sabotage during our acceptance checks. Cables or wires were not secured, were improperly attached, scratched or had even been visibly cut."

These issues were typical of many new aircraft being delivered to German front line units.

The available statistics for the aircraft examined here, regardless of their origin, do not include measurements for some of the most important aspects of performance either – such as manoeuvrability, rate of turn, rate of roll or dive speed. For these, anecdotal evidence must suffice.

In addition, several of these aircraft were only available in tiny numbers and so were unable to make any real impact on the outcome of the war – such as the Heinkel He 162 and Focke-Wulf Ta 152. Some types, such as the Me 163 Komet, were of greater value for the fear they instilled in Allied bomber crews and Allied intelligence than for the pitifully small number of aircraft they were actually responsible for shooting down.

Had they been urgently needed, jets such as the Gloster Meteor F.3 and Lockheed P-80 Shooting Star could have been rushed to the front line and brought into action far sooner – hence their inclusion here. Similarly, the Bell P-63 Kingcobra was delivered to the French too late to see combat and was supposedly only used on the Western Front in small numbers by the Soviets. It was available in 1945, however, and did see combat against Luftwaffe types.

The aim here is simply to provide a statistical comparison between the most powerful and advanced aircraft available in Europe. Five British types have been chosen for inclusion – the Supermarine Spitfire LF.IX, the Spitfire Mk.XIV, the Hawker Typhoon Mk.1b, the Hawker Tempest V and the Gloster Meteor F.3. The four American types are the North American P-51D Mustang, the Republic P-47D Thunderbolt, the Lockheed P-38L Lightning and the Lockheed P-80A Shooting Star.

The four Soviet types are the Lavochkin La-7, the Yakovlev Yak-3, the Yak-9U and the Bell P-63A Kingcobra – an American fighter but initially flown almost exclusively by the Russians. Finally, seven German machines are included: the Focke-Wulf Fw 190 A-9, the Ta 152 H-1, the Fw 190 D-9, the Messerschmitt Bf 109 K-4, the Me 262 A-1a, the Me 163 B-1 and the Heinkel He 162 A-2.

Some contemporary types, such as the Bell Airacomet, are omitted because they were never considered for front line duties, and others, such as the Hawker Tempest II and De Havilland Vampire, have been left out because they were simply not yet ready for action.

Supermarine Spitfire LF.IX

The Merlin 66-engined Spitfire LF.IX was the workhorse of the RAF's fighter squadrons from its introduction in 1943 through to the end of the war. The original Mk.IX was introduced as early as mid-1942.

Compared against a captured Bf 109 G-6/U2 with GM-1 nitrous oxide injection by the Central Fighter Establishment in late 1944, the LF.IX was found to be superior in every respect except acceleration in

a dive. Manoeuvrability was "greatly superior" and it was noted that the LF.IX "easily out-turns the Bf 109 in either direction at all speeds".

By 1945, the LF.IX was beginning to show its age. Figures given for its top speed vary but it was undoubtedly among the slowest of the 20 aircraft being assessed here in a straight line. It could out-climb and fly higher than most of its opponents, however, even out-performing many of the most advanced German types.

There were few to rival it for manoeuvrability either, making it worthy of inclusion here, and explaining why it remained on the front line for so long even when more 'advanced' types were becoming available to replace it.

Later production models of the Spitfire LF.IX were fitted with the pointed tail fin that was also a feature of the Spitfire XVI. Production of the Mk.IX continued until the end of the war and it was the most numerous type of Spitfire built.

A line-up of Spitfire LF.IXs at an advanced landing ground on the Continent in late 1944.

Flying Officer George Lents of 341 Squadron pictured in front of his Spitfire LF.IX in Sussex, June 1944. By 1945, the Spitfire IX had been completely outclassed in straight line speed by newer types, but it could still climb faster and manoeuvre better than many of its opponents.

Supermarine Spitfire Mk.XIV

Combining the Spitfire Mk.VIII airframe with a two-speed, two-stage supercharged 2220hp Rolls-Royce Griffon 65 engine resulted in the Mk.XIV. Introduced in 1943, in appearance it was similar to the Spitfire XII with normal wings but with a five-bladed propeller. The rudder was also enlarged and an extra internal fuel tank was fitted.

The huge increase in power meant the XIV was a match for most of its piston-engined contemporaries, the only exception being the Ta 152, and the two are believed never to have met in combat. Its range was short and its manoeuvrability was inferior to that of the Spitfire LF.IX, but nevertheless the XIV was one of the best fighters of the war's final months.

Flight Lieutenant Ian Ponsford, who shot down seven

enemy aircraft while flying a Spitfire Mk.XIV with 130 Squadron, remembered: "The Spitfire XIV was the most marvellous aeroplane at that time and I consider it to have been the best operational fighter of them all as it could out-climb virtually anything.

"The earlier Merlin-Spitfire may have had a slight edge when it came to turning performance, but the Mark XIV was certainly better in this respect than the opposition we were faced with. The only thing it couldn't do was keep up with the Fw 190 D in a dive.

"It could be a bit tricky on takeoff if one opened the throttle too quickly as you just couldn't hold it straight because the torque was so great from the enormous power developed from the Griffon engine.

"One big advantage that we had over the Germans

was that we ran our aircraft on advanced fuels which gave us more power. The 150 octane fuel we used was strange looking stuff as it was bright green and had an awful smell – it had to be heavily leaded to cope with the extra compression of the engine."

During the Arab-Israeli War in 1948, Israeli pilots flew both Mk.IX and Mk.XIV Spitfires bought from Czechoslovakia against Egyptian Spitfires and concluded that the IX was better due to its superior manoeuvrability.

The Spitfire XIV sacrificed some manoeuvrability for raw speed but was still capable of out-turning and out-climbing almost any opponent.

Sporting a large five-bladed propeller, the Spitfire XIV was tricky on takeoff due to the enormous torque produced by its Rolls-Royce Griffon 65 engine.

— Hawker Typhoon Mk.1b —

The history of the Typhoon is too long and troubled to detail in full here, suffice to say that it was a failure in the high-altitude interceptor role for which it was designed. Although it was the RAF's first fighter capable of more than 400mph, climbing speed was regarded as inadequate and a series of structural failures in the fuselage caused significant delays in its production.

Having entered service in 1941, it is one of the oldest of the 20 aircraft examined here and was beginning to struggle against more advanced competition by 1945. Pilots had to wear an oxygen mask from the moment the engine was switched on due to heavy carbon monoxide contamination in the cockpit, and the level of noise and vibration made life at its controls doubly uncomfortable.

Nevertheless, as history shows, it proved to be a deadly fighter-bomber when armed with rockets or bombs, and many Fw 190 pilots were unpleasantly surprised to discover that despite its size and weight – being one of the largest and heaviest single-engined aircraft here – it had a very short radius of turn and rolled well.

It could also carry a heavy load with relative ease, which meant it could be fitted with four powerful 20mm Hispano Mk II cannon – a weapon originally designed as an anti-aircraft gun – in addition to its bombs/rockets.

Typhoon MN686 was one of Hawker's development machines, photographed here in late 1944. The Typhoon was fast but poor in a climb.

It was uncomfortable to fly but the Typhoon was agile at low level despite being a large aircraft and could carry a heavy weapons load, making it particularly useful as a fighter-bomber.

— *Hawker Tempest V* —

Big, heavy and fast, this thin-wing upgrade of the Typhoon design was undoubtedly one of the best fighters of the Second World War and at low altitudes could give either of the two Spitfires detailed here a run for their money.

It had the same Napier Sabre IIA engine as the Typhoon but range was extended by moving the engine forward 21in to make room for a 76 gallon fuel tank. Tail surfaces were enlarged and a four-bladed propeller was fitted. While the first 100 built had the Typhoon's four Hispano Mk II cannon, the Series II Tempest V got the Hispano Mk V cannon – the weapon's ultimate wartime development.

The first Tempests reached squadrons in January 1944 and they were initially used to combat Fieseler Fi 103 V-1 flying bombs. When they were moved on to the Continent, it quickly became clear that below about 8000ft the Tempest dramatically outperformed the very best aircraft that the Luftwaffe could throw at it – such as the Fw 190 D-9 and the Bf 109 K-4. Tempest pilots were also responsible for shooting down a number of Me 262s.

According to Hubert Lange, a pilot who flew 15 missions in Me 262s with JG 51, the Hawker Tempest was the German jet's most dangerous opponent, "extremely fast at low altitudes, highly manoeuvrable and heavily armed".

LEFT: Hawker Tempest Vs from 501 Squadron pictured in 1944. The Tempest V had a quartet of 20mm cannon, giving it a deadly punch, and at low level was capable of overmatching even the Luftwaffe's finest fighters.

BELOW: Similar to the Typhoon, the Tempest's redesigned wing and enlarged tail were big improvements. These 486 Squadron Tempests are pictured at Lübeck shortly after the war's end.

— *Gloster Meteor F.3* —

Powered by a pair of Rolls-Royce Derwent I jets with a static thrust of 2000lb each, the Meteor F.3 began to enter service in early 1945. Deliveries of its predecessor, the F.1, had begun in June 1944.

While the first Meteors were actually slower than the fastest piston-engined fighters then available, such as the Spitfire XIV, the F.3 offered much higher performance.

It was field tested from bases in Belgium with 616 and 504 Squadrons during the last weeks of the war primarily in the fighter reconnaissance and ground-attack roles. It never met the Me 262 in aerial combat but some were shot down by Allied flak due to their superficial resemblance to the German machine.

As a result, Meteors were given an all-white paint scheme to make them more easily recognisable to friendly units.

Like all in-service jets in 1945, the Meteor was at the cutting edge of performance, and in good weather handling was described as "pleasant". But the F.3 suffered from 'snaking' – directional instability – which made it more difficult to target an aerial opponent effectively.

A report from the Central Fighter Establishment noted: "The failure of the Meteor to come within an acceptable standard is due to the directional snaking which occurs in operational conditions of flight so far experienced and the heaviness and consequently slow operation of the ailerons to bring the sight back on to the target.

"This snaking tends to increase with increase of speed and once it has commenced it is impossible to correct it within the limits of time available during an attack."

Whether this would have proved to be a fatal flaw in actual combat or merely an annoyance to the type's pilots will never be known.

It says a lot about the fortunes of Britain in the war and the role of the Meteor that a large section of the CFE report is devoted to how difficult it would be to fly in formation. It is impossible to imagine the Germans, desperate to rush their jets into action, bothering to do the same for the Me 262.

The first Gloster Meteors on the Continent during 1945 were painted white to avoid 'friendly' fire. The jet's handling was described as pleasant but it suffered from directional snaking, particularly in poor weather.

A Meteor in flight. The type was Britain's first operational jet fighter and while its performance on paper was not dramatically dissimilar to that of the Me 262, the Meteor's handling was probably inferior.

North American P-51D Mustang

Flown in huge numbers while escorting American bombers, the Mustang is widely accepted as having been the USAAF's most successful air superiority and escort fighter.

In P-51D form its performance was excellent at high altitude. Powered by a Packard-built version of the Rolls-Royce Merlin engine and featuring a bubble canopy, it boasted a good though not sparkling rate of climb and exceptional visibility.

It retained a good measure of agility even above 400mph and was a very stable aircraft with few vices to punish the inattentive. At low altitude and in low speed encounters with enemy aircraft however, its large turn radius became a real disadvantage.

In addition, as a high performance long-range escort, it was lightly built and poorly armoured – rendering it vulnerable to even slight battle damage. Many American pilots using the Mustang for strafing ground targets found that even a light flak hit could be fatal.

In encounters at high speed and altitude, the Mustang was able to reach its full potential and there was little to match it in this, its own stomping ground – as Fw 190 and even Me 262 pilots discovered.

LEFT: North American P-51D-5-NA Mustang serial 44-13926 serving with the 375th Fighter Squadron. The famous 'Cadillac of the sky' was America's best regarded fighter of the war. It was capable of flying huge distances and performed exceptionally well at high to medium altitude. BELOW: Beloved of its pilots, the P-51D was an excellent air superiority fighter, though it was poorly armoured and could be a handful at low level. This is serial number 44-14955 'Dopey Okie' of the 487th Fighter Squadron, part of the 352nd Fighter Group.

— *Republic P-47D Thunderbolt* —

Faster and higher flying than even a Mustang, the P-47D Thunderbolt was a big, heavy aircraft – the Tempest to the Mustang's Spitfire. As such, it could also soak up more battle damage and could carry a heavier weapons load too.

On paper, the Thunderbolt seemed to have the edge over the Mustang, but pilots told a different story. The Mustang was simply more agile – it handled better and was easier to fly well. Against German fighters, the Thunderbolt seems to have been just as effective at all altitudes. In the end, the Thunderbolt lost out simply because fewer were used in situations where they were likely to enter aerial combat with German fighters.

One source gives the total number of enemy aircraft shot down by the P-47 as 3662 compared to the P-51's 5944. General der Jagdflieger Adolf Galland's Me 262 was shot down by a P-47 Thunderbolt though, not a P-51.

Against the Spitfire XIV, neither the P-47 nor the P-51 could be said to have had a clear advantage. Both were slower, less manoeuvrable at all altitudes and less able to climb at speed – but they had the capacity to keep up with high-flying B-17s and B-24s long after a Spitfire XIV would've had to turn for home.

P-47D-30 Thunderbolt 44-32760 'Shorty Miriam' of the 354th Fighter Group. The Thunderbolt was a huge, powerful fighter and in the right circumstances could beat the Messerschmitt Me 262. It gave continual mechanical problems, however, and was less able than the P-51D.

Like the Hawker Typhoon, the P-47 achieved great success as a fighter-bomber, though it was also a superb fighter. Pictured here is P-47D-25 42-26641 'Hairless Joe' of the 56th Fighter Group.

— *Lockheed P-38L Lightning* —

The oldest of the three piston-engined American fighters featured here, the P-38, had matured by 1945 and had been available in its definitive P-38L form since June 1944.

Its twin engines made it heavy and gave it a very broad wingspan, but since these were set back from the cockpit they also allowed the pilot an excellent view in all directions.

LEFT: A Lockheed P-38L Lightning in flight. Thanks to its powerful twin engines, the 'L' could climb at an incredible rate and it boasted cutting edge technology – but it was behind the P-51 and P-47 in manoeuvrability.

It wasn't astonishingly fast in a straight line but the Lightning had an exceptional rate of climb. And its counter-rotating propellers meant there was no torque effect in flight and enabled the Lightning to turn equally well to the left or the right. In addition, it had cutting edge features such as power boosted ailerons and electrically operated dive flaps.

However, the Lightning was complicated and pilots had to manage twice the number of engine controls while watching twice the number of gauges. Also it's armament, while a good average for a late war fighter, was not exceptionally heavy.

It therefore must come last when compared against its American contemporaries.

RIGHT: The P-38L was used by fighter squadrons of the 1st Fighter Group in Europe. Pilot 2nd Lieutenant Jim Hunt of the 27th Fighter Squadron sits atop P-38L 'Maloney's Pony'. The aircraft was never flown by its namesake, 1st Lieutenant Thomas Maloney, because on August 19, 1944, his P-38 (a different one) was forced down on the French coast. While walking along the beach to find help, he trod on a landmine and was badly injured – spending the next three and a half years in and out of hospital.

— *Lockheed P-80A Shooting Star* —

Just two pre-production YP-80A Shooting Stars saw active service during the Second World War, operating briefly from Lesina airfield in Italy with the 1st Fighter Group. Another two were stationed at RAF Burtonwood in Cheshire for demonstration and test flying.

Powered by a single General Electric J-33-GE-9 jet engine mounted centrally in its fuselage, the Shooting Star was aerodynamically clean and was therefore able to reach an impressive 536mph in level flight at 5000ft – though only when fully painted and without wingtip fuel tanks.

In natural metal finish and with those range extending tanks, performance tests carried out by the USAAF's Flight Test Division showed top speed to be just over 500mph – placing it behind all of its jet-powered contemporaries.

Many postwar comparisons of wartime jets have been overly favourable towards the P-80 and tend to take their figures from later, improved versions.

The aircraft available during the last four months of the war was somewhat less impressive. Without wingtip tanks, its range was that expected of a short-distance high-speed interceptor – 540 miles – yet with them its range improved but its best rate of climb was down to just 3300ft/min.

Armament was six .50 calibre machine guns – the same as that of a Mustang – but these were concentrated in the nose, giving it a more effective fire pattern.

The faster of the two XP-80A Shooting Star prototypes, 44-83021 'Gray Ghost'. While this aircraft was given an all-over pearl grey paint job, the other XP-80A, 'Silver Ghost', was left in bare metal finish for comparative tests. These showed that just painting the Shooting Star had the effect of increasing its top speed. The P-80 was quicker than Gloster's Meteor but still failed to beat the Me 262.

Lockheed P-80A-1-LO Shooting Star 44-85004 in flight. The production P-80A was fitted with wingtip fuel tanks which extended its range but resulted in performance-sapping drag.

— *Lavochkin La-7* —

Based largely on the earlier La-5 fighter and powered by an air-cooled 1850hp ASh-82FN radial engine, the La-7 incorporated more alloys in place of the original wooden structure. The cockpit got a rollbar, the landing gear was improved and a better gunsight, the PB-1B(V), was installed along with a new VISh-105V-4 propeller and an enlarged spinner to improve streamlining.

Unfortunately, the bigger spinner meant less air reached the engine for cooling so a fan was fitted behind it.

Visibility was excellent and either a pair or trio of 20mm cannon gave good though not exceptional firepower.

The Soviets at the time honestly believed that the La-7 was the best fighter in the world for dogfighting and it was certainly faster and more manoeuvrable than the older marques of Fw 190 A that it typically faced on the Eastern Front.

In company such as that discussed here, however, it fails to make the grade. The latest and last Fw 190, the D-9, outperformed it in most areas when using MW-50. Small and lightweight, the La-7 had to be flown at low level because it simply couldn't manage at high altitude.

It was available in big numbers though that the Germans were simply unable to match.

The Russians believed that the Lavochkin La-7 was the world's best piston-engined fighter aircraft in 1945.

It boasted a powerful radial engine which gave it a performance advantage over older Luftwaffe types but the La-7 was falling behind as the war ended.

— *Yakovlev Yak-3* —

The Russians did their best to develop small lightweight fighters that could be produced in huge numbers and this design philosophy had its greatest success in the form of the Yak-3.

Work on it commenced in 1941 but was seriously hampered by first a lack of aluminium and then the German invasion which resulted in design work actually being halted.

As the tide of battle turned, Yakovlev picked up where it had left off and produced the Yak-1M, a

The diminutive Yak-3 in flight. The aircraft was primitive in comparison to other nations' fighters but could still skirmish effectively at low altitude.

A Yak-3 pictured in Poland during 1945 beside the carcass of a Bf 109. Its high power to weight ratio meant that it handled extremely well with an expert pilot at the controls.

lighter, shorter-winged version of the Yak-1. This embodied many technological advances such as a mastless radio antenna, reflector gunsight and better armour. It was meant to have a 1600hp Klimov M-107 V12 engine but this was unavailable and the 1300hp M-105 had to be used instead.

Even with this relatively small powerplant fitted, the redesignated Yak-3 was still 40mph faster than the Yak-9, which despite its name actually entered service first.

The fact that the Yak-3 can be found somewhere towards the bottom of every table associated with this comparison belies its greatest strength – its ability to out-turn both the Bf 109 and the Fw 190 below 20,000ft. Pilots who were new to the Yak-3 found it easy to fly but its true potential was only realised in the hands of an experienced flyer.

Against the best of the Luftwaffe's machines, performing at their best, the Yak-3 would have been found sorely lacking but it was ideal for low-level skirmishing and could face standard German types on an even footing.

— *Yakovlev Yak-9U* —

The first Yak-9s off the production line were fitted with the same Klimov M-105 as the Yak-3 and being substantially heavier paid a big price in performance. Top speed was just 367mph – about the same as that of a Spitfire Mk.I in 1939.

However, when the Yak-9 was fitted with the Klimov M-107A, which delivered 1650hp, its performance dramatically improved. Like the Yak-3, it offered excellent all-round visibility but armament was somewhat lacking – with just a single 20mm cannon firing through its propeller hub and a pair of .50 calibre machine guns mounted in its engine cowling.

Like the La-7 and the Yak-3, the Yak-9U did its best work at low altitude. It was heavy only when compared to the Yak-3 and even with the more powerful M-107A it could still be considered underpowered in this company.

It was manoeuvrable and had better armour than the Yak-3 but it was still no match for the likes of a Fw 190 D-9 or a Bf 109 K-4 on a good day.

A Yakovlev Yak-9U of the 151st Guard Air Fighter Regiment at Yambol in Bulgaria. The original Yak-9, fitted with a Klimov M-105, was a poor performer, but once it had the Klimov M-107A it joined the front rank of fighters available in 1945.

Visibility from the Yak-9U's cockpit was good and it manoeuvred well at low altitude but its performance was unremarkable compared to its more powerful peers.

— *Bell P-63A Kingcobra* —

The Americans did not think too highly of Bell's Kingcobra. They had thought even less highly of its predecessor, the Airacobra, largely because it had been designed to fly with a turbosupercharger but was put into production without one.

The Soviets, however, who received hundreds of Airacobras from the Americans on a lend-lease basis, rather liked it. Much has been written about the Airacobra's strengths as a ground-attack aircraft, even though the Soviets themselves never regarded it as such and tended to use it for air-to-air interception missions instead.

The Kingcobra saw the turbosupercharger finally installed and the overall design modified to incorporate technological advancements – such as laminar flow wings, a redesigned tail and a four-blade propeller. The first XP-63, a converted XP-39E, was first flown on December 7, 1942.

From the outset, the Soviets were involved in the development process to the extent of supplying personnel to fly the prototypes at Bell's factory.

Overall Kingcobra production ran to 3303 examples and 2397 of them were supplied to the Soviet Union.

No Kingcobra ever saw combat with a USAAF squadron, which is not surprising since the P-63's range was limited and its performance was poor at high altitude – making it useless as an escort fighter.

At low level, however, where the Soviet fighter pilots flew, it was effective. Like the other high performance fighter aircraft flown by the Soviets, its top speed and rate of climb were by no means sparkling but it was highly manoeuvrable below 8000ft.

Row upon row of P-63 Kingcobras lined up at the Bell factory prior to delivery to the Soviet Air Force.

Pilots of the Soviet 66th Fighter Wing take a break beside their Bell P-63s. More than two-thirds of all Kingcobras built went to the Russians.

Focke-Wulf Fw 190 A-9

Based largely on the earlier La-5 fighter and powered by an air-cooled 1850hp ASh-82FN radial engine, the La-7 incorporated more alloys in place of the original wooden structure. The cockpit got a rollbar, the landing gear was improved and a better gunsight, the PB-1B(V), was installed along with a new VISh-105V-4 propeller and an enlarged spinner to improve streamlining.

Unfortunately, the bigger spinner meant less air reached the engine for cooling so a fan was fitted behind it.

Visibility was excellent and either a pair or trio of 20mm cannon gave good though not exceptional firepower.

The Soviets at the time honestly believed that the La-7 was the best fighter in the world for dogfighting, and it was certainly faster and more manoeuvrable than the older marques of Fw 190 A it typically faced on the Eastern Front.

In company such as that discussed here, however, it fails to make the grade. The latest and last Fw 190, the D-9, outperformed it in most areas when using MW-50. Small and lightweight, the La-7 had to be flown at low level because it simply couldn't manage at high altitude.

It was available in big numbers though that the Germans were simply unable to match.

LEFT: The Fw 190 A-9's BMW 801S (TS) engine was a compromise but still produced a respectable 2000hp. Note the bubble canopy and the broad paddle blades of the VDM-9 propeller on this example.

BELOW: A Fw 190 A-9 leads a line-up of captured Focke-Wulf machines shortly after the war's end. The A-9 might have been produced in greater numbers had BMW not been so heavily bombed. As it is, a lack of production figures for 1945 means it will never be known precisely how many were made.

— *Focke-Wulf Fw 190 D-9* —

German pilots were largely thrilled by the performance of the Fw 190 D-9 – a stretched Fw 190 A powered by the Junkers Jumo 213 A-1 which could be boosted up to an output of 2000hp with MW-50 injection.

The 'long nose' D-9 lost some of the Fw 190 A's handling and manoeuvrability as the trade-off for its increased speed, however.

Focke-Wulf designer Kurt Tank never intended the D-9 to be the next step in the Fw 190's evolution – that was the Ta 152. Instead he was on record as saying that the existing airframe simply needed an alternative powerplant since BMW's factories were being so heavily targeted by Allied bombing.

There was some suggestion that without water-methanol injection, the D-9's top speed was around 390mph. The Soviets who tested examples they captured intact but without MW-50 were certainly deeply unimpressed by the performance of its Jumo 213 A engine.

The long nose restricted forward and downward visibility, which became a problem because the aircraft had a high wing loading – its wings were the same as those used on the A-8 – and it therefore needed a fast landing and stalled easily. Having to put the aircraft down fast and being unable to see where you were going was a bad combination.

Even so, German pilots still considered the D-9 easier to land and take off in than any Bf 109 variant due to its wide-track landing gear.

Armament was a pair of wing-mounted 20mm cannon and two .50 calibre machine guns in the engine cowl – not outstanding but still sufficient, particularly against lightly armoured opponents such as the Soviet types.

The Fw 190 D-9 was regarded by those who flew it and those who flew against it as a development of the Fw 190 A. In fact, it was simply Focke-Wulf's attempt to provide an alternative engine for the Fw 190 airframe in case the supply of BMW units was disrupted. This example, WNr. 210051, has just rolled off the production line at Bremen-Neuenlanderfeld. It was later delivered to III./JG 54.

An early production Fw 190 D-9 stands out in the snow prior to delivery to III./JG 54, the first unit to operate the type, in September 1944. In combat, the D-9 was fast with MW-50, particularly in a dive. Its performance surpassed that of the Fw 190 A types but Allied types such as the Mustang still eclipsed it.

— *Focke-Wulf Ta 152 H* —

The Ta 152 was effectively brought into being on the same day that its predecessor, the Ta 153, was cancelled. At a meeting on August 13, 1943, Tank suggested that the same benefits of the Ta 153, which was almost entirely a new machine, could be achieved by simply extending the wings and fuselage of the existing Fw 190 airframe with inserts. The Ta 152 would be only 10% new and as such was approved for development. The Fw 190 D-9 was an even simpler conversion.

Bringing the Ta 152 to production took longer than expected due to delays in the development of the engines that were to power it. In the end, the Ta 152 C standard fighter version only reached the prototype stage and just a handful of high-altitude Ta 152 Hs were built and saw combat.

Powered by the long-delayed but finally sorted supercharged Junkers Jumo 213 E-1 engine, the 152 H was the fastest piston-engined aircraft to see combat during the war by a considerable margin. It also had a decent rate of climb, the highest ceiling of any piston-engined fighter of the war and a remarkable wingspan of 47ft 4½in.

Even its armament was good – two 20mm cannon in the wings and a single 30mm cannon in the nose – though in practice problems were encountered with jamming. There was no chance of development work to resolve the issue since by this stage the factories that built the Ta 152 H were overrun by Soviet troops.

Precisely how manoeuvrable the production Ta 152 H-1 was is largely based on speculation. After the war its surviving pilots defended its reputation to the hilt – standing by their claim that it was better than almost anything else in the sky by the end of the war.

However, there are no flying examples available today

and even while the type was briefly in service it was prone to sudden and mysterious failures which, on a couple of occasions, resulted in the death of the pilot.

It seems to have enjoyed mixed fortunes in combat against the excellent Hawker Tempest V and somewhat more success against Yak-3s but it never faced a Mustang or Thunderbolt in their high altitude area of operations, as far as is known. If it had done, it might have faced them on at least an equal footing.

Focke-Wulf Ta 152 H W.Nr. 110003 of JG 301 as it appeared having been captured by the Allies and shipped to America with the Foreign Equipment number 112. The abilities of the Ta 152 H remain difficult to assess since so few were made. On paper it was, perhaps, the best piston-engined fighter of the war.

Messerschmitt Bf 109 K-4

The final production version of the long-serving Bf 109 design was the K-4. The first production examples of the type, conceived in the mid-1930s as a lightweight highly manoeuvrable fighter, flew in 1937, making it easily the oldest type here.

The Bf 109 that saw a vast increase in production alongside the Fw 190 A-8 was the Bf 109 G-6 and later versions were produced in progressively smaller numbers. Shortly before the war's end, Willy Messerschmitt was preparing his company to wind up production of the 109 in preparation for a wholesale switch to the Me 262 and its projected successors.

The K-4 was an attempt to give the basic design a clean-up using all available technological advances to produce something close to the ultimate Bf 109. It was also a move intended to remove the need for the bewildering variety of sub-variants spawned as part of the Bf 109 G series.

Further K series 109s were projected beyond the K-4 but none made it to production.

The K-4's cockpit canopy was altered to the less-heavily framed Erla/Galland design to provide improved visibility and a powerful Daimler-Benz

DB 605 DC engine was installed, producing 1800hp during takeoff, rising to an incredible 1973hp with MW-50; this in an aircraft that was lighter than any of the lightweight Soviet designs.

At its best, the Bf 109 K-4's performance figures were nothing short of astounding. Its boosted top speed of 440mph put it in the same league as the Spitfire XIV and P-51 Mustang, and a climb rate of 4500ft/min was among the very best.

Armament was a problem, however. The K-4's standard load was a 30mm MK 108 firing through the propeller hub and a pair of MG 131 .50 calibre machine guns mounted in the engine cowling. There were difficulties in getting the MK 108 to work properly in this configuration, which meant the gun jammed easily if attempts were made to fire it while manoeuvring.

In practice, many Bf 109 K-4s reached the front line without their MW-50 kits fitted or with some other defect whether as a result of deliberate sabotage or simply poor craftsmanship on the part of the forced labourers who built many of their components. The type was therefore seldom able to reach its dazzling full potential in combat.

The ultimate development of the Messerschmitt Bf 109 to actually reach front line service was the K-4. It was a remarkable upgrade of the type but was often let down by shoddy workmanship and sabotage. This one is WNr. 330230 'White 17' of 9./JG 77 at Neuruppin in November 1944.

Messerschmitt Bf 109 K-4 WNr. 330130 at a Messerschmitt factory during the autumn of 1944. In all-round performance the K-4 surpassed the final development of its great rival, the Fw 190 A-9, but still suffered from its antiquated narrow track undercarriage and small wings.

Messerschmitt Me 262 A-1a

The Me 262 was the first operational jet fighter anywhere in the world when it equipped Erprobungskommando 262 and then KG 51 in May-June 1944 and entered combat against Allied aircraft.

Some American writers such as Robert F Dorr have attempted to advance the claim of the Bell P-59A Airacomet to being the first operational jet fighter – since it entered 'service' in late 1943, but in practice this was little more than part of the development process.

The Me 262 was a high performance combat machine that could outrun anything short of a rocket-powered Me 163. It was armed with four 30mm cannon and potentially R4M air-to-air rockets – making it the most heavily armed aircraft here – and could handle sufficiently well to make good use of its other virtues.

Its design was futuristic – those swept-back wings were revolutionary – and a lengthy period of development before it entered even service testing meant many, though by no means all, of its early foibles were worked out and eliminated.

In combat it was by no means indestructible and its engines had a very limited operational lifespan before they needed to be removed and overhauled. Its nosewheel was notoriously weak, acceleration was slow, landing speed was high and the aircraft was so fast in combat that pilots unfamiliar with jets – in other words, most of its pilots – struggled to hit their targets.

But still, the Me 262 was a deadly opponent for any Allied fighter. It could be outmanoeuvred by a Spitfire but it was very difficult to catch. Even its cruising speed, 460mph, was above anything the Allies could match except in a dive.

It has been endlessly opined that had the Me 262 been built in much larger numbers – or fractionally sooner – the war might have had a different outcome. In reality it was at the very edge of what was technologically possible for 1945 and its engines were the source of its worst problems. They simply could not be made good enough fast enough.

The first jet fighter to begin combat operations anywhere in the world, the Me 262, was an engineering masterpiece and remains a design icon. Not only that, it was also an excellent fighter. One of the best known Me 262s, the unpainted WNr. 111711, was surrendered to the Americans by Messerschmitt company pilot Hans Fay at Rhein-Main airfield on March 30, 1945.

The Me 262 took years to develop but the end result, when its engines had been freshly reconditioned and everything was working correctly, was spectacular. Pictured here is Me 262 A-1a 'White 4' of JG 7 at Achmer in Germany towards the end of 1944.

Messerschmitt Me 163 B-1

The first rocket-powered aircraft in the world was the tailless Ente or 'duck' – a glider designed by Alexander Lippisch powered by an engine produced by rocket pioneers Max Valier and Friedrich Sander at the behest of car company publicist Fritz von Opel.

After Opel left Germany in 1929 and Valier was killed in 1930, Lippisch went to work for the DFS – the German glider research organisation. Here he produced several revolutionary tailless designs and in 1940 these were fitted with a powerful liquid rocket engine designed by Hellmuth Walter, the HWK 109-509, and the Messerschmitt Me 163 was created.

Filled with volatile explosive chemicals that provided enough thrust for only seven and a half minutes of powered flight and lacking even a proper undercarriage once it had been glided back to the airfield, the Me 163 was as much a danger to its pilots as it was to the enemy.

The tiny lightweight interceptor had two 'fuel' tanks, one filled with a methanol, hydrazine hydrate and water mixture known as C-Stoff and the other with a high test peroxide known as T-Stoff. When combined, these volatile liquids produced a powerful jet or sometimes a catastrophic explosion.

This was enough for just seven and a half minutes of powered flight, although during that time the aircraft could reach a speed of nearly 600mph and an altitude of nearly 40,000ft. This performance put every other Second World War aircraft in the shade but it was also the Me 163's undoing as a fighter.

It was armed with a pair of 30mm MK 108 cannon – sufficient to destroy any aerial target, bomber or fighter, with only a couple of hits – but the Komet closed so rapidly on its target that it was very difficult for the pilot to hit anything.

There was usually only enough time and fuel for a couple of passes at enemy bombers before the Me 163 was forced to begin its unpowered glide back to base – often at the mercy of Allied fighters.

For all its years in development, the deaths of several of its pilots and the huge efforts required to maintain it in service, the Me 163 is believed to have achieved only nine aerial victories.

Heinkel He 162 A-2a

More so than the Me 163 – which had actually been in development when the Third Reich was at its peak – the Heinkel He 162 was a product of desperation.

Its overall layout was informed by experiences of the Me 262, with its single BMW 003 jet mounted above the fuselage so that when it crashed the precious engine had a better chance of survival. In addition, its major structural elements were made mostly out of wood.

An ejection seat was fitted but this was ineffective at low altitude. Design work was started by Heinkel as the P 1073 in July 1944 and submitted as the company's attempt to meet an RLM requirement for a cheap jet that was easy to build and easy for a novice to fly, a people's fighter, or Volksjäger, two months later. Once it was declared successful on September 23, 1944, the Heinkel design was modified and rushed into production. The first test flight took place on December 6, and efforts to bring it into front line service were being made as the war ended.

The He 162 had a hidden problem, however. The design should have used Tego film plywood glue – which was in common use with other German

aircraft types – but the factory that made it at Wuppertal was destroyed in an RAF bombing raid and an alternative was needed to ensure He 162 production could go ahead.

The replacement glue, unbeknownst to Heinkel, had a gradual corrosive effect on wood and the He 162s that were produced began to suffer from mysterious

The very first He 162 V1, W.Nr. 20001. When it remained in one piece, the He 162 was a fine fighter aircraft, yet it still matched the speed and hitting power of the Me 262.

Most photographs fail to capture just how small and light the He 162 was – this image of a captured one taking off at Muroc Flight Test Base, California, shows the test pilot, Bob Hoover, looking surprisingly large in relation to the machine.

structural failures. It didn't help that the BMW 003 wasn't ready for service either and was prone to flameouts.

When the He 162 was working properly and not falling apart in the sky, pilots regarded it as an excellent aircraft with light controls that was stable at high speed. While its speed couldn't match that of the Me 262, or even the Meteor F.3, it could out-climb either of them.

Its armament of two MG 151/20 autocannon was relatively light but the small aircraft simply wasn't up to housing the twin MK 108s originally projected.

Given more time and better glue, the He 162 might conceivably have been a contender but in the event it was a non-starter.

SO WHICH WAS THE BEST?

From among the 20 aircraft examined here, there are some obvious dropouts when it comes to deciding which was best. The British Hawker Tempest V was a better fighter than the Typhoon, so the latter can be safely ruled out.

The same applies to the Focke-Wulf Ta 152 and both of the Fw 190 A types. The A-9 and the D-9 can be ditched. Similarly, the Me 262 would have been the better fighter even if the He 162 could have been made to work flawlessly so the notorious Volksjäger has got to go. The Me 163's endurance was too brief to make it an effective fighter so it can also be taken out of contention.

The slowest of the American types was the P-38 Lightning. It climbed well but was surpassed as a dogfighter, therefore it too has to go.

Though they were good at low-level fighting they were not superior to the most exceptional of their contemporaries, so all four of the Soviet types can be excluded too.

This leaves a top 10 of the Tempest V, Spitfire IX and XIV, Meteor F.3, P-47 Thunderbolt, P-51 Mustang, P-80 Shooting Star, Me 262 A-1a, Ta 152 and Bf 109 K.

The non-operational Meteor F.3 and P-80 can probably be ruled out due to ongoing development issues, the Bf 109 K could not be said to have surpassed the Ta 152 in performance, the P-47 Thunderbolt was less manoeuvrable than the P-51 and the Spitfire IX lacked the raw speed to keep up with the new German jets, so a reasonable top five would be the Tempest V, Spitfire XIV, P-51 Mustang, Me 262 A-1a and Ta 152.

Here, narrowing down gets more difficult. The Ta 152 was designed as a high altitude fighter and relied heavily on its complex engine to give it an amazing turn of speed. Its guns were prone to jamming and its reputation rests on only a handful of accounts by decidedly partisan witnesses. It ought therefore to be excluded.

The Tempest V was fast and deadly but it lacked performance at high altitude and straight line speed. Would it have been able to best a Spitfire XIV in a dogfight? Maybe, maybe not.

The choice really comes down to three machines – the Spitfire XIV, the P-51 Mustang and the Me 262 A-1a. All three were potent dogfighters, loved by their pilots and feared by their enemies. The P-51 was the best aircraft in the world for its particular role – escorting bombers over long distances at high altitude – but was it the best fighter of the three finalists?

It lacked the speed of either the Spitfire or the Messerschmitt and its rate of climb was significantly below that of the other two. Its manoeuvrability was excellent but it did not surpass that of the Spitfire.

The Me 262 represented the future of air combat. It could outrun almost anything and its armament was second to none – yet it had serious problems in operational service.

Built by dedicated German engineers rather than slaves, flown in numbers from well-defended airfields and kept well supplied with fuel and fresh engines, it would undoubtedly have had the edge over the Spitfire, but in reality Germany's war situation, coupled with its own design flaws, served to handicap the world's first truly successful jet fighter.

In the final analysis, there have to be joint winners – the British Supermarine Spitfire XIV and the German Me 262. The Spitfire Mk.XIV was faster than any other piston engine aircraft bar the Ta 152, its manoeuvrability was outstanding, it could perform exceptionally at any altitude and its rate of climb was stupendous. Its short range made it unsuitable for escort missions but in a straight fight it was simply very hard to beat. Nevertheless, in one-on-one combat, a Spitfire Mk.XIV pilot would have found it very difficult to best a Me 262 – particularly with the latter able to fly 93mph faster. The Spitfire pilot would have enjoyed greater horizontal manoeuvrability and acceleration but would still have had to surprise the Me 262, or the Me 262 pilot would have had to make a fatal error.

After the war, former Luftwaffe General of Fighters and Me 262 pilot Adolf Galland said: "The best thing about the Spitfire XIV was that there were so few of them."

CLAIMED TOP SPEED

1.	Me 163 B-1	596mph
2.	Me 262 A-1a	540mph
3.	P-80A Shooting Star	536mph
4.	Meteor F.3	528mph
5.	He 162 A-2	522mph
6.	Ta 152 H-1	462mph
7.	Spitfire Mk.XIV	447mph
8.	P-47 Thunderbolt	443mph
9.	Bf 109 K-4	440mph
10.	P-51 Mustang	437mph
11.	Tempest V	432mph
12.	Fw 190 D-9	428mph
13.	La-7	418mph
14.	Yak-9U	417mph
15.	P-38L Lightning	414mph
16.	Typhoon 1b	412mph
17.	P-63 Kingcobra	410mph
18.	Spitfire LF.IX	409mph
19.	Fw 190 A-9	404mph
20.	Yak-3	398mph

CEILING

1.	Ta 152 H-1	49,540ft
2.	Meteor F.3	46,000ft
3.	P-80A Shooting Star	45,000ft
4.	P-38L Lightning	44,000ft
5.	Spitfire Mk.XIV	43,500ft
6.	P-47D Thunderbolt	43,000ft
7.	P-63A Kingcobra	43,000ft
8.	Spitfire LF.IX	42,500ft
9.	P-51D Mustang	41,900ft
10.	Bf 109 K-4	41,000ft
11.	Me 163 B-1	39,700ft
12.	He 162 A-2	39,400ft
13.	Fw 190 D-9	39,370ft
14.	Me 262 A-1a	37,565ft
15.	Tempest V	36,500ft
16.	Fw 190 A-9	35,443ft
17.	Typhoon 1b	35,200ft
18.	Yak-3	35,000ft
19.	Yak-9U	35,000ft
20.	La-7	34,285ft

RATE OF CLIMB

1.	Me 163 B-1	31,000ft/min
2.	Spitfire Mk.XIV	5100ft/min
3.	Spitfire LF.IX	5080ft/min
4.	La-7	4762ft/min
5.	P-38L Lightning	4750ft/min
6.	He 162 A-2	4615ft/min
7.	Bf 109 K-4	4500ft/min
8.	Tempest V	4380ft/min
9.	Yak-3	4330ft/min
10.	Fw 190 D-9	4232ft/min
11.	P-80A Shooting Star	4100ft/min
12.	Meteor F.3	3980ft/min
13.	Ta 152 H-1	3937ft/min
14.	Me 262 A-1a	3900ft/min
15.	Fw 190 A-9	3445ft/min
16.	Yak-9U	3280ft/min
17.	P-47D Thunderbolt	3260ft/min
18.	P-51D Mustang	3200ft/min
19.	Typhoon 1b	2740ft/min
20.	P-63A Kingcobra	2500ft/min

RANGE (without drop tanks)

1.	P-51D Mustang	950 miles
2.	P-47D Thunderbolt	800 miles
3.	Ta 152 H-1	745 miles
4.	Tempest V	740 miles
5.	Me 262 A-1a	646 miles
6.	He 162 A-2	602 miles
7.	Fw 190 A-9	569 miles
8.	P-80A Shooting Star	540 miles
9.	Fw 190 D-9	520 miles
10.	Typhoon 1b	510 miles
11.	Meteor F.3	504 miles
12.	Spitfire Mk.XIV	460 miles
13.	P-38L Lightning	450 miles
14.	P-63A Kingcobra	450 miles
15.	Spitfire LF.IX	434 miles
16.	Yak-9U	420 miles
17.	La-7	413 miles
18.	Yak-3	405 miles
19.	Bf 109 K-4	404 miles
20.	Me 163 B-1	25 miles

WINGSPAN

1.	P-38L Lightning	52ft
2.	Ta 152 H-1	47ft 4½in
3.	Meteor F.3	43ft
4.	Typhoon 1b	41ft 7in
5.	Me 262 A-1a	41ft 6in
6.	Tempest V	41ft
7.	P-47D Thunderbolt	40ft 9in
8.	P-80A Shooting Star	38ft 9in
9.	P-63A Kingcobra	38ft 4in
10.	P-51D Mustang	37ft
11.	Spitfire Mk.XIV	36ft 10in
12.	Spitfire LF.IX	36ft 8in
13.	Fw 190 A-9	34ft 5in
14.	Fw 190 D-9	34ft 5in
15.	Bf 109 K-4	32ft 9½in
16.	La-7	32ft 2in
17.	Yak-9U	31ft 11in
18.	Yak-3	30ft 2in
19.	Me 163 B-1	30ft 7in
20.	He 162 A-2	23ft 7in

EMPTY WEIGHT

1.	P-38L Lightning	12,800lb
2.	Meteor F.3	10,517lb
3.	P-47D Thunderbolt	10,000lb
4.	Tempest V	9250lb
5.	Typhoon 1b	8840lb
6.	Ta 152 H-1	8640lb
7.	P-80A Shooting Star	8420lb
8.	Me 262 A-1a	8366lb
9.	Fw 190 D-9	7694lb
10.	P-51D Mustang	7635lb
11.	Fw 190 A-9	7055lb
12.	P-63A Kingcobra	6800lb
13.	Spitfire Mk.XIV	6578lb
14.	Spitfire LF.IX	6518lb
15.	La-7	5743lb
16.	Yak-9U	5526lb
17.	Yak-3	4640lb
18.	Bf 109 K-4	4343lb
19.	Me 163 B-1	4200lb
20.	He 162 A-2	3660lb

RAM THEM!

❖

April 7, 1945: Sonderkommando 'Elbe' is unleashed on the Eighth Air Force

Adolf Galland's Great Blow never landed but his idea was not forgotten. Influential ex-bomber pilot Oberst Hans-Joachim 'Hajo' Herrmann gave it a novel twist – why not send up fighters en masse and have their pilots simply ram them into the bombers? The attack went ahead, though not exactly as planned…

One of the Luftwaffe's rising stars and a keen ideas man, Oberst Hajo Herrmann was appointed Luftwaffe Inspector of Aerial Defence in December 1943, aged 30, after pioneering the innovative but risky Wilde Sau or 'wild boar' night fighter technique.

This involved day fighters, unequipped or only lightly equipped for night-time operations, being sent up into enemy bomber 'streams' to find their own targets independent of radar guidance – seeking to make visual contact by the glare of specially directed searchlights or the glow of burning buildings below.

Herrmann himself took part in more than 50 Wilde Sau missions – practising what he preached.

In late 1944, the seeds of another idea began to grow. What if he could recruit a large force of idealistic if inexperienced young pilots – volunteers – to participate in an attack en masse against the American bomber force?

Given the Luftwaffe's burgeoning supply of newly built fighters, such a force could be equipped without difficulty, he reasoned, and launched together in a single one-off assault.

So far, so like Adolf Galland's Great Blow. But where Galland's force actually was trained to attack bomber formations with their fighters' weapons, Herrmann's force would not require even this basic instruction.

The attack would be carried out with Messerschmitt Bf 109s fresh off production lines – Bf 109 G-10s, G-14s and K-4s – but with their engine cannon and one machine gun removed. The remaining MG 131 machine gun would have just 60 rounds of ammunition, compared to the usual 300. All armour protection would also be removed and a metal propeller was fitted rather than a wooden one. The standard Revi 16 gun sight was also removed.

Lightened to this degree, the Bf 109's qualities as a fast and manoeuvrable high performance machine would be considerably enhanced – giving it a greater top speed and allowing it to achieve a higher service ceiling.

With such an aircraft, even a novice ought to be able to catch up with waves of high-flying bombers and then… crash into one of them.

When he put the idea to Hermann Göring, the Reichsmarschall gave it a lukewarm reception. But early in 1945 he finally gave it his backing. With this in hand, Herrmann secured a promise of 1500 fighter aircraft from General der Flieger and Luftwaffe chief of staff Karl Koller.

Next, at 3.25pm on March 8, 1945, he sent out an appeal for volunteers to all units of Luftflotte Reich – the home defence force – 'signed' by Göring. It read: "The fateful battle for the Reich, our people and our homeland has reached a critical

Famous or perhaps infamous for an unconventional approach to warfare, Oberst Hajo Herrmann was the mastermind behind the ramming attacks carried out on American bombers by Luftwaffe pilots on April 7, 1945. *Bundesarchiv*

stage. Almost the whole world is against us.

"They have sworn to destroy us in battle and, in their blind hate, to wipe us out. With one final effort we must stem this threatening wave.

"As never before in the history of the Fatherland, we are facing a final destruction from which there can be no rebirth. This danger can only be averted by preparing to fight in the highest German tradition. I turn to you, therefore, in these deciding moments.

"I ask you to rescue, with one conscious effort, the life of your nation from a final downfall. I call you to an operation from which there is little possibility of returning. Those of you who are called will be sent immediately to flight training.

"Comrades – a place of honour in the glorious history of the Luftwaffe will be yours. You will give the German people in this hour of grave danger a hope of victory and you will be an example for all time."

These stirring words elicited 2000 volunteers – more than the absolute maximum number of aircraft that would be available.

It seemed that Herrmann's operation, now named Elbe, had all the right ingredients but the big problem was fuel. With operational Luftwaffe units having struggled for months to exert maximum effort on all fronts as shortages bit deep, there was precious little to spare. Koller first reduced the total of fighters due to participate in Elbe to 1000, then down to 350.

The list of volunteers was correspondingly pared back and those selected began arriving at Stendal airfield – about 60 miles directly west of Berlin – for training on March 24. Prior to briefing his men, Herrmann visited the Luftwaffe test centre at Rechlin to get an idea of how a Bf 109 might best approach a B-17 Flying Fortress or B-24 Liberator, and how it might cause maximum damage by ramming it.

Aircraft such as this Messerschmitt Bf 109 G-10AS were used in the Elbe attacks of April 7. This machine is marked up as belonging to IV./JG 301 but was captured at the Elbe base, Stendal, on April 27, 1945.

shattered, proved to be a more difficult question to answer.

Pilots were given the option of jettisoning their canopy before the attack or leaving it on and hoping to get it open afterwards.

This 'training' lasted for 10 days. Although some Luftwaffe pilots belonging to the earlier Sturm units, which specialised in attacking bomber formations, had successfully rammed their targets, little or no real research had been carried out on the topic. Much of what the young pilots were presented with was guesswork.

Training ended on April 4, and on April 6 Herrmann told his men they would go into action the following day. Unfortunately many of the specially stripped aircraft had not yet been delivered to Sonderkommando Elbe's airfields – Stendal itself, Gardelegen, Sachau, Delitzsch and Morlitz, plus Klecan and Rucin on the outskirts of Prague in Czechoslovakia to the south.

On a more positive note, the experienced Me 262 pilots of JG 7

Serious consideration was also given to how a Messerschmitt's pilot might possibly escape its crippled remains in the immediate aftermath of the crash.

It was decided that the best option was for the pilot to dive on to his target and use his aircraft's propeller as a saw to cut through control surfaces on the tail or wings – or even to chop the rear end of the fuselage off completely. How best to get out of the fighter as it fell away with, at the very least, its propeller

Damaged Messerschmitt Bf 109 G-10s of JG 301 hidden among the trees close to Stendal airfield. Bf 109s used in the Elbe attacks are believed to have been unmarked and were modified to make them lighter and faster. Those machines that survived would probably have been pressed into service with other units.

Bf 109 G-14 WNr. 465805 abandoned at Prague-Rucin airfield in May 1945. Rucin was one of two airfields on the outskirts of Prague in Czechoslovakia that served as a reserve station for the Elbe attack.

Probably the first American aircraft destroyed by a ramming attack on April 7 – B-24L-5-FO 44-49254 'Palace of Dallas'. It was named after its skipper Lieutenant Bob Dallas and as the leading B-24 of the 389th Bomb Group, the 'Sky Scorpions', was hit head-on by the Bf 109 of Unteroffizier Heinrich Rosner at around 12.30pm.

On board Lieutenant Bob Dallas's B-24 was the commander of the 389th Bomb Group, Lieutenant Colonel John B Herboth Jr. He, Dallas, and everyone else on board was killed when the bomber was rammed and veered off course into a second B-24, B-24L-10-FO 44-49533 flown by 1st Lieutenant Walter R Kunkel.

and KG (J) 54, and the Fw 190 pilots of JG 301, were instructed to provide support for the Elbe mission by attacking escort fighters that might otherwise prevent the 'rammers' from doing their job.

April 7 saw a total of 1314 bombers and 898 fighters – the full might of the Eighth Air Force – sent against targets in central and northern Germany.

More than half of the 974 B-17s involved, 529 of them, were to attack airfields at Kaltenkirchen and Parchim, the oil depot at Buchen

and a munitions centre at Gustrow, with secondary targets of the rail marshalling yards at Neumunster and Schwerin.

Another 442 B-17s were to hit airfields at Wesendorf and Kohlenbissen plus an oil depot at Hitzacker. The secondary target was Lundeburg. Three more B-17s were involved in scouting missions.

The other heavy bombers, B-24s, were despatched to destroy explosives plants at Krummel and Duneburg.

At around 11am, the leading bombers were flying over Holland and it was possible for Luftwaffe staff to plot their likely course targets. It was apparent they were heading into northern Germany and could soon become targets for Herrmann's Elbe force. Herrmann gave the order and his plan swung into action.

He wanted to have Elbe forces to the north and south of the bomber stream so the chances of interception were increased. Their rallying points were to be above Domitz to the north and Magdeburg to the south.

Even now, however, the pilots at Stendal had no aircraft to fly. At the last moment, 16 aircraft held in readiness elsewhere were ferried over to them. This still left 40 pilots effectively grounded. There were enough aircraft at Delitsch, 30 Bf 109s, but they were still being refuelled and there was a shortage of drop tanks.

A force of 24 aircraft was available at Morlitz and 20 at Gardelegen. Sachau was the only station to field 30 fully prepared machines. Altogether, around 120 Bf 109s set off from the five bases to intercept the Americans at about 11.15am. Shortly after takeoff, the pilots were surprised to find the Nazi party's official anthem, Horst-Wessel-Lied, and Deutschlandlied, the German national anthem since 1922, were being played directly to them on their radio sets.

This was eventually replaced with the sound of a woman's voice speaking to them. It told them to "remember the women and children burned under the ruins of our towns" and to "save the Fatherland".

The 60 fighters at Klecan and Rucin near Prague were also ordered to take off, even though they were probably too far away to reach the bombers.

It has been estimated that out of the 180 fighters that should have taken off, for one reason or another, only 143 actually did.

The Elbe pilots were now expected to climb to an altitude of 10,000 metres – 32,800ft – where the air was thin and the temperature was about –40°C. This would put them above the bombers and in an

Pictured left is 2nd Lieutenant Robert F Bare of the 563rd Bomb Squadron with his crew. On only their second mission, their aircraft, B-17G-95-BO 43-38869 'Paula Sue', was hit by the Bf 109 of Oberfeldwebel Werner Linder, formerly of training unit Ergänzungs-Jagdgeschwader 1. Linder, Bare and all his crewmen were killed.

Unnamed B-17G-40-BO 42-97105 of the 388th Bomb Group. Flown by 2nd Lieutenant Lew A Hickman Jr on April 7, it was hit by an Elbe rammer but was not immediately destroyed. Five crewmen managed to parachute to relative safety in captivity, but the other four were killed when the bomber went down.

ideal position to dive on them when the opportunity arose.

By midday, around 70 Elbe machines had assembled over Magdeburg, ready for action. Herrmann, realising that the fighters from Prague were not going to be of much use at this point, recalled them.

Even now, several American fighter units began to make contact with Bf 109s flying alone or in pairs at extreme high altitude. North of Celle at 11.55am, one was shot down by 2nd Lieutenant Charles McBath, flying a P-47 of 'Household White' flight of the 63rd Fighter Squadron.

Another was destroyed by P-51 pilot 1st Lieutenant James W Ayers of the 334th Fighter Squadron's 'Cobweb Blue' flight at 12.15pm.

There were soon more sightings and more battles but before long a Bf 109 managed to get through and strike a B-24 of the 330th Bomb Squadron a glancing blow, taking two feet off the port wingtip and damaging the No.1 engine. Another B-24 of the 467th Bomb Squadron had the fin and rudder from its starboard vertical stabiliser sliced off by a Bf 109. Both bombers were able to limp home.

At just after 12.30pm, Elbe pilot Unteroffizier Heinrich Rosner managed the unit's first major success of the day – slamming his aircraft into the cockpit of the leading B-24 of the 389th Bomb Group, the 'Sky Scorpions'.

This was B-24L-5-FO 44-49254 'Palace of Dallas' flown by Lieutenant Bob Dallas but with Lieutenant Colonel John B Herboth Jr, the commander of the 389th, also on board. Dallas and Herboth were both either killed or incapacitated by the attack and the stricken 'Palace of Dallas' careered to one side and crashed into the second aircraft in the formation, B-24L-10-FO 44-49533.

This was a radar-equipped pathfinder flown by 1st Lieutenant Walter R Kunkel, with Major James

ABOVE and BELOW: The damaged tail of B-17G-90-BO 43-38514 'E-Z Goin' of the 100th Bomb Group. The vertical slash marks were made by the Elbe Bf 109 that crashed into it.

F Tolleson on board as command pilot. Both were in the cockpit when the aircraft began to disintegrate around them – the rest of the crew unable to bail out. Abruptly, the cockpit itself came apart and both Kunkel and Tolleson were thrown clear. They parachuted to the ground and were taken prisoner.

The rest of the crew were killed, along with Dallas, Herboth and all but two of their crew members, who also survived as PoWS.

Remarkably, Rosner himself managed to bail out after the crash and survived the attack by taking to his parachute as his ruined Messerschmitt fell away.

At around the same time, B-17s of the 388th Bomb Group came under

attack from Elbe fighters. The first hit was B-17G-95-BO 43-38869 'Paula Sue' of the 563rd Bomb Squadron flown by 2nd Lieutenant Robert F Bare. Oberfeldwebel Werner Linder, formerly of training unit Ergänzungs-Jagdgeschwader 1, crashed his Bf 109 into it, causing fatal damage and a fire which rapidly engulfed it.

Unlike Rosner there was no escape for Linder, whose body was recovered from the Hüttensee, a collection of small lakes just outside Meissendorf, a few days later. All of the 'Paula Sue' crew members were killed – it was only their second mission.

A moment later a second bomber from the 388th BG was rammed, this time an aircraft from the 561st BS – the unnamed B-17G-40-BO 42-97105 flown by 2nd Lieutenant Lew A Hickman Jr. This time the damage was severe but not immediately catastrophic and five crew members managed to parachute to safety – Hickman himself, navigator 2nd Lieutenant Arnold Wolf, bombardier Staff Sergeant Cawthon B Perdue Jr, ball turret gunner Sergeant Albert W Vawter and right waist gunner Sergeant Herman R Meyer. All were taken prisoner on the ground.

The other four crewmen were killed – co-pilot Second Lieutenant John A Hughes, top turret gunner Sergeant Elwood P Eisenhawer, radio operator Sergeant Jim F Martin and tail gunner Sergeant Bob W Wetzel.

Following on behind the 388th came another large formation of B-17s, those of the 452nd BG. They were also set upon by Elbe fighters, seemingly from every direction. The first casualty came quickly when B-17G-15-BO 42-31366 'Old Outhouse – Never a Dry Run', aka 'Snake Eyes' of the 731st BS flown by Dave Owens, suffered a head-on collision. The entire fuselage forward of the top turret was completely destroyed. After

The crew of B-17 'E-Z Goin' stand where the horizontal part of its tail should be.

wavering for a second, the remains of the aircraft crashed down, and all nine crew members died.

Another bomber, B-17G-95-BO 43-38868 of the 728th Bomb Squadron, was sliced in half by a Bf 109, its front and tail sections falling separately to earth. Eight of its crew were killed but two were thrown clear and managed to get their parachutes open. They were bombardier Technical Sergeant Vance P Urban and radar counter measures operator Staff Sergeant Stephen A Kiss.

Two more B-17s suffered damage that eventually resulted in the aircraft being brought down. B-17G-75-VE 44-8634 'Ida Wanna' of the 731st BS, flown by Dabney W Sharp, suffered substantial damage, including having its number four engine knocked out by an Elbe attacker. It crashed near Heide, killing all but two of its crew – top turret gunner Technical Sergeant Arris D Stephenson and radio operator Technical Sergeant Ralph W De Celle.

Most of the crew of B-17G-70-VE 44-8531 'Miassis Dragon' of the 728th BS were more fortunate. When an Elbe machine wrecked the number two engine and set the port wing on fire, pilot 2nd Lieutenant Bill H Gill gave the order to bail out. Everyone managed to get out safely except for tail gunner Sergeant Bill E Costley, whose parachute snagged on the aircraft's tailwheel and dragged him down to his death.

At 1.04pm, the action resumed with an attack on B-17G-55-VE 44-8225 'Hard To Get'. The 579th Bomb Squadron, to which it belonged, was part of the 390th BG which had so far avoided any fighter attacks. This time though, it was a Me 262 of I./KG(J) 54 which dealt the killing blow – a ruined and burning number four engine. Flames spread up the wing and quickly threatened to set the whole aircraft ablaze.

Pilot 2nd Lieutenant Bill Kotta from San Francisco told his crew to abandon ship and all nine men managed to get down safely, while the vacated bomber, actually loaded with leaflets rather than ordnance, hit the ground near Celle.

Another bomber shot down at this time – by a Bf 109 or Fw 190 – was 2nd Lieutenant Warren P Whitson Jr's unnamed B-17G-100-BO 43-39070. The damage inflicted made the aircraft unflyable but there was enough time for Whitson and his nine-strong crew to take to their chutes before it went down. All 10 survived as prisoners of war.

It was well after 1pm when the B-17s of the 100th BG, the 'Bloody 100th', first came under attack. The Elbe pilot who crashed into B-17G-40-BO 42-97071 'Candy's Dandy' of the 418th BS, flown by Lieutenant Arthur R Calder, was unlucky. His terrific strike succeeded in igniting the bomber's load of six 1000lb bombs and both B-17 and Bf 109 were instantly annihilated in a huge fireball that ripped through the sky.

At around the same time, the crews of bombers flying with the 385th BG saw fighters closing in on their formations. Four Bf 109s flew in close, attempted some head-on attacks and then pulled away without making contact. Four Fw 190s made similarly unenthusiastic attempts to fire into the bombers, swerving away before any real damage was done.

Then a Bf 109, flying on its own, plunged out of the clouds above the 385th and sped down through the bombers, apparently taking hits from several gunners before crashing into the unnamed B-17G-80-VE 44-8744 flown by 2nd Lieutenant George E Burich Jr. The heavily damaged bomber began to fall out of formation but it only got a few hundred feet before, like 'Candy's Dandy', it exploded, killing all nine crewmen on board.

Attacks on the 490th BG began at 1.13pm and an unusually well-equipped Elbe Bf 109, believed to have been flown by Leutnant Hans Nagel, formerly of IV./JG 102, accounted for B-17G-80-BO 43-38082 'Lady Helene' by shooting it down with its machine guns.

One crew member, navigator 2nd Lieutenant Jack F Knox, was killed in action but the other eight survived. Pilot Lieutenant Dick L Druhot, radio operator Staff Sergeant Bob M Campbell, ball turret gunner Edgar L Plaeger, right waist gunner Sergeant Ralph F Hogan and Jim Kyser were all taken prisoner.

Three men evaded capture however. These were co-pilot 2nd Lieutenant Chas W Bowers, bombardier Staff Sergeant Carmen B Francis and top turret gunner Staff Sergeant Jim A Bobo. 'Lady Helene' came down over Stolzenau, west of Hannover, which was very close to the Allied front line on April 7.

After putting 'Lady Helene' out of action, Nagel then targeted a second B-17, presumably having now run out of ammunition, and rammed it in the right waist gunner's position. This machine, B-17G-75-BO 43-38058 flown by 1st Lieutenant Carroll D Cagle, reportedly shuddered as Nagel's machine was briefly dragged down the fuselage, opening a 6ft rent along its side, caught on the ball turret and then span away, ripping the supercharger from one engine and smashing the propeller from another as it went.

Somehow, Cagle managed to coax the machine to a forward air base in France and land it successfully. The only crewman injured was the turret gunner, who suffered a broken arm.

A group of civilians, who had witnessed Nagel's battle with the B-17s, saw the remains of his fighter tumbling away and rushed to the crash site. His body was swiftly recovered and identified from its papers before he was buried with full honours in a village cemetery.

At 1.23pm, the 'Bloody 100th' was targeted again. B-17G-90-BO 43-38514 'E-Z Goin' was singled out by another Elbe volunteer. In an article for the 100th Bomb Group Foundation, the co-pilot of 'E-Z Goin', Hank Cervantes, remembered: "Caarraash! The nose yawed left, we skidded right and the plane waggled like a dog shaking water off itself.

"Instinctively Carl (pilot 1st Lieutenant Joe Carl Martin) and

ABOVE and RIGHT: Inspecting the damage done to B-17G-90-BO 43-38514 'E-Z Goin'. To make matters worse, the aircraft's No. 1 engine was accidentally shot up by a gunner aboard a nearby B-17. It had to fly home on only three engines – the damaged tail causing them to struggle against tremendous extra drag.

BELOW: Even seen from the opposite side, the damage to 'E-Z Goin's tail still looks severe.

I kicked hard right rudder – both pedals disappeared under the instrument panel then returned to dangle uselessly; the control columns were violently jerking back and forth, the number one engine was streaming white smoke and all

The final moments of B-17G-105-BO 43-39163 'Happy Warrior'. Missed by the Elbe rammers, the aircraft nevertheless had the double misfortune to be hit by bombs from above and by flak gunners on the ground. Six of its 10-strong crew survived, two of them reaching the ground safely but then being killed by German soldiers or civilians.

the radios including the intercom were dead.

"We had no way to ascertain the crew's condition or to get their damage assessments. However, like the stubborn old war horse unwilling to give up the fight, 'E-Z Goin' seemed to still want to fly, so we stablilised the rocking and rolling with the ailerons and hung on.

"At 1.28pm over the target, toggler (bombardier) Ralph Spada released the bombs and the nose lurched up sharply. Carl rolled the elevator trim wheel forward to add nose-down trim, but the wheel spun ineffectively. Now we were on a collision course with a B-17 in the squadron above.

"Quickly we exerted our combined strength to push the control columns forward. But it was insufficient and at the last possible moment Carl retarded the throttles. 'E-Z Goin' shuddered into a stall and the B-17 slid by close enough for us to see the startled look on the tail gunner's face.

"By trial and error, we found that 'E-Z Goin' was most stable at an airspeed of 105-110mph. This is just above the stall speed at that altitude, but although we could not understand the reason at the time, drag induced by the damaged tail was causing the engines to labour even at that airspeed.

"As the strung-out remnants of the 100th disappeared into the haze, we wallowed through the sky alone. Now the number one engine oil pressure was dropping rapidly; to prevent a friction-induced fire in the engine, we feathered the propeller and shut it down.

"This put an additional strain on the three functioning engines. The battle ended and flight engineer William 'Dude' Dudecz toured the ship to assess our condition. He reported back: 'Everyone's okay. Paul (tail gunner Paul Gerling) says that a Me 109 crashed into us; it just missed hitting him. The

left elevator and the top half of the rudder are gone. There are two big gashes in the fuselage aft of the left gunner's window and the flight control cables and electric wire bundles are cut there. What's left of the tail is flapping up and down so hard that it looks like it might break off. Oh dear, there are bullet holes in the left side of the nose. We think a gunner in another B-17 shot out the number one engine and the master radio control box, that's why the radios are dead.'

"On a B-17, the tips of the horizontal stabilisers are visible from the pilots' side windows, and I looked back to determine what was causing the control wheels to jerk back and forth so violently. 'Carl,' I said, 'Dude's right. The tail's really bobbing up and down on my side. What's yours doing?' Carl checked his and asked, 'Are you sure we're supposed to be able to see the tail from here?' 'Yeah, I'm sure.' 'I don't have one.'

"Dude tapped me and asked, 'Do you want to come back and take a closer look at the damage?' 'No Dude,' I replied, 'I'm needed here. How's Paul doing? Is he still in the tail?' 'No, I ordered him out of there. He says that when parts from the plane went flying back, they knocked off the left horizontal stabiliser on another B-17 behind us. They're back there somewhere.'"

The 'E-Z Goin' remained in one piece all the way back to the 100th BG's base at Thorpe Abbotts in Norfolk but the landing gear had to be manually cranked down.

Cervantes wrote: "Carl made a perfect two-point landing, and as everyone held their breath, we gently lowered the tail-wheel to the runway. 'E-Z Goin' screeched, grated and groaned in protest (picture a giant beer can being scrunched on the sidewalk), but she held together and a fleet of emergency vehicles trailed us to our hardstand.

"Five hours had elapsed since the collision, but no one cheered, embraced or shook hands – we were all barely into our twenties and at that age everyone thinks he is going to live forever."

Flying close to 'E-Z Goin' had been another B-17 of the 100th, B-17G-60-VE 44-8334, with Lieutenant Bill E Howard at the controls and Lieutenant Genaro Delgado as co-pilot.

Seconds after the attack on 'E-Z Goin', Delgado noticed that 44-8334's starboard wing was burning. Exactly what caused the damage is unclear – it may have been debris from another aircraft, bullets from a Bf 109 or even bullets from the gunner of another B-17. Whatever the cause, the aircraft's No. 3 engine was on fire.

Howard banked 44-8334 sharply out of formation and ditched the load of bombs it was carrying. He tried various manoeuvres to put the flames out but failed. Then the main wheel beneath the engine caught fire and began to produce a stream of thick black smoke. As the wing itself began to buckle, Howard set his autopilot and ordered his crew to abandon ship.

All nine men managed to get out and dropped to the ground beneath their parachutes. They all hit the ground safely too, but on his way down Howard was fired on by shotgun-wielding civilians. They missed but it gave the pilot a taste of what was to come. Quickly captured by armed civilians, he was beaten before being dragged to the local village hall where he had stones and mud thrown at him by an angry mob.

Already at the village hall was navigator 2nd Lieutenant Doug Jones, who had suffered a broken jaw during his beating. They were eventually taken to a Luftwaffe detention centre with four of their fellow crewmen but the other three were nowhere to be seen.

Much later, after the war, the bodies of the missing men were found – sergeants Mike A Maty, Lou A Lehrman Jr and George F Thomas had been killed after landing but their killers were never found.

There were more casualties when the bombers finally reached their targets. B-17G-70-VE 44-8528 'Flak Sack' was destroyed, not by flak, but by bombs dropped from another B-17. Eight of its 10-strong crew survived and were taken prisoner. Top turret gunner Staff Sergeant Roland R Fricault evaded capture and the 10th, right waist gunner Staff Sergeant Tom G McMahon, was killed in action.

Another aircraft, B-17G-105-BO 43-39163 'Happy Warrior', had the double misfortune of being hit by bombs from above and by flak gunners on the ground. From a crew of 10, six men survived to be taken prisoner. Two others reached the ground alive but were subsequently killed.

In addition to the B-17s rammed or otherwise shot down, many more suffered varying levels of damage which forced them to land on the Continent rather than flying back to their bases in England – in the 303rd BG alone, three aircraft had to get down as quickly as possible: the unnamed 43-38763, 42-97944 'Daddy's Delight' and 44-6309 'The Duchess' Granddaughter'.

The raid was judged a success, with 1257 bombers successfully dropping their ordnance on target out of the 1311 that set off (not including the three B-17s on recon duties) – a total of 3446 tons of bombs. Some 850 people were killed on the ground, four airfields were badly damaged, rail infrastructure targets were destroyed and oil production at two sites was disrupted.

A report on the day's action produced for the Eighth Air Force's director of intelligence, Brigadier Charles Y Banfill, stated: "After

Despite the best efforts of Sonderkommando Elbe, the vast majority of Eighth Air Force bombers deployed on April 7, 1945, returned home safely. Some, such as 42-97944 'Daddy's Delight', were not shot down but suffered damage severe enough to force an early landing at Allied airfields on the Continent.

a lapse of several weeks during which conventional single-engined enemy aircraft have largely been non-active partners in the air war, and even when encountered have shown very little fighting spirit, today in excellent flying conditions the Luftwaffe put up a force of some 115-130 single-engined fighters supplemented by 50-plus jets.

"From all reports it appears that this was a desperate attempt on the part of the enemy, and although enemy aircraft fought aggressively and made determined efforts to get through to the bombers, our losses were comparatively light while more than half the enemy force was destroyed or damaged.

"Signs of desperation are evidenced by the fact that Fw 190 pilots deliberately rammed the bombers, bailing out before their planes went into the formations and making fanatical attacks through the murderous hail of fire.

"Tactics were thrown to the wind and attacks were made from all positions, mainly in ones and twos."

Banfill added: "The desperation of the enemy attacks and the closeness and abandon with which they were pressed seemed to be evidence of 'suicidal ramming'. They were not suicidal ramming attacks, but in each case were aircraft clearly out of control either through injury to pilot or structural failure of attacking aircraft.

"The closeness of attack has given rise to rumours of ramming but review of complete division experience fails to substantiate the ramming theory."

Eighth Air Force fighter pilots claimed to have shot down 67 enemy aircraft on April 7, 1945. When Me 262s, Fw 190 Ds, probables, a case of 'friendly fire' and multiple claims are removed, this boils down to 47 claimed victories. Bomber gunners claimed a further six Bf 109s shot down, making a total of 53. Given the likelihood of overclaiming, this probably amounts to about 30 Elbe aircraft being shot down before they reached their intended targets.

It has been estimated that around 40 Elbe fighters managed to attempt a ramming attack on the American bombers. Some 10 bomber losses, two B-24s and eight B-17s were directly attributed to ramming by enemy fighters, with overall losses to all causes of 17. Or sources have claimed anywhere between eight and 14 B-17s were destroyed by Elbe attacks.

Herrmann hoped to carry out further attacks the following day but it was not to be. No further Elbe attacks were ordered and he turned his attention to his final wartime scheme – Sonderkommando Bienenstock or 'Beehive'.

This involved using Fieseler Fi 156 Storch light aircraft to carry demolition teams behind enemy lines where they could carry out attacks on Allied static targets such as bridges, supply depots and parked-up tanks.

The order to establish Bienenstock was given on April 14

and 15 personnel were ready for action four days later. Five aircraft took off for operations on April 25 with only four returning and no concrete results.

The following day, nine Storchs took off between 1.45am and 2.30am, carrying two-man demolition teams. Two bridges were blown up but five of the aircraft and their crews were lost. Finally, on April 28, three Fi 156s took off to attack supply depots in south east Germany but none returned.

8

WHEN 'WEE WILLIE' RAN OUT OF LUCK

❖

April 8, 1945: Boeing B-17G 42-31333 is destroyed

One of the iconic images of the American daylight bombing campaign is a photograph showing a B-17 Flying Fortress with one wing blown off, plummeting to its doom on April 8, 1945. But which Fortress was it, where had it been and who was on board?

The 302nd Boeing B-17G to roll off the production line at Boeing Plant 2, King County, Washington, was serial number 42-31333. It was the second aircraft of the fourth production block of B-17Gs and was therefore one of a hundred B-17G-15-BOs.

Like all the early B-17Gs, it was painted up in camouflage colours before being flown to United Airlines' completion and modification centre at Cheyenne, Wyoming, on October 22, 1943. Here its turrets received minor adjustments and guns were calibrated.

Next, 42-31333 was flown to Grand Island Army Airfield in Nebraska, a journey east of some 360 miles, on November 3. Six days later, it was transferred to Memphis and on December 20, 1943, it arrived at USAAF Station 121, aka RAF Bassingbourn in Cambridgeshire.

Coded LG-W and referred to in reports as 'aircraft #333', 42-31333 was assigned to the 322nd Bombardment Squadron of the 91st Bombardment Group (Heavy) 'The Ragged Irregulars' and was immediately prepared for its operational debut.

The first pilot to take 42-31333 into action was 2nd Lt Robert L Gough. The mission, on Christmas Eve 1943, was an attack on German installations under construction south of Andres, near Calais, in France. Gough and his crew took off at 11.12am along with seven other B-17 crews. They hit the target area with sixteen 300lb bombs from 21,000ft at 1.41pm and returned home safely at 4.36pm.

Results could not be observed due to poor visibility and no enemy fighters were encountered but flak over the target was intense. 42-31333 came through unscathed, though one of the other B-17s suffered minor damage.

The next mission for Aircraft #333 saw a different pilot take the controls – 2nd Lt Paul D Jessop. This time it was a New Year's Eve raid on the Bordeaux-Merignac Aerodrome, five miles west of Bordeaux in France. The base was home to the Luftwaffe's Kampfgeschwader 40, operating anti-shipping Focke-Wulf Fw 200 Cs and Junkers Ju 88s.

This time 42-31333's payload was 21 M47 incendiaries. Heavy cloud cover over Bordeaux-Merignac, however, resulted in the raid being diverted to Cognac-Chateaubernard, also used by KG 40 and its Fw 200 Cs. The airfield was hit from 18,000ft and the results were reported as "good".

This time, however, the B-17s were met by 15 to 25 German aircraft, including Messerschmitt Bf 109s, Focke-Wulf Fw 190s and Junkers Ju 88s. None of the bombers were lost but of the seven aircraft from the 322nd involved, six were damaged including #333.

From this point on 42-31333 became Jessop's regular ship and he named it 'Wee Willie', having a cartoon image of a baby standing atop a bomb painted on the side by line mechanic and nose artist extraordinaire Sgt Anthony 'Tony' Starcer – the same man who painted the 'Memphis Belle's' famous telephone girl.

More missions followed on January 7 and 21, 1944, Jessop having flown a different B-17 on January 14 while 'Willie' was undergoing repairs and maintenance.

He flew Willie once again on January 24 before being promoted to 1st Lieutenant on January 26. He next flew Willie on January 30 but during the following mission, to Wilhelmshaven in Germany on February 3, 1944, Willie suffered major flak damage. Bombing altitude was 29,500ft but nevertheless Willie suffered a bad hit. Waist gunner Sergeant Henry F Osowski was wounded and the aircraft was out of commission for more than two weeks while repairs were made.

It was to be the last time that Jessop would fly 42-31333. That May he was promoted to captain, completed the last of the 25 missions he and his crew were required to undertake, and went home to the US. 'Wee Willie' now passed from one pilot's hands to the next. During its service career a total of 37 men including Gough and Jessop took it into action, with dozens of different crewmen occupying the various positions inside the fuselage.

After brief stints with lieutenants Clarence N Pingel, Edward Robertson and Bernard W Hayen, 'Wee Willie's' second long-term pilot was Lieutenant Edward L Mooney.

Mooney joined the 322nd on April 28, 1944, and his first mission, on the 29th, saw him flying as a co-pilot for the first of two 'check rides' with pilot 2nd Lieutenant Edward Waters over Berlin.

Mooney's second mission to Lyon, France, saw him once again in the co-pilot's seat as the marginally more experienced pilot 1st Lieutenant Lester W Duggan commanded Mooney's crew.

It was the third mission to Troyes, France, where Mooney commanded his own crew in combat as the pilot.

Mooney was eager to get his 25 missions done. His crew's tail gunner, John F Coyne, said Mooney "offered our services for every available fill-in" because his wife Eileen was pregnant and he "wanted to be home for the grand occasion".

It is equally possible that he simply wanted to get himself and his men home and out of danger; every time they climbed into a B-17 they had about a one-in-five chance of not making it back.

In the end, he managed all 25 and 12 more – toward the end, 35 missions were required and Mooney did 37 (two being aborted with no credit given) – in roughly 12 weeks.

In doing so, he and his crew flew in numerous B-17s, including

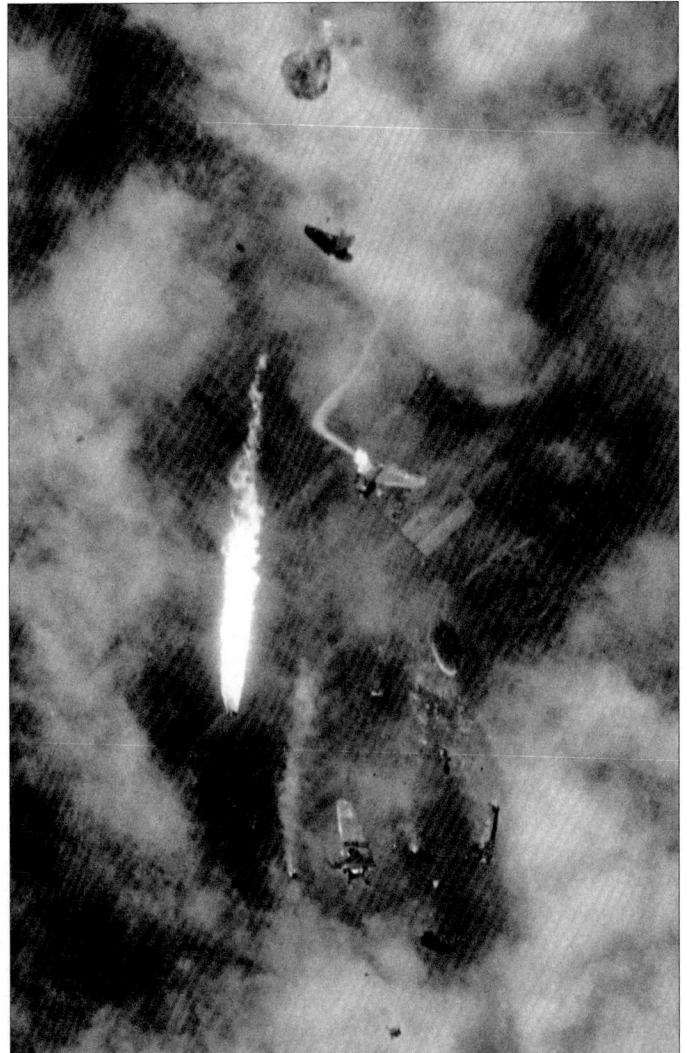

LEFT and ABOVE: Three photographs taken by the automatic bomb strike camera of a Boeing B-17 show the final 18 seconds of 42-31333 'Wee Willie' on April 8, 1945, over Stendal, Saxony-Anhalt, Germany, after it was hit by an 88mm flak burst. In the first, Willie's port wing has already sheared off and is spinning over its tail, gouting flames. The second photograph, frequently used to show the horrors faced by American air crews during the daylight bombing campaign over Germany, shows the aircraft during the final seconds of its death dive. All nine crew members are still inside. In the last photograph, 'Wee Willie' has exploded. Fragments of debris, wings, tail and fuselage fall burning to the ground.

'Fifinella' twice, 'The Bloody Bucket' once, 'Boston Bombshell' twice, 'Heavenly Body' once, 'Lassie Come Home' three times, 'The Liberty Belle' once, 'Red Alert' once, 'Bachelor's Bride' once, 'Man O War II' once, 'My Baby' twice, 'Superstitious Aloysius' three times, 'Texas Chubby' five times, 'Chowhound' once – and 'Wee Willie' 13 times.

Every Fortress that Mooney flew was eventually shot down – none survived the war.

Mooney's first acquaintance with 'Wee Willie' came on May 20, 1944, when elements of the 322nd were sent to join a bombing run on Villacoublay airfield in northern France, which was being used by fighter units of Luftflotte 3. Willie suffered minor damage, with holes in the nose and waist.

He flew Willie to Berlin on May 24 but despite heavy enemy opposition the aircraft suffered only one flak hit.

May 25 saw him fly to Nancy-Easey, France, to bomb a target without flak or fighter attacks taking place.

On June 3, he flew Willie against coastal gun emplacements at Hardelot in the Calais area – part of the pre-D-Day tactics of convincing the Germans that the invasion would arrive there rather than in Normandy.

Next, on D-Day itself, June 6, 1944, Willie bombed a radar station close to La Riviere. This was part of the Gold Beach landing area – where at 7.25am, 13 minutes after the B-17 attack, British troops began to wade ashore.

D-Day +1, June 7, saw Willie and Mooney in action again, this time attacking the Ju 88 C fighters of V./KG 40 based at Kerlin-Bastard on the Brest peninsula. There was flak over the target but no fighters.

On June 8, Willie took minor flak damage to its nose during a raid on a railway bridge over the Loire river, about six miles east of Tours, but otherwise came through unscathed.

June 11, 12, 13, 15 and 18 saw still more raids on airfields and an oil refinery in Hamburg. June 19 was Mooney's final mission with 'Wee Willie', an attack on the KG 40 aerodrome at Merignac in Bordeaux.

Good results were observed, the runway having been rendered unusable with 100lb bombs. Thus ended Mooney's 'one month with Willie' tour.

The frenetic activity of June had taken its toll on the bomber, and it did not fly again until June 28. During that mission, to attack a railway bridge over the Oise canal at Anizy Le Chateau, eight miles

south-west of Loan, pilot Lt Louis M Walton was forced to turn back due to mechanical problems with two of its engines.

More repairs followed and it was not until July 8 that Willie was back in the air, this time with a third long-term pilot in the hot seat – Lt Roy A Hammer. He had the aircraft for just seven missions in 20 days but during that time he and his crew attacked the Junkers aircraft factory, Messerschmitt's Augsburg facility and the hydrogen peroxide plant at the Peenemünde research facility.

Another pilot, John M Hamilton, then flew Willie for a single mission to attack Lechfeld where pilots were being trained to fly Germany's first operation jet and rocket fighters. Hammer returned on July 24 for a ground support mission against German troop formations south of St Lo ahead of Operation Cobra – the breakout from the Normandy beachhead.

His association with Willie ended after another mission on July 28 and five more pilots took Willie up for a handful of missions: lieutenants Dale N Brant, Thomas P Burne, Russel H Brown, Howard Mitchell and William H Trent.

Lt Louis G Starks flew the aircraft for six missions in a row from August 24 to September 8 but it would be one of his predecessors, from the five, who would go on to become the most prolific Willie pilot of them all by a considerable margin – William H Trent.

After a single mission attacking a heavy gun position on the Brest peninsula on August 11, 1944, Trent returned to Willie on September 19, 1944, for an attack on the rail marshalling yards at Hamm, Germany, and again on September 25 for a rail on the Frankfurt rail yards. During this mission Trent's tail gunner S/Sgt Dennis J Moore was hit in the left eye by

The first regular crew of B-17G-15-BO 42-31333 'Wee Willie'. They are, back row from left, co-pilot 1st Lt John A Moeller, navigator 2nd Lt Harry Lerner, waist gunner SSGT Robert Kelley, ball turret gunner SSGT Sidney D Martin, bombardier Lt Joe Gagliano, pilot 1st Lt Paul D Jessop. Front row from left, waist gunner SSGT Robert C Elroy, radio operator SSGT Berchel L Shope, flight engineer/top turret gunner SSGT Walden P Southworth and tail gunner SSGT Joe Zastinchik.

Two men gaze into the forward crew access hatch of 'Wee Willie' at Bassingbourn in Cambridgeshire. The photograph is undated. *Library of Congress*

The four bomb markings on the nose of 42-31333 indicate that this photograph was probably taken between January 21 and January 24, 1944. It seems likely that it was taken to commemorate the nose art newly painted on to the aircraft by mechanic Anthony 'Tony' Starcer.

Boeing B-17G 42-232095 LG-L Ack Ack Annie was a contemporary of 'Wee Willie' flying with the 322nd Bombardment Squadron. The pair flew together on more than 60 missions and 'Ack Ack Annie' was there on April 8, 1945, when Willie was destroyed.

Lt Edward L Mooney was the second longest serving pilot of 'Wee Willie', in terms of missions flown. He took the aircraft into action over Normandy before, during and after the D-Day landings.

a piece of flak debris and needed three stitches.

Trent was promoted from second to first lieutenant the same month and on October 9 he flew Willie during an attack on the ball bearing factory at Schweinfurt. Five days later, he took Willie out over Cologne, then it was Brunswick's turn on October 22 and the oil plant in Hamburg's dockyard area on October 25. More than a month after its first visit, 42-31333 returned to Hamm's rail yards, though contrails from other aircraft got in the way and necessitated bombing from 28,900ft.

Sturmbock attack
The aircraft's greatest challenge to date came with a mission to the Leuna oil refinery at Merseberg on November 2, 1944, with Trent again at the controls.

The 322nd provided 13 of the 693 B-17s sent to attack the target and they were part of the high squadron of the bombing group. Former Willie pilot Roy A Hammer, now

Another contemporary of 'Wee Willie' with the 322nd was 43-38901 LG-T Star Dust. It was also flying nearby when Willie was fatally damaged on April 8.

a captain, was flying the leading aircraft, 44-8208 'My Baby II'.

The target was hit as planned and the formation turned around to return westwards. As they were passing Hamburg the B-17s were

bounced by a formation of between 50 and 75 enemy aircraft. Many of these were Fw 190 Sturmbock bomber killers but there were also Me 163 interceptors and Me 262 jets involved in the attack.

The Sturmbocks, heavily armoured and fitted with 30mm cannon, moved in on the B-17s in formation, line abreast, and hit them at close range. The effect was devastating but not quite as devastating as the Germans would have liked.

According to the official 322nd Bombardment Squadron report: "After the first pass the attack was continued by individual aircraft and formations up to five aircraft from all directions. The attacks covered a period of about 20-25 minutes. Friendly fighters were engaged at the time by large formations of enemy aircraft including a few Me 163s and Me 262s.

"The group lost 13 aircraft to flak and fighter attacks, the worst loss suffered to date. Of these the 322nd lost six ships. Captain Hammer's aircraft #208 was last seen off to the left of formation apparently under control but with fire observed in the radio room and behind #3 engine due to enemy action.

"Lt Burne in aircraft #212 flying on Captain Hammer's left wing was observed peeling off from the formation, losing altitude but apparently under control with no visible damage. Lt Russel H Brown in aircraft #298 in the number three position of the high element was last seen lagging about 1000ft behind the formation under control and with no apparent damage.

Two of 'Wee Willie's' pilots appear in this badly faded photograph. Lt William H Trent is seated in the aircraft's cockpit while Captain Roy A Hammer is in the front row on the right. Also pictured are, back row, radio operator S/Sgt Emile Freeman, the only member of Hammer's crew killed when his B-17, 'My Baby II', was shot down over Merseburg on November 2, 1944; Hammer's engineer S/Sgt William Nagy and Sgt John Baird. Beside Hammer on the front row is his navigator Lt Raphael Czepkiewicz. When the photograph was taken Trent was Hammer's co-pilot. It is possible that the aircraft shown is in fact 'Wee Willie' during Hammer's tenure in July 1944. *Library of Congress*

"Lt Hare flying number three of the low element in aircraft #083 was last seen under control but with his left wing on fire and under persistent attack by six to eight Fw 190s. Lt Brant in the flying spare #202 was lost at the time of the enemy aircraft attack but no observations were made of the circumstances.

"Lt Hamilton, flying aircraft #102 in the number four position of the low element, was last observed under control but losing altitude rapidly and burning fiercely in

both wings at the number two and number four engines.

"The tail gunner S/Sgt Wayne W Ritchie, ball turret gunner, S/Sgt Thomas R Giordano, and S/Sgt Joseph M Wirtz Jr, on Lt Sparkman's crew, distinguished themselves during the attack by continuing to fire their guns in spite of severe damage to their aircraft and wounds sustained by them."

On a single mission, five former 'Wee Willie' pilots were lost – Captain Hammer and lieutenants Burne, Brown, Brant and Hamilton. Hammer and seven of his crew were taken prisoner when 'My Baby II' crashed at Micheln, Germany. The ninth man, Emile Freeman, was killed.

Tom Burne and four of his crew died when 43-38212 'Gal O'My Dreams' had its intercom shot out and bomb bay set on fire by the German fighters. It crashed at Gross Oesingen and the four survivors became PoWs.

Russel Brown and five of his crew died and their aircraft, 44-6298 White Cargo, crashed at Neugattersleben.

The only known photograph of 42-31333 'Wee Willie' in flight before the photographs taken during its destruction. *USAF*

The three survivors were captured. Dale Brant managed to get out of his aircraft, 43-38202 'Miss Slipstream', over Marbitz, near Halle, but he and his navigator John F Gustavson were shot dead near the crash site. His other seven crew members were taken prisoner.

Hamilton, his co-pilot, the tail gunner and a waist gunner aboard 42-98012 'Cannon Ball Too' were killed. The other five crewmen managed to jump from the stricken aircraft and were taken prisoner. The aircraft crashed at Haideburger.

Despite being hit by a Me 163 during the attack, 'Wee Willie', Trent and his crew made it back to Bassingbourn in one piece. Three days later they were back in the air and heading for the rail marshalling yards at Frankfurt. The mission seemed to go as planned but when the 322nd's aircraft returned and photographs of the bombing run were analysed, it was found that they had actually dropped their bombs over the western edge of Offenbach, a town five miles east of the target.

Another raid on November 9 was even further off target due to faulty navigational gear. Trent and the Willie crew, among 12 aircraft allocated to the raid from the 322nd, were meant to hit a fortress four miles south east of Metz in support of American ground forces. Instead, they ended up dropping their bombs six and a half miles away.

Eventually, after three unsuccessful runs at the target, the B-17s, including 'Wee Willie', were forced to land at a captured airfield in France for refuelling before they could return home.

A third failure followed on November 16. It was another raid in support of ground forces, this time fighting in the Aachen area. There was little flak and radio beacons were functioning properly for guidance but there was heavy cloud over the target and little was achieved by the 322nd.

There was another attack on the Merseburg oil plant on November 21 but this time the 322nd's objective was the flak battery protecting it. Very low cloud forced the B-17s down to 19,500ft and on the way back from the target Willie was forced to make another unscheduled stop on the continent, this time due to mechanical failure. Trent put it down on an airfield in Belgium for repairs.

Five days later, Willie was part of a group attacking a railway viaduct at Altenbeken and on November 27 Trent flew it on a mission to attack a bridge at a railway marshalling at Offenburg. Cloud cover was a problem again, however, and the pilots decided to make their bombing run entirely on instruments. When the photos were later examined, it was found that the bombs had been dropped two and a half miles away from the target.

Trent ended a month of almost non-stop action with another raid on Merseburg at the controls of 'Wee Willie' on November 29.

An automatic bomb strike camera image showing just that – bombs hitting the synthetic oil production facility at Merseburg during the raid on November 2, 1944. It was during this attack that four former pilots of 'Wee Willie' were killed and a fifth was taken prisoner.

An unidentified later crew of 'Wee Willie'.

According to the 322nd report: "Visual sighting was done and good results obtained on the hangar line. On return, persistent fog at base forced our aircraft to land at Bury St Edmunds."

From a German perspective, the 'good results' were anything but. I./JG 2 was taken completely by surprise. All five waves of bombers hit the airfield and turned it into a cratered wasteland. Most of the station buildings on the north side were destroyed too, though only two German personnel were killed and only one Fw 190 was destroyed. It took until December 31 to make the airstrip usable again.

Before then, on December 28, Trent flew 'Wee Willie' to attack the railway bridge at Remagen over the Rhine. Another mission, to hit a German communications centre at Wittlich, followed on December 29 – it was Trent's last with Willie and the last of his operational tour.

The next generation

With almost all of Willie's previous pilots now dead or gone home, a new generation took over sporadically. First to take the helm was Lt James

An attempt to bomb the Soest railway marshalling yard near Kassel on December 4 failed due to poor weather conditions. Neither 'Wee Willie' nor Lt Trent took part in a raid on Berlin the following day – the first attack on Berlin by the 322nd since June. However, another ex-Willie pilot did fly the mission: Howard Marshall in his now regular aircraft, the unnamed 43-38693.

After the mission, the official report stated: "Anti-aircraft fire was accurate and consisted of both barrage and tracking fire. Our aircraft #693, Lt Mitchell pilot, was last observed at 1058 hours with number one prop windmilling. Six chutes reported."

In fact, only five men survived. Mitchell and three of his crew were killed.

'Wee Willie' was flown by Lt Robert L Schuck on December 9 for a mission against the railway marshalling yards at Stuttgart but Trent was back in command on Christmas Eve 1944. This time

Willie was to attack the airfield at Merzhausen near Frankfurt where the Fw 190 A-8/R6s and new Fw 190 D-9s of I./JG 2 were based. A total of 198 B-17s joined the attack in five waves.

Another unidentified crew with Willie. The number of mission markings on the fuselage, around 105, tends to indicate that the pilot might be Lt Wayne F Swegle, who flew the aircraft on eight occasions around this time.

L Ashlock Jr for another attack on a communications centre, this time at Bitburg on New Year's Eve. The raid was relatively successful but no results could be observed due to heavy cloud cover.

December 14 saw the arrival with the 322nd of new pilot Lt Robert E Fuller, from Hollywood, California, and his first mission was to bomb Cologne on January 3, 1945. 'Wee Willie' took part in the uneventful mission but was flown by another newcomer as of December 4, Lt Robert Marlow. Lt Edward E Chase had joined the unit in the same intake as Fuller and he flew Willie for the first and only time on January 5, also against Cologne.

Lt Ashlock flew Willie again on January 10 during a mission to bomb Ostheim aerodrome, home to elements of JG 11, and Lt Arthur Ernst took a turn flying Willie on January 14 for an attack on the Deutsch bridge over the Rhine at Cologne. It was Ashlock again on January 15 and 20 for bombing runs on rail yards at Ingolstadt and a bridge over the Rhine at Ludwigshaven respectively.

Lt Harold L Reinhart flew Willie on January 21 – more marshalling yards, this time at Aschaffenburg – and Lt Fuller finally took his first turn on February 1 to hit still more rail yards at Mannheim.

The rest of February saw five more unfamiliar faces flying 'Wee Willie' for brief periods – Robert W Roach, Marvin L Pearson, Wayne F Swegle, Robert H Miller and Nelson D Van Blarcom.

From February 14 to 21, 1945, Swegle flew Willie for four missions in a row. The first of these would have seen Willie bombing Dresden – the city already burning from a night of incendiary attacks by the RAF – however, a diversion to avoid an unexpected front of bad weather saw the 322nd's aircraft diverted to bomb Prague instead.

On the way home, the squadron

Another automatic bomb strike camera shot, this time showing bombs falling on the rail yards at Stendal on April 8, 1945. Just minutes later, 'Wee Willie' was destroyed.

encountered heavy flak over Munster and seven aircraft suffered damage. B-17G #027, with Fuller at the controls, was the worst hit, and Fuller was wounded.

Rather than attempt to reach Bassingbourn, Fuller turned his aircraft in the direction of Advanced Landing Ground A-83, Denain in northern France. After jettisoning the ball turret, Fuller made a belly landing and was taken to hospital.

Swegle's other missions with Willie, including another four in early March 1945, were uneventful, with little or no damage taken to any 322nd aircraft, including 'Wee Willie'.

After March 7, Willie was taken off the roster until March 19, when it was sent back into action with yet another pilot, Lt Leroy B Hansen, against the Bohlen synthetic oil plant. Lt Gerald G Kranch flew Willie for two missions on March 22 and 23, then it was Joseph J Troccoli's turn for a single mission on March 24.

Having finally been passed fit for service, Fuller's first mission back

in action after his injury was on March 30, 1945, flying 'Wee Willie' once again. The objective was the shipyards at Bremen and the 322nd encountered heavy flak, though Willie came through unscathed and was back in action the following day, with Fuller taking it on a raid over a locomotive depot at Halle.

Several missions in early April were scrubbed so Willie's first outing of the month was to the airfield at Reinsehlen on April 4. No enemy opposition was encountered but then cloud cover was so thick that no positive identification of the target could be made and the 322nd brought their bombs back to Bassingbourn. Fuller flew Willie again on April 7 against airfields at Fassberg and Kohlenbissen, the group achieving "excellent results".

Raid on Stendal
It was business as usual the following day, April 8, 1945, when Fuller flew 'Wee Willie' as part of a 73-bomber raid on the locomotive repair shops at Stendal in Saxony-

Anhalt, Germany. The mission was carried out using H2X 'Mickey set' ground search radar to identify the target – although the lead and high squadrons, the latter including 'Wee Willie', could actually see it anyway.

The mission was a great success, the 322nd's official report noting: "The high squadron was furnished by the 322nd, led by Lt Johnson. Strike photographs for the high squadron's bombs show an excellent concentration of hits covering the aiming point.

"Almost the entire concentration lies within a 1000ft circle over the MPI. Meagre to moderate tracking AA fire on the bomb run which was extremely accurate resulted in minor damage to 13 aircraft and major damage to four in the group.

The high and lead squadrons each lost one aircraft in the target area from flak damage."

The aircraft lost from the lead squadron, the 401st, was B-17G-50-BO 42-102504 Times A-Wastin', flown by Lt Peter Pastras. Its demise was witnessed by Lt Mike Fodroci, a navigator aboard another B-17. He saw the four gun batteries on the ground tracking bursts of flak through the lead formation, getting closer and closer to Times A-Wastin' until the fourth one went directly into the aircraft's still-open bomb bay.

In his report he states: "The pilot must have been killed instantly; for the ship pulled up and veered to the right, climbing directly over our ship. Captain Shelby put our

ship into a dive so steep that I was thrown up against the astro hatch of the ceiling in the nose – seems I hung there for a brief second or two.

"I also observed that a bad fire was burning on the aircraft's forward bomb bay area and that the co-pilot was trying to climb out of the small window with his back pack on. Somehow, we saw three chutes emerge from #504 as she spun toward the earth."

Times A-Wastin's co-pilot, Bob Morris, was killed when the B-17 exploded in mid-air, along with all but two of its crew, engineer Lyle Jones and radio operator Bob A Smith, who were taken prisoner on the ground.

The aircraft lost from the high squadron was 42-31333 'Wee Willie'.

B-17G-50-BO 42-102504 'Times A-Wastin" was blown apart by a direct flak hit at around the same time as 'Wee Willie' over Stendal. This colour image shows an earlier 'Times A-Wastin" crew.

In the Missing Air Crew Report S/Sgt George Little, a gunner aboard a 401st B-17, states: "I observed 42-31333 receive a direct flak hit approximately between the bomb bay and the number two engine. The aircraft immediately started a vertical dive. The aircraft fuselage was on fire and when it had dropped approximately 5000ft the left wing fell off.

"It continued down and when the fuselage was about 3000ft from the ground it exploded, and then exploded again when it hit the ground. I saw no crew members leave the aircraft or parachutes."

There was another witness to 'Wee Willie's' end that was able to offer an even more accurate account of what happened. About a third of the B-17s flying on any given mission were equipped with bomb strike cameras. These were fitted under the floor in the radio room and the lens cone was exposed to the elements.

The cameras were automatically operated from 'bombs away' until they ran out of film or automatically stopped after a predetermined number of exposures. They took an exposure every six seconds, with the mechanism then winding the film on, ready for the next shot.

In this way, the success or failure of a mission could sometimes be determined by examining the photographs.

The automatic camera on another B-17, flying beside or below 'Wee Willie', captured the aircraft's violent final 18 seconds in three photographs.

Shortly before the last of the three, Willie was torn apart by an explosion that ripped right through the fuselage and blew Lt Robert E Fuller clear out of the cockpit. Somehow, he managed to get his parachute open and survived the descent. The remainder of his crew were all killed.

Although he is recorded as having been taken prisoner, Fuller's final fate remains unknown and in some sources he is listed simply as 'killed in action' alongside his crew.

'Wee Willie' had completed 127 missions and was destroyed on its 128th.

9

WORLD'S FASTEST MESSERSCHMITT

❖

April 9, 1945: Hans-Guido Mutke's controversial dive

Whatever might be said about its other abilities and
frailties, there is no denying that the Messerschmitt
Me 262 jet fighter was fast. Extremely fast. Little was
known for certain about the sound barrier in 1945, but did
one German pilot manage to push his Me 262 through it?

For every famous pilot who flew the Me 262 in the last days of the war, there are a dozen more that history has all but forgotten.

Fähnrich Hans-Guido Mutke looked certain to be just such an unremembered and uncelebrated pilot.

Born in Neisse, Germany, on March 25, 1921, he became a medical student but was called up to join the war effort. After pilot training he joined Nachtjagdgeschwader 1 in 1942, flying Messerschmitt Bf 110s and Dornier 217s against British bombers.

Then, in the March of 1945, he was transferred to 10./EJG 2 (Ergänzungsjagdgeschwader 2 or 'Operational Fighter Training Group 2') at Lechfeld for retraining on the Me 262, since his experience with twin-engine fighters made him an ideal candidate.

On April 9, Mutke was ordered to carry out a training mission at high altitude and therefore climbed to just over 36,000ft – close to the Me 262's ceiling of 37,565ft. He was at this near-maximum altitude when he overheard a flight controller warning that a P-51 Mustang was about to intercept one of his fellow trainees and decided to fly down to help.

He pushed his Me 262 'White 9' over into a steep 40-50° left bank with both engines on full power and plunged downwards.

In just a few seconds, the aircraft began to shudder violently.

Mutke himself recalled: "The airspeed indicator was stuck in the red danger zone, which is over 1100kph. I noticed that rivets began popping out of the tops of the wings. The aircraft began vibrating and shaking wildly, banging my head against the sides of the cockpit.

"I moved the stick wildly around the cockpit. For a brief moment, the aircraft responded to controls again, then went back out of control. The aircraft still did not respond to pressure on the stick so I changed the incidence of the tailplane.

"The speed dropped to 500kph, the aircraft stopped shaking and I regained control. After diving about three miles I was able to return to base. On the runway the mechanics were very surprised by the appearance of the aircraft, which looks as though it had been shaken by the hand of a giant."

In another interview, Mutke stated: "What happened had never happened to another pilot as I entered a very dangerous realm without knowing it. I had no idea what was happening. I thought there was something wrong with the aircraft."

The mechanics may have been bewildered by the state of Mutke's jet fighter but his superiors were not impressed.

He said: "When I landed, the commander was furious and

Towards the end of his life, former Luftwaffe pilot Hans-Guido Mutke claimed that during the Second World War he had flown his Messerschmitt Me 262 faster than the speed of sound. Pictured here during the 1960s, Mutke, who stood 6ft 2in tall, became a gynaecologist after returning to Germany.

Swiss ground crew attempt to tow Hans-Guido Mutke's Me 262 A-1a/R1, 'White 3' W.Nr. 500071, after he landed near Zurich on April 25, 1945. Presumably they have taken heed of the printed notice on the forward landing gear door not to tow the aircraft by its nosewheel. *Bundesarchiv*

demanded to know what I had done with the aircraft, and demanded to know if I had gone above the red mark of 950km.

"I said, 'Of course not. You know, this might be a Monday production'. That means it was made the day after the workers had been drinking."

Mutke soon discovered that the comrade to whose aid he had been rushing got shot down anyway, but had managed to parachute to safety.

And that might have been the end of the story.

Two weeks later, on April 23, Mutke was ordered to go to Fürstenfeldbruck to join 7./JG 7 but the following day American tanks advanced to within 30 miles of the airfield and the unit was transferred to Bad Aibling. On the same day the unit's leader, the famous ace Major Heinz Bär, left to join Adolf Galland's 'squadron of aces' JV 44.

At the last minute, with almost everyone already en route, it was realised that one particularly well dispersed Me 262 had been forgotten about – W.Nr. 500071 'White 3' which was sitting under cover in woodland just over a mile from the airfield.

Since Mutke was available, he was ordered to collect it and fly it to join his new comrades at Bad Aibling.

When he got out on to the airfield he discovered that the only personnel in sight were a trio of soldiers who had no idea how to service a Me 262.

Mutke later recalled: "I didn't even know how long the Me 262 had been standing there and if it was filled up with fuel or not.

"I called the three soldiers, but all the efforts to start the aircraft were in vain. So we decided to try it again next morning. On the morning of April 25, we succeeded in starting the Messerschmitt. It was a high risk, because I didn't know where the aircraft had come from and how long it had been standing there.

"We found out that the fuel tanks were almost empty. We towed it to the petrol station and in order to reduce the time of filling the fuel tanks, the pump attendant put two fuel hoses into it, one in each of the two fuel tanks."

Just as the fuel was flowing, Mutke looked up and saw 25-40 B-26 Marauders approaching the airfield. He ordered the attendant to pull out the hoses, fired up the aircraft's twin engines and took off. The bombers, seeing him become airborne, flew into a bank of cloud and by the time he gained enough altitude to give chase he could see no sign of them.

Checking his fuel, he saw that he did not have enough to reach Bad Aibling and resolved to fly to Lake Constance and ditch in it instead.

When he reached it, he decided to attempt a landing over the border in Switzerland. However, he had no

When Mutke landed in Switzerland, his aircraft was carefully examined by Swiss engineers and photographed from every conceivable angle. As an R1, W.Nr. 500071 was equipped to fire salvos of R4M rockets, although it wasn't fitted with any when Mutke flew it on April 25, 1945.

idea whereabouts in Switzerland he could put the aircraft down. Reaching the southern shore of the lake, his fuel gauge showed zero.

He flew over what appeared to be a Swiss airfield and was soon being escorted down by four Swiss fighters. Mutke was taken prisoner and his aircraft was handed over to the Swiss military for testing before being put in storage.

From October 1945, Mutke was treated as an interned civilian and returned to his medical studies. In later years he moved to Argentina and then Bolivia, working as a pilot for civilian airlines flying DC-3s.

A move back to Germany followed and Mutke took up a position as a gynaecologist in Munich.

In 1957, the Swiss authorities handed Me 262 W.Nr. 500071 over to the Deutsches Museum in Munich.

During a conference to mark the 50th anniversary of jet powered flight in 1989, Mutke mentioned

A rear view of Mutke's Me 262 as engineers tinker with an access panel on its nose.

his experiences of April 9, 1945, to some of the experts present and they discussed with him the possibility that he might in fact have broken the sound barrier some two years earlier than Chuck Yeager – who officially became the first man to go supersonic on October 14, 1947.

The precise details of Mutke's flight, the suitability or otherwise of the Me 262 for passing through the sound barrier, the accuracy of its in-flight instruments and the technical difficulties of proving or definitively disproving the pilot's story have occupied the minds of Me 262 enthusiasts and the aircraft's detractors ever since.

Those who support his claim – he died on April 8, 2004, donating his body to anatomist Gunther von Hagens – cite a handbook on the Me 262 written by the USAAF in January 1946 based on tests of captured aircraft.

This states: "At speeds of 950 to 1000kph the airflow around the aircraft reaches the speed of sound, and it is reported that the control surfaces no longer affect the direction of flight. It is also reported that once the speed of sound is exceeded, this condition disappears and normal control is restored."

Computer simulations carried out at Munich Technical University in 1999 concluded that the Me 262 might have been able to go supersonic.

Professor Otto Wagner told Reuters, which was reporting on Mutke's claims in 2001: "I don't want to exclude the possibility but I can imagine he may also have been just below the speed of sound and felt the buffeting, but did not go above Mach 1."

In addition, engineers recreating the Me 262 at the time in the US, using modern engines in a replica airframe, said they believed Mutke might have been right.

Jim Byron of the Me 262 Project said: "We met with Herr Mutke and having listened to his story, we believe he could have accomplished this in the severe dive and engine flameout."

Wartime flight tests by Messerschmitt engineers determined the Me 262 would become uncontrollable beyond Mach 0.86, leading to an ever steepening dive that could not be corrected by the pilot. Higher speeds would then result until the airframe came apart due to high G loads.

Some believe that Mutke's changing the tailplane incidence enabled him to overcome the steepening dive and level out to regain control briefly at just above supersonic speed.

Sceptics have pointed to the unreliability of German measuring equipment during the later stages of the war and compressibility in pitot tubes that resulted in

Another view of W.Nr. 500071 under tow. The aircraft was involved in the second controversial episode for which Hans-Guido Mutke is primarily remembered.

inaccurate readings close to the speed of sound.

Also counting against the Me 262 was its fuselage, designed without knowledge of the area rule, which would have resulted in very high drag at transonic speeds. Nevertheless, it is acknowledged that engine thrust combined with the pull of gravity during a steep dive might have supplied sufficient force to push the Me 262 through the sound barrier and into supersonic flight.

In all likelihood, while the air passing over Mutke's aircraft might have exceeded Mach 1, his jet probably did not. However, it will never be known for certain just how fast he really went.

10

CANADIANS AGAINST THE KOMET

❖

April 10, 1945: Leutnant Friedrich Kelb achieves the final rocket fighter victory of the war

As the Allies advanced into Germany, Bomber Command continued to target German rail infrastructure. On April 10, it was the turn of the marshalling yards at Engelsdorf and Mochau near Leipzig. The mission was almost routine but one of the defenders the bombers faced when they got there most definitely was not.

It was planned that two waves would strike the rail yards – one during the early evening and one that night.

In the first wave were 134 Lancaster bombers – 110 from 6 (RCAF) Group's 419, 424, 427, 428, 429, 431, 433 and 434 Squadrons and another 24 from 8 (Pathfinder) Group – plus 90 Halifaxes from 408, 415, 420, 425, 426 and 432 Squadrons and six Mosquitos of 105 Squadron.

Having taken off from their bases in England between about 2.30pm and 3pm, the bombers linked up with their escort, RAF Mustang IIIs, and reached their target by about 6pm. The skies were blue with patchy cloud.

In the meantime, one Halifax from 408 Squadron became lost and turned for home, while another four Halifaxes and two Lancasters suffered mechanical trouble and went back to base early, running on three engines.

There was heavy flak as the bombers prepared to release their loads at between 15,500ft and 19,000ft, and several aircraft were hit – including Lancaster I PB903, BM-F, of 433 Squadron, flown by Flying Officer Robert Grisdale. He feathered the starboard inner engine after it took damage.

A 425 Squadron Halifax had a hole measuring 2sq ft blasted through the wireless operator's compartment, wrecking the oxygen system. Then the Mosquitos dropped their target indicator flares.

An air gunner with 433 Squadron, Cameron Clare Campbell, wrote in his diary: "This was a good raid but we were towards the rear of the formation and took a dreadful pounding from slipstreams all the way to the target.

"There was heavy predicted flak close to the target. With predicted flak, the Germans would fire a burst and from observing the blast could make a correction on the next shot which would be closer, then make a correction on the second burst and usually the third burst had your number on it.

"The secret was to change your height or heading after the first blast. Just as we were about to drop our bombs, I heard Chris ask the bomb-aimer who was flying F Freddy because he was on fire. Just as Plaskett answered him telling him it was Grisdale's crew, the bombs and the plane blew up. I never saw the explosion as it was slightly ahead of us and to the right

Veteran Messerschmitt Me 163 B Komet rocket fighter pilot Leutnant Friedrich 'Fritz' Kelb of I./JG 400 in the cockpit of his aircraft. Kelb was sent up to attack the Allied bomber formation targeting rail yards near Leipzig on April 10, 1945, using a new weapon over which he had only indirect control. The SG 500 Jägerfaust was fitted in the aircraft's wings and triggered automatically by a daylight sensor.

but we felt the blast and saw the debris as we passed."

According to the official RCAF report: "This Lancaster was hit by flak, the starboard inner was seen to be feathered. Then a small explosion was seen, the aircraft flipped onto its back and spiralled to the ground. No parachutes were seen."

At this point several crews saw small dark shapes flitting among their aircraft and were quick to identify them as Messerschmitt Me 163 B-1 Komet rocket-propelled point defence interceptors.

The pilot of 415 Squadron Halifax VII RG447 'S', Flying Officer R Jupp, spotted an enemy fighter at 6.02pm at 16,500ft, 4500ft off the port bow. The Halifax's mid upper gunner told the Jupp: "Corkscrew starboard" and opened fire with the Me 163 some 2400ft away. The rear gunner joined in at 2100ft and the Me 163 reportedly broke away.

At around the same time, 6.02pm, the crew of 425 Squadron Halifax NP937 'T' saw a Me 163 attacking a Lancaster bomber. They reported seeing flames coming from the Lanc's rear turret and no combat manoeuvres being undertaken by the bomber. NP937's mid-upper gunner fired at the Me 163 and reportedly saw it stall, roll onto its back and go into a steep dive.

That Lancaster was ME315 'LQ-K' of 405 Squadron – a Lancaster III. The pilot was Squadron Leader C H Mussels. The official report on what happened stated: "In the target area, immediately following release of target indicators, Lancaster aircraft 'K' ME315 was attacked by an enemy fighter Me 163. The attacking aircraft approached from the rear and above, and with one burst completely shot away the rear turret, rudder and elevator.

"Damage was also caused to the H2S set and mid-upper turret. The rear gunner, Flight Lieutenant Mellstrum, was in his turret when the attack commenced

Lancasters flying in large formation during daylight was a rare sight for most of the war – but the attack on railway marshalling yards near Leipzing on April 10 took place just after 6pm. Sunset would have been at around 7.45pm. This switch to daylight bombing made the Allied aircraft a viable target for the Me 163 point defence interceptors of I./JG 400.

and is believed killed. This officer is missing, no further information available.

"A number of Mustangs who were acting as fighter escort moved in closer to the disabled aircraft and covered it until it reached the front lines. The pilot, due to the fact that he had only partial control of the aircraft, ordered the crew, except for the mid-upper gunner, to bale out over RAF station Woodbridge.

"Had not the mid-upper gunner been injured the whole crew would have baled out. The pilot was successful in making a reasonable landing at RAF station Woodbridge. All members of this crew, with the exception of the rear gunner, are back at this unit."

One of the RAF Mustang pilots, Flying Officer Johnny 'Slops' Haslope of 165 Squadron, claimed to have destroyed the Me 163 during the attack. His report stated: "I was flying as Green 1 when at approx. 6.05pm I noticed a bomber begin to smoke and something appear to fly off it. This resolved itself into a Me 163 which climbed vertically at great speed.

"I reported the aircraft and dropped my overload tanks and gave chase at full throttle. The Me 163 turned towards me and I had a shot at him in a right-hand turn, range about 900 yards and 30 degrees defection, but observed no strikes.

"The Me 163 then spiralled into a vertical dive which I followed, firing several bursts of about 2-3 seconds observing strikes on four occasions on the wing roots and several small pieces came off.

"These strikes were observed by Flying Officer Rae flying Green 2, Flying Officer Lewin, Green 3, and Flight Lieutenant Kelly 64 Squadron. I overshot rapidly at 3000ft and had to pull up to avoid collision, wrinkling the wings as I did so.

"The Me 163 continued on down and was observed by Squadron Leader Potocki of 315 Squadron

The small size and unusual shape of the Me 163 B-1 rocket fighter are evident in this photo showing 2./JG 400's Unteroffizier Rolf Glogner, pictured right, and his machine. Glogner proved that the Me 163 could be effective in the right circumstances by shooting down a de Havilland Mosquito on March 16, 1945. After the disbandment of JG 400, he served with Leutnant Kelb in JG 7 on the Eastern Front flying Me 262s.

This still from a propaganda film shot between August 21 and September 9, 1944, shows Me 163s on the apron at I./JG 400's base at Brandis airfield, near Leipzig.

and Flying Officer Wacnik of 306 Squadron to hit the ground and explode near an airfield believed to be either Brandis or Manstorf.

"I turned away from the aerodrome and climbed back with Green 2 to rejoin my squadron, followed by 40mm flak from the aerodrome."

It is believed that his Mustang III, KH557 SK-Z, was so damaged by his power dive in following

the German aircraft that it never flew again.

Precise records are lacking but it is believed that three Me 163 B-1s from 1./JG 400 had been sent up to attack the bombers, one of them flown by Lt Friedrich 'Fritz' Kelb of 1/JG 400. He took off from Brandis airfield near Leipzig with the express purpose of field-testing a new weapon. His aircraft was one of three Me 163s to have been equipped with the SG 500 Jägerfaust weapon and was the only one to see action. This was also the last time that Me 163s would see action.

The SG 500 was designed and patented in 1944 by Oberleutnant Gustav Korff and consisted of a number of rifled steel tubes, each loaded with a single projectile and mounted vertically in the carrier aircraft.

The single shot tubes were linked to an optical sensor mounted on the upper portion of the carrier aircraft which when it sensed the substantial difference in light caused by flying underneath a bomber, into its shadow, fired the tubes automatically.

The tubes themselves were ejected beneath the aircraft as the projectiles flew upwards, cancelling out any hazardous recoil and simply leaving a series of holes in the carrier aircraft. A 20mm version of the weapon was tested on a Fw 190 before the production 50mm version was built for the Me 163.

On the Me 163, four tubes were fitted to each wing, with the optical sensor being installed in the port wing where there was already a suitable access panel.

Signals officer with 2./JG 400, Feldwebel Hans Hoever, saw what happened when Kelb took the weapon into combat: "I watched Kelb attack a formation of about

150 Lancasters that were bombing Leipzig and the city's outskirts on April 10. I had just finished my shift and was standing on the observation tower of the fighter control command post next to the Würzburg radar when I heard over the loudspeaker that Leutnant Kelb was about to take off with his special aircraft.

"I heard the rocket motor and saw Kelb climb above the trees at the end of the runway south of where I was standing. I followed him with the aid of the long-range flak telescope and saw him head towards the lead aircraft of the bomber formation which was flying at a height of about 8000m.

Lancasters of 405 Squadron, like this one, were pathfinders for the main bomber force on April 10. During the attack, two bombers were lost but the only 405 Squadron machine to suffer heavy combat damage and remain airborne, Lancaster III ME315 'LQ-K', made it home, albeit without its tail gunner. Several witnesses saw ME315's tail section being hit by a Me 163.

A I./JG 400 Me 163 B under full rocket power over Brandis, near Leipzig, in 1944. The unit became operational at the airfield in July 1944 and remained there until its dissolution a fortnight before the war's end.

An Avro Lancaster bomber belonging to 433 Squadron. The Canadian unit was based at RAF Skipton-on-Swale in North Yorkshire and flew Handley Page Halifaxes for over a year before re-equipping with Lancasters for the last three months of the war. On April 10, 433 Squadron's Lancaster I PB903, BM-F, flown by Flying Officer Robert Grisdale was shot down over the unit's rail yard target.

This low quality shot purportedly shows the underside of a Me 163 wing fitted with SG 500 firing gear. The white block with the vertical row of four holes in it gives more visible evidence of the positioning of the unusual weapon.

The wreckage of a Me 163 modified to fire the 50mm SG 500 weapon. The only visible evidence of this is on the machine's port wing. A series of small black holes run in a straight line through the centre of the white Balkenkreuz from front to back. With the weapon installed, the tips of four metal tubes would have been visible protruding from the holes. When the SG 500 was fired, the tubes were ejected from the bottom of the wing, while the projectile shot upwards, leaving just the holes, four in each wing.

"I thought he wanted to ram it but just at the moment he passed about 100m below the aircraft, the bomber exploded in a cloud of smoke and flames. I had never before seen a bomber so easily destroyed as that attack by Leutnant Kelb.

"Just after the bomber exploded I noticed that the escort fighters had spotted Kelb. My first thought was that he had enough fuel left, at least enough for 15 seconds, to reignite his engine. I was pleased to see the motor spring to life just as the fighters swarmed down to attack him and Kelb shoot through them to a height 2000m above them.

"My telescope allowed me to follow the ensuing fight. With his fuel spent, Kelb turned and dived past a fighter that was close to him with such a speed that the fighter was not aware of what had happened."

North American Mustang IIIs of 315 Squadron in Europe in the spring of 1945. The unit's Squadron Leader Wladyslaw Potocki witnessed a Me 163 attacked by Flying Officer Johnny 'Slops' Haslope, of 165 Squadron, hit the ground and explode on April 10, 1945.

A German report on the use of the Jägerfaust on April 10, made on April 12, stated: "The first and also the last operational trial of the Jägerfaust was made over Leipzig on April 10, 1945. At about 6pm a strong formation of enemy bombers appeared over the city. A Me 163 B with 'vertical armament' went into action.

"The aircraft came unheeded below the enemy machines. The armament was immediately discharged. A bomber at once fell out of the sky like a burning torch, none of the crew being able to make their escape. Two other aircraft were so badly damaged that they also crashed after flying over out airfield. Our aircraft was able to draw away still unobserved by the enemy, and was only located and attacked by Mustang and Thunderbolt fighters when it had arrived back over our airfield.

"The anti-aircraft defences were able to keep the enemy aircraft

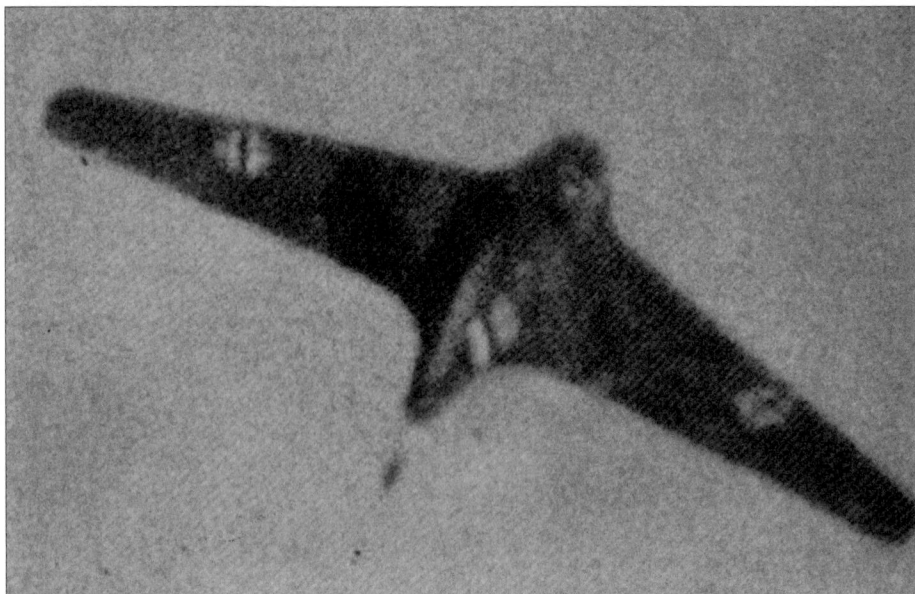

Gun camera footage of a Me 163 in flight and under attack. The distinctive 'bat wing' shape was enough to strike fear into the hearts of bomber crews wherever it appeared. Though the type is believed to have been responsible for destroying only 16 Allied aircraft, 12 of them were four-engined bombers.

at a distance while a smooth landing was made with no damage to our aircraft. These were the last successes obtained with the Me 163 B."

Flight Lieutenant Melborn Leslie Mellstrum was the tail gunner in 405 Squadron Lancaster III ME315 'LQ-K' when it suffered severe damage during a Me 163 attack. His turret torn open, his body fell to the ground. It was recovered by the Germans and buried three days later by a party of British PoWs.

Veteran assault glider pilot Hauptmann Wilhelm Fulda was the commander of I./ JG 400 on April 10, 1945. The unit was disbanded just nine days later.

Aftermath

Kelb was killed in action less than three weeks later, on April 30. After the disbandment of JG 400, he joined I./JG 7 flying the Me 262. During a fighter sweep he was apparently attacked by a pair of fighters from the 358th Fighter Group flown by Lieutenant Joseph Richlitzky and Captain James H Hall, each claiming a Me 262 damaged. Another version of events suggests that he was hit by flak near the Focke-Wulf facility at Cottbus.

Every crewman aboard Grisdale's Lancaster I PB903, BM-F, was killed and their remains were buried in Berlin War Cemetery. Another bomber went down during the same raid, Halifax BIII NA185, 6U-B, which was reportedly hit by bombs from another aircraft. All of its crew were killed too.

Nothing of the tail gunner of Lancaster III ME315, LQ-K, of 405 Squadron, Flight Lieutenant Melborn Leslie Mellstrum, remained in his turret when the crippled aircraft arrived at Woodbridge, but he had not disappeared completely as a surprising number of men did during the war.

A British prisoner of war, Gunner Robert David Williams of the 11th (HAC) Regiment, Royal Horse Artillery, reported on June 24, 1945 that he had been at Stalag IVG at Engelsdorf during April 1945, when a chaplain asked him to join a funeral service for two British servicemen – one of them another PoW killed during an air raid, and the other an airman whose body had been found by the Germans.

After he was liberated, he told the British military authorities: "The burial took place in the evening of April 13 at the cemetery of the Luthren Evangelical Church at Engelsdorf about 10km east of Leipzig.

"The bearers and all the burial party were from Lager 29. The men were under the command of Lance Sergeant Frank Cole. They slow-marched from outside the mortuary to the grave. The coffins were draped with the Union Flag. They were lowered into the grave simultaneously by two different parties.

"After the service the men saluted. The Germans were unable to supply the usual firing party as the Americans were just outside Leipzig and the guns could be heard constantly. We ourselves were evacuated by the Germans at 3am the following day."

Williams asked after the airman's identity following the service and several hours later was told that it was Melborn Leslie Mellstrum.

To this day, it is unclear precisely which aircraft Kelb hit with his novel upwards firing weapon. If he was alone, then it would make sense that Lancaster ME315 was badly damaged by him. If there were indeed two other Me 163s with him, the flak hit on Lancaster PB903, Grisdale's machine, may in fact have been the result of his SG 500 – the effects of which would have been very like a flak strike.

The machine that blew Mellstrum from his turret and was then followed to its destruction by Haslope's Mustang might have been one of Kelb's comrades, rather than Kelb himself.

It is a mystery unlikely to ever be satisfactorily resolved.

11

THE GRASSHOPPER THAT KILLED A STORK

❖

April 11, 1945: Piper L-4H v Fieseler Fi 156 Storch

One of the oddest air-to-air actions of the war took place
on April 11. Often wrongly cited as the 'last dogfight' in the
European theatre, it nevertheless spoke volumes for the
courage of US airborne artillery spotters.

American tanks of the 5th Armored Division were rolling across central Germany in the direction of Berlin by April 11, 1945, and on the front line was the 71st Armored Field Artillery Battalion.

Equipped with M7 self-propelled 105mm howitzers and M4 Sherman tanks, the unit drove east and south along the Weser river before crossing at Hamlin and continuing to push east.

According to the official history of the battalion, Fire Mission: The Story of the 71st: "The old familiar tactics of bypassing heavy resistance by using secondary roads and passing through only small villages were put to use again.

"Sixty and 70-mile marches were standard operations during the passing of those lightning fast days. The deeper we drove into the Reich the longer our supply lines were stretched and the more difficult the job of service battery became."

And on April 11: "That day German air activity increased over the column. All sizes and types either roared or limped past. Our ack-ack would pull off to the side of the road at the slightest pause."

Since landing at Utah beach on July 28, 52 days after D-Day, the 71st's progress had been guided by spotter pilots flying ahead over enemy territory. Equipped with tiny two-seat 65hp Piper L-4 Grasshoppers, the spotters flew long hours in often hazardous conditions.

One of the 71st's most experienced Grasshopper pilots was 24-year-old Merritt Duane Francies of Wenatchee, Washington. Known as Duane, or sometimes 'Doc' because he took some pre-med courses at college and was often called upon to give first aid for minor injuries, Francies had been with the 71st from the start of the European campaign.

Pilot Lieutenant Duane Francies, left, and observer Lieutenant William Martin in front of Piper L-4J 44-80699, serial number 12965, G-54 – one of three L-4s used by observers for the 71st. Another, J-54, was named Miss Me!? by Francies.

Lieutenant William Martin, left, and Lieutenant Duane Francies with the Fieseler Storch they forced down on April 11, 1945.

He flew an L-4H called 'Miss Me!?' He said: "I named my plane 'Miss Me!?' Because I wanted the Germans to do that, the reason for the exclamation point, but I also wanted someone back home to 'miss me', so there was the question mark."

April 11 saw Francies and his observer Lieutenant William Martin flying ahead of the 5th Armored about 100 miles west of Berlin. Not far from the 5th's advancing vehicles, on a side road, they noticed a German motorcycle and sidecar speeding along. Moving in to get a closer look, they then saw a Fieseler Fi 156 Storch observation aircraft flying at about 700ft above some trees.

Abandoning the motorcycle outfit, Francies and Martin decided they needed to do something about the Storch, and fast, before it had a chance to report on the 5th's positions.

Afterwards, Francies wrote: "The Storch had an inverted eight Argus engine. It was also a fabric job and faster and larger than the 'Miss Me!?'. It spotted us and

The Fieseler Storch is a physically larger, tougher and more powerful aircraft than the Piper L-4 but only 3000 or so were built, compared to 20,000 L-4s. *Tony Hisgett*

One of the lightest aircraft to see action during the war, the Piper L-4's diminutive size made it a difficult target to hit and meant it used fuel only sparingly – allowing it to remain aloft to extended periods. *Pete Markham*

we radioed: 'We are about to give combat.'

"But we had the advantage of altitude and dove, blasting away with our Colt .45s, trying to force the German plane into the fire of waiting tanks of the 5th. Instead, the German began circling."

Flying slightly above and across the German aircraft, Francies and Martin had opened their aircraft's side doors and emptied their pistols into the Storch. They saw hits on its windscreen, fuel tank and right wing. Francies then gripped the Grasshopper's control column between his knees while he reloaded. He wrote: "The two planes were so close I could see the Germans' eyeballs, as big as eggs, as we peppered them."

Trying to avoid the American aircraft that dogged its every move, the Storch went into a low turn

– too low – and its right wing tip struck the ground. It span around, cartwheeling, its right wing and undercarriage coming apart, before finally coming to rest right side up.

Francies set down close by and he and Martin ran to the wreck. The German crew had stumbled, dazed, from their machine. When they saw the Americans approaching, the pilot jumped behind a pile of sugar beet to hide and the observer dropped to the ground, defeated.

Seeing that the observer had been hit in the foot, Francies ran over and went to help. He pulled off the man's boot and a .45 bullet fell out. Martin, his gun now also reloaded, fired a warning shot and the pilot came out with his hands up.

Francies took the pilot's uniform insignia and a German flag they found inside the Storch. He wrote:

"I never found out their names. They could have been important, for all I know. We turned them over to our tankers about 15 minutes later, after the injured man thanked me many times for bandaging his foot. I think they thought we would shoot them."

Not long after their aerial victory, Francies and Martin were scouting ahead of the 5th when elements of the division reached the Elbe. They flew over the river and landed on the other side, only to be approached by a group of Soviet soldiers wearing grey greatcoats and riding steppe ponies.

The Russians backed off when they saw the Grasshopper's white star insignia but were not friendly and later the Americans got back in their aircraft and flew back to the 71st. They had not realised that they were supposed

The Piper L-4's large glass windows – ideal for artillery spotting and reconnaissance – are clearly illustrated in this colour photograph of 236389.

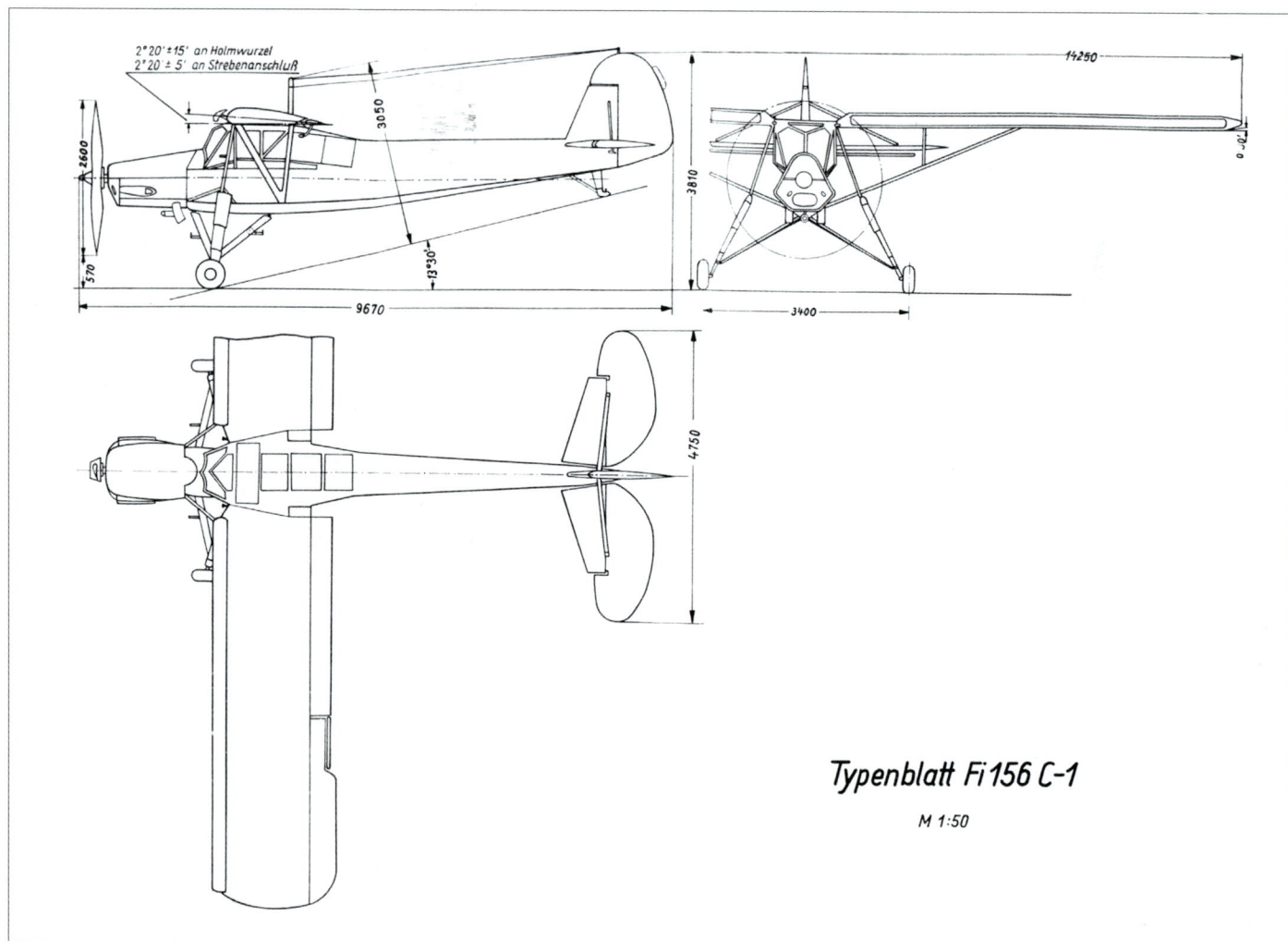

Typenblatt Fi 156 C-1

M 1:50

A three-view drawing from an original brochure for the Fi 156, specifically the C-1 model. The aircraft looks unusual even for its time since its form was largely dictated by its function.

to remain on the 'American' side of the Elbe.

When the war ended, Francies had twice been recommended for the Distinguished Flying Cross but had not received it. Years passed and the recommendations were forgotten about. Francies served during the Korean War before becoming a commercial pilot. In 1966, historian Cornelius Ryan wrote about his exploits in his book The Last Battle. A US senator, Harry Jackson, pressed for Francies' achievements to be recognised and finally, the following year, Francies got his DFC.

GRASSHOPPER V STORCH

	Piper L-4 Grasshopper	Fieseler Fi 156 Storch
Crew:	2	2
Length:	22ft 5in	32ft 6in
Wingspan:	35ft 3in	46ft 9in
Height:	6ft 8in	10ft
Empty weight:	765lb	1900lb
Loaded weight:	1220lb	2780lb
Powerplant:	1 x Continental A-65-8 air-cooled four-cylinder, 65hp	1 x Argus As 10 air-cooled inverted V8, 240hp
Maximum speed:	87mph	109mph
Range:	220 miles	240 miles
Service ceiling:	11,500ft	15,090ft
Rate of climb:	450ft/min	945ft/min

12

PISTON ENGINE ZENITH

❖

April 14, 1945: Oberfeldwebel Willi Reschke destroys a Hawker Tempest V

Focke-Wulf's Ta 152 fighter barely entered service in time to see the end of the war. Nevertheless, it was flown in combat and its most notable success was in the hands of Oberfeldwebel Willi Reschke against arguably the most powerful British fighter then in service – the Hawker Tempest V.

The Ta 152 was the ultimate development of the Focke-Wulf Fw 190 and came about as the result of a novel idea.

Work on developing the Luftwaffe's next generation of piston engine fighters was already well under way by early 1943, with two evenly matched contenders in the frame to replace the Messerschmitt Bf 109 and the Focke-Wulf Fw 190 – the Me 209 and the Ta 153, the latter having been known as the Fw 190 D until its re-designation in July 1943.

Both of these designs were to be powered by a Jumo 213 engine and were projected to offer very nearly the same level of performance. The only differences were the Me 209's very slight speed advantage and the Ta 153's ability to carry a slightly heavier weapons load.

This unusual parity made it very difficult for the RLM and the Luftwaffe to choose between them. A meeting chaired by Generalfeldmarschall Erhard Milch on August 10, 1943, attended by several dozen concerned parties including Willy Messerschmitt, Kurt Tank and Adolf Galland representing the Luftwaffe's fighter force, failed to reach a decision.

A second meeting was arranged for August 13, giving Messerschmitt and Tank 72 hours to make adjustments which might tip the scale in favour of their design.

At the beginning of the meeting, Messerschmitt explained how the Me 209 could be modified to accept the same weaponry as the Ta 153 without any effect on performance. He further argued that the Me 209 could be ready sooner since 40-50% of it was built out of existing components. The Ta 153, although at first glance looked similar to the Fw 190, was nearly a completely new design, less than 20% of it being existing components.

When his opportunity came, Tank turned the tables on Messerschmitt – and stunned Milch – by telling the assembled dignitaries that the performance advantages of the Ta 153 could be achieved by making a single simple addition to the existing Fw 190. The existing Fw 190 airframe was easily modified to accept the Jumo 213 and the resulting centre of gravity problem could be solved by inserting a tubular 50cm section into the tail. Some 90% of existing components would be retained.

Once he understood what Tank was proposing, Milch immediately cancelled the Ta 153, approved the Me 209 for development and ordered Tank to prepare a full presentation on his 'new' design. He told Tank he could call this design anything he liked and a month later, in a summary of this meeting's minutes, the design is described as the 'Fw 190 neu (Ta 152)'.

Almost from the beginning, Tank began making alterations to his 'simple' concept which would lower the percentage of pre-existing components. The earliest Ta 152

Oberfeldwebel Willi Reschke flew Ta 152 H-1 W.Nr. 150168 on April 14, 1945, when he shot down the Hawker Tempest V, SN141, of New Zealander W/O Owen James Mitchell. He was one of only a handful of pilots ever to fly the type.

was to have wing inserts, giving it a slightly longer wingspan than the original Fw 190.

By September 9, 1943, the basic Ta 152 concept had been adapted to produce a longer-winged high-altitude version as the Ta 152 H, replacing the nascent high-altitude Fw 190 Ra-6 design which had briefly been given the designation Fw 190 H.

And a document of September 17 shows three engines being planned for the Ta 152 – the Jumo 213 A, DB 603 G and Jumo 213 E. The standard Ta 152 would have a wingspan of 36.1ft and a wing area of 210sq ft. The Jumo 213 A aircraft would weigh 10,141lb with a top speed of 430mph using GM1 boost, the DB 603 G aircraft would weigh 10,218lb with a boosted top speed of 426mph and the Jumo 213 E aircraft would weigh 10,362lb with a boosted top speed of 450mph.

By December 15, 1943, it was decided there should be three versions of the Ta 152 – the Ta 152 A, powered by the Jumo 213 A, the Ta 152 B powered by the Jumo 213 E, and the Ta 152 H, also powered by the Jumo 213 E but with a 47ft 3in wingspan, compared to the standard Fw 190 A's 34ft 5in, and a pressure cabin.

Just as the Ta 152 was moving increasingly further away from the initial concept, a report of November 12, 1943, shows another new design was being worked on. It was exactly what Tank had originally promised at the August 13 meeting – a re-engined standard Fw 190 with a tail insert. This was initially known simply as 'Fw 190 with Jumo 213 A' but by December 15 received the revived designation Fw 190 D-1, shortly thereafter to become the D-9 so that it would correspond to the current model of Fw 190 A, the A-9.

By the end of February 1944, it was decided that the Ta 152 A offered no real advantage over the Fw 190 D-9 and it was dropped –

leaving the Ta 152 B as the standard fighter and the Ta 152 H as the high-altitude version, both powered by the Jumo 213 E. However, by May 8, 1944, as development of the Daimler-Benz DB 603 L engine came closer to fruition, another Ta 152 variant was conceived to accommodate it – the Ta 152 C.

It soon seemed that the DB 603 L would overtake the Jumo 213 E in development and the Ta 152 C overtook the Ta 152 B in development priority as the 'standard fighter' – though work on the Ta 152 H continued. Design work on both the Ta 152 C and Ta 152 H progressed into prototype construction.

Ta 152 H into service

The war situation was deteriorating rapidly by the autumn of 1944, but sufficient testing had been done for the Ta 152 H to enter full production in late November.

Neuhausen, near Cottbus in Brandenburg, on the far eastern edge of Germany, was chosen as the Ta 152 production centre and work began slowly. While the facilities were available for mass production, the materials and components were not. There were continuous delays

The enormous wingspan of the Ta 152 H is shown in this photo of 'H' prototype Fw 190 V30/U1 GH+KT.

at the factory as missing parts were tracked down for the first run of Ta 152 H-0 aircraft.

Focke-Wulf chief test pilot Hans Sander flew the first machine off the production line, W.Nr. 150 001 CW+CA, on November 24, 1944. The second machine was first flown on November 29 and the third on December 3. A total of 21 H-0s were completed by the end of December. These had no wing fuel tanks or MW-50/GM 1 boost.

Production was in full swing during January but on January 16, a group of 40 USAAF Lightnings and Mustangs attacked the airfield at Neuhausen, where the new Ta 152s had been gathered prior to delivery to III./JG 301, the first

unit intended to operate them. Fourteen brand new 152s were completely destroyed and another was damaged.

The Ta 152 C programme forged ahead but was still in the prototype stage of development by the end of January 1945. Another 20 Ta 152s, H-0s and H-1s would be completed that month and three more in February before production ceased, giving a total of 44 production machines, plus 11 prototype/experimental airframes.

Pilots working from the Rechlin-based unit had been flying the aircraft since November 2, 1944, but the first unit to operate it was III./JG 301. The Gruppe was withdrawn from front line operations to begin

The only known photograph of Ta 152s actually in service with III./JG 301. The image was taken at Alteno on January 27, 1945, immediately after the unit's pilots took delivery of 12 aircraft.

conversion to the type on January 27, 1945. Four days earlier, the order had been given to redesignate the test unit Stabsstaffel JG 301 but in practice the Erprobungskommando took no part in front line activities.

III./JG 301 pilots were taken to Neuhausen by truck in the early hours on January 27 and when they arrived were presented with 12 Ta 152s parked in three rows of four. After a technical briefing lasting half an hour they flew the aircraft to nearby Alteno. One of those pilots was Oberfeldwebel Willi Reschke. He recalled: "The first unpredictable surprises occurred during practice flights over the airfield in the Ta 152, when aircraft from other Staffeln were encountered. Such encounters often proved problematic, for the outline of the Ta 152 was virtually unknown to German pilots.

"In such encounters pilots also reacted very differently. The vast majority immediately displayed defensive reactions or offensive intentions, but there were also pilots who reacted to the encounter with panic and tried to flee to safety. The pilots of the Ta 152 had to deal with these reactions until the end of the war."

He said the Ta 152 gave a sense of "tremendous power" and gave impressive acceleration. It was also able to perform well above 30,000ft, where the Fw 190 A-8 would lose power and behave sluggishly.

After the initial 12 were transferred, III./JG 301 received a further four Ta 152s over the next two months but none thereafter. It therefore only had 16 in total, though it had been planned that it would receive 35. The first was lost on February 1 when Unteroffizier Hermann Dürr's machine entered a flat spin and crashed near Alteno.

As the conversion continued into the middle of February, all of III./JG 301's pilots flew the Ta 152, while also continuing offensive operations with the unit's Fw 190 A-8s and A-9s. On February 19,

An unusual view of a Ta 152 H-1, W.Nr. 150067, from above and behind, showing its broad paddle-like propeller blades.

Another shot of Ta 152 H-1 W.Nr. 150067 showing the type's elongated fuselage. It was captured by the Americans in flyable condition at Erfurt-North on April 15, 1945. It is believed to have been selected for conversion to Ta 152 H-10 standard – a high-altitude reconnaissance version originally designated Ta 152 E-2.

The aircraft flown by Oberfeldwebel Willi Reschke during his combat with 486 Squadron Tempest Vs, W.Nr. 150168, after its capture by the British.

Oberfeldwebel Josef 'Jupp' Keil was the first pilot to shoot down an enemy aircraft with a Ta 152.

Ta 152 H pilot Oberfeldwebel Sepp Sattler was killed when his aircraft crashed shortly before his comrades engaged in combat with a pair of RAF Hawker Tempests. The cause of his aircraft's crash was never discovered.

Oberfeldwebel Willi Reschke was awarded the Knight's Cross on April 20, 1945, six days after his combat over Ludwigslust.

III./JG 301 was forced to abandon Alteno as Soviet forces advanced towards it, relocating to Sachau west of Berlin.

Stab./JG 301 in combat

It was while based at Sachau that the Ta 152 nearly made its first 'kill' – a Boeing B-17 Flying Fortress claimed shot down by III./JG 301's Oberfeldwebel Josef 'Jupp' Keil. In fact, no B-17s were lost that day, though some were damaged.

Another Ta 152 was destroyed after stalling too close to the ground during the unit's first few days at Sachau, killing pilot Oberfähnrich Jonny Wiegeshoff.

Keil tried again on March 1, this time claiming a North American P-51 Mustang shot down. This seems more likely, since the US 8th Air Force lost seven Mustangs that day.

On March 2, 1945, during a mission escorting Fw 190 A-8 and A-9 Sturmbocks towards an American bomber formation, a unit of Bf 109s attacked III./JG 301's Ta 152s and forced them to take evasive action – aborting the mission.

The remaining Ta 152s were formed up into a Stabsschwarm (staff flight) at Stendal on March 13, away from their comrades at Sachau. They moved again on April 10, this time to Neustadt-Glewe air base – hidden by woodland in a secluded area.

Their first mission from this new home, on the same day of the move, was to attack American forces that had just overrun Stendal. While providing top cover for this mission, Oberfeldwebel Keil claimed an American P-47 as a 'probable' kill in his Ta 152, though over the decades since this has proved hard to verify.

By April 14, Soviet forces had crossed the River Oder and were advancing on Berlin. In the late afternoon, two Hawker Tempests were spotted attacking the railway line from Ludwigslust to Schwerin and three Ta 152s were sent up to intercept them – flown by Oberfeldwebel Sepp Sattler, Oberfeldwebel Willi Reschke and Oberstleutnant Fritz Auffhammer.

Reschke, who flew Ta 152 H-1 W.Nr. 150168, wrote in his autobiography: "As our takeoff

was in the same general direction as the railway line, we reached the Tempests' attack area shortly after leaving the airfield. I was flying as number three in the formation, and as we reached the area where the Tempests were I saw Sattler's Ta 152 go down for no apparent reason. Now it was two against two, and the low-level battle began.

"As I approached my opponent pulled up from a low-level attack and I attacked from out of a left-hand turn. Both pilots realised that this was a fight to the finish, and from the outset both used every tactical and piloting ploy in an attempt to gain an advantage. At that height neither could afford to make a mistake, and for the first time I was to see what the Ta 152 could really do.

"Twisting and turning, never more than 50m above the ground, I closed the range on the Tempest. At no time did I get the feeling that my machine had reached the limit of its performance. The Tempest pilot quite understandably had to undertake risky manoeuvres to avoid a fatal burst from my guns. As my Ta 152 closed in on the

Tempest, I could see that it was on the verge of rolling the other way: an indication that it could not turn any tighter.

"The first burst from my guns struck the Tempest in the rear fuselage and tail. The Tempest pilot reacted immediately by flicking his aircraft into a right-hand turn, which increased my advantage even further. There was no escape for the Tempest now. I pressed the firing buttons again, but my guns remained silent. Recharging them did no good: my guns refused to fire a single shot.

"I can't remember whom and what I cursed at that moment. Luckily the Tempest pilot was unaware of my bad luck, for he had already had a sample. He continued to twist and turn, and I positioned my Ta 152 so that he always had a view of my machine's belly.

"Then came the moment when the Tempest went into a high-speed stall: it rolled left and crashed into a wood. This combat was certainly unique, having been played out at heights which were often just 10m above the trees and rooftops.

"Throughout I never had the feeling that my Ta 152 had reached its performance limit, instead it reacted to the slightest control input, even though we were practically at ground level. Oberstleutnant Auffhammer also gained the upper hand against his Tempest, but in the end the enemy succeeded in escaping to the west.

"As the combat had taken place just a few kilometres from the airfield, in the late afternoon we drove out to the scene and discovered that Oberfeldwebel Sattler's Ta 152 and my Tempest had crashed within 500m of each other. The treetops had absorbed some of the force of the crash and the Tempest looked like it had made a forced landing.

"The damage inflicted by my cannon shells was clearly visible on the tail and rear fuselage and

the pilot was still strapped in the cockpit. It turned out that he was a New Zealander, Warrant Officer Owen James Mitchell of 486 Squadron, Royal Air Force. The next day the two fallen pilots were buried with military honours in the Neustadt-Glewe cemetery."

What 486 Squadron saw

W/O Mitchell had in fact been flying one of four, not two, Tempest Vs on April 14 in the Ludwigslust area. The section was led by the 122 Wing Leader, Wing Commander Richard Edgar Peter Brooker, Pink 1, and consisted of 486 Squadron pilots W/O William John 'Bill' Shaw, Pink 2, F/O Sydney John 'Sid' Short, Pink 3, and Mitchell, a new pilot with the squadron, who was Pink 4.

They had taken off from Advanced Landing Ground B-112, at Hopsten, Westphalia, Germany, at 6.25pm and later split up into two sections of two – Brooker and Shaw, and Short and Mitchell. At 7.30pm, the former pair saw a lone Fw 190

The leader of 122 Wing, Wing Commander Peter Brooker, was flying with three 486 Squadron pilots during an armed reconnaissance mission on April 14 when his men were involved in air-to-air combat with Ta 152s of Stab./JG 301.

and shot it down after a brief battle.

Short and Mitchell had been strafing ground targets when they were set upon by three other fighters. While Mitchell, flying Tempest V SN141 SA-U, was shot down and killed, Short, in NV651 SA-R, claimed to have damaged one of his attackers – which he believed to have been a Bf 109 E.

Short's official report of the combat states: "I was flying Pink 3 on an armed recce of the Perleberg-Ludwigslust area and together with my No. 2 W/O Mitchell was pulling up from attacking Met north of Ludwigslust when we saw two Me 109s at 1000ft and another four 109s at about 3000ft. The two 109s were coming in to attack us from port rear-quarter.

"I called up and advised my No. 2 and instructed him to drop his tanks. I broke port but could not quite get onto the tail of the leading 109, who started turning with me. A climbing turning match ensued and after three turns I was able to give the 109 a burst with about 45° off. The 109 flew through and I observed four strikes aft of the cockpit.

"I was unable to observe further results because I had one 109 on my tail and another positioning to attack. The last I saw of my No. 2 was from 6000ft, when I saw him turning at deck level with some 109s. Cine camera used. I claim one Me 109 damaged."

Meanwhile, Shaw and Brooker were not far away. Shaw, who was flying Tempest V NV753 SA-J, reported: "I was flying Pink 2 and while diving to attack Met on a road about 10 miles east of Ludwigslust I saw a single Fw 190 flying east at deck level. I reported this to Pink 1 who ordered me to follow him in to attack.

"The 190 broke when we were out of range and as I could see that my No. 1 would be unable to attack I dropped my tanks and climbed for height. As the enemy aircraft

A Tempest V of 486 Squadron, NV763 SA-Z, in flight during 1945, though after hostilities had ended. *Gerald Trevor Roberts via John Roberts*

straightened out east I dived on it passing my No. 1. This time the 190 broke rather later and again to port and I was able to pull my bead through until he disappeared beneath my nose.

"It was a full deflection shot and I opened fire when I judged I had two radii deflection on him. I fired a long burst and then broke upwards to observe the results. As the 190

came in sight again I saw the flash of a strike just forward of the cockpit.

"An instant later flames appeared from the port side and, enveloped in flames, the 190 went down in a gradual straight dive to the deck. I saw it crash in a field and explode. Cine camera used. I claim one Fw 190 destroyed."

It is almost certain that the 'Me 109' damaged by Short was

a Ta 152. It is also very likely that the Fw 190 claimed by Shaw was Oberfeldwebel Sattler's Ta 152.

Though he was a relative newcomer to 486 Squadron and front line combat, having been posted to the unit in early March 1945, Mitchell was not a rookie pilot. He joined the RNZAF in 1942 straight from university, where he had been an engineering undergraduate, and transferred to England where he completed his training.

He then flew with various Operational Training Units as both pilot and instructor, and racked up 700 hours before he converted to the Hawker Tempest V in early 1945.

Aftermath

More than two years after his death, in September 1947, Owen James Mitchell's body was recovered by the Missing Research and Enquiry Unit. The official report stated: "We visited the area (now in the Russian Zone) and found Body No. 1. This

A group of 486 Squadron RNZAF pilots in conversation with their commanding officer at Advanced Landing Ground B60 in Belgium. The man who appears sixth from left, with his eyes shadowed by his cap, is Pilot Officer Sid Short, who was flying with Warrant Officer Owen Mitchell when he was shot down by Willi Reschke.

body was found to be clothed in khaki battledress and had New Zealand marked on the shoulder. The socks were RAF blue and the boots RAF escape type flying boots. On a handkerchief found in the pocket I found the name Pettitt in print letters, about a quarter inch high on the hem."

The body was reinterred at the British Military Cemetery in Heerstrasse, Berlin.

Reschke continued flying the Ta 152 for only 10 more days after shooting down Mitchell. On April 21, 1945, the Stabsschwarm's Ta 152s encountered their first Yak-9s during a mission to cover Fw 190 As flying fighter-bomber missions against Soviet targets on the eastern side of Berlin. Oberfeldwebel Keil claimed two of them shot down.

It was Reschke's turn three days later. On April 24, he found himself facing a group of Yak-9s. He recalled: "Having never encountered Russian fighters before, I was unfamiliar with their tactics, but figured that if I got in trouble I could still climb up into the clouds. The Russians held their tight formation, consequently I was at first unable to turn as tightly as I would have liked.

"I soon went from being in front of the enemy fighters to behind them, further proof of the Ta 152's manoeuvrability. Only after I shot down the number four aircraft did the Russian formation split up, and each tried to get me on his own.

"Only one of the Russians had the will to carry on, however, and the other two withdrew. The remaining pilot was probably the leader of this small fighter unit, but his Yak-9 was hopelessly inferior to my Ta 152. In the end he went down trailing smoke."

This was the last known flight of the Ta 152 in service and the British captured his machine shortly afterwards.

13

TWO SHOTS TO THE HEAD

❖

April 16, 1945: The murder of Captain Chester E 'Coggie' Coggeshall Jr

It was a strafing mission much like any other. Tudor Red
flight of the 343rd Fighter Group were shooting up the
airfield at Ainring near the Austrian border at around
3.45pm and each of the four P-51 pilots claimed a Focke-
Wulf destroyed on the ground. Then things went badly
wrong for Red Leader...

The 343rd were having a field day. During one of their regular freelance strafing missions they had stumbled upon a large selection of German aircraft parked out in the open and were doing their best to fill them full of holes.

The attack turned out to be not quite the turkey shoot the Americans were expecting. Tudor Red flight consisted of Red Leader Captain Chester E 'Coggie' Coggeshall Jr in his P-51D 44-15608 CY-T 'Cape Cod Express', with 2nd Lieutenant George A Apple in 44-15735 as Red 2, 1st Lieutenant Walter Strauch in 44-72362 CY-B as Red 3 and 2nd Lieutenant Jack A Bevington in CY-L as Red 4.

Strauch reported of the combat: "I was flying Tudor Red 3 on the mission of April 16. We passed over Ainring aerodrome in the vicinity of Salzburg.

"About 25-30 aircraft of all types were seen to be parked around the field. Red Leader, Captain Coggeshall, decided to attack the field, so we came in to the field out of the hills to the south of it, making our pass from south to north.

"I saw Red Leader and his wingman, Lt Apple, firing at 190s. I picked a Focke-Wulf Fw 189 and my wingman, Lt Bevington, chose another 190. I got a good concentration of hits on my target and saw it burst into flame.

"When we pulled up off the field I saw Capt Coggeshall in a shallow dive attempting a crash landing. Since I had also been hit by flak we did not attempt any further attacks on the field. However, on looking back over the field after Capt Coggeshall had gone in, I could see that there were four distinct fires burning."

In the Missing Air Crew Report filed on Coggeshall, he reported: "We drove down to strafe an airfield west of Salzburg and when we pulled up to about 1000ft I noticed Red Leader Capt Coggeshall

Captain Chester E Coggeshall of the 343rd Fighter Squadron, 55th Fighter Group.

making a very gentle turn to the left and losing altitude.

"I immediately started over toward him and noticed his airplane was covered with oil, and about this time he made a fast belly landing, dug a wing in and cartwheeled. I went back to investigate and saw where the plane had hit a small brick building. There was no fire but the airplane was completely demolished."

Strauch's wingman, Lt Bevington, reported: "When we came across the field from out of the south, I was trailing behind the rest of the flight.

"I picked out a Fw 190 for my target and fired a short burst at it. The strikes were pretty well concentrated about the engine and nose of the aircraft. It had begun to smoke badly when I passed over it. I did not get a chance to look back at it since the flak was pretty heavy and our flight leader, Capt

Coggeshall, had been hit and was attempting a crash landing."

Bevington also contributed to Coggeshall's MACR. He wrote: "We went down to strafe an aerodrome just west of Salzburg. I was last man across the airfield and after pulling up I noticed Capt Coggeshall's ship smoking. He started to pull up, then went into a slow turn, losing altitude.

"Just before hitting the ground he straightened the ship up and attempted to belly land at high speed. His right wing dug in, after sliding three quarters of the way across an open field, and he cartwheeled through a small building at the opposite end of the field. Although the ship did not burn it was completely demolished."

Coggeshall crash-landed at Sillersdorf, Germany, just over three miles west of Freilassing. When his shattered Mustang came to rest, he was conscious and struggled to extract himself from the cockpit. Four French PoWs, who had been working in the fields nearby, ran over to help, along with a German civilian.

Fighting to remain conscious, Coggeshall asked them: "Friend or foe?" They told him: "Friend."

Not long after the crash, however, Freilassing policeman Joseph Lohmeir received a telephone call about it and drove to the scene in an armoured car. When he arrived, he found the meadow with the wrecked aircraft lying in it. Fifty metres away from that, Coggeshall was lying on a stretcher on the ground and standing beside it were the four PoWs and the German civilian.

Lohmeir asked the men for the pilot's papers and they handed them over, along with a box, a map, some flight manuals books, a small dictionary, a booklet and a number of other small items.

He asked them to help him take Coggeshall to the nearest farmhouse. Lohmeir said later: "At the railroad station we put down the stretcher and then I saw exactly that one eye was swollen. I think the right eye and somewhere on his side there was a wound and he didn't say anything."

He asked the Frenchmen if the pilot had been conscious and they said he had been for a short time, describing the encounter.

Lohmeir asked the farmer's wife for some water and Coggeshall took a small sip but coughed and blood came out of his mouth. After calling for the local ambulance and being told that it was unavailable, Lohmeir put the stretcher, with Coggeshall strapped to it, on top of the armoured car and drove him to the police station at Freilassing.

When he arrived there, Lohmeir was told to take the American to the temporary military post inside the local school house. He got back in the car and drove the short distance over, followed by a growing crowd of 20-30 curious civilians.

Lohmeir tried to report to the company commander, Leutnant

Pilot Chester E Coggeshall Jr during his days as a P-38 pilot early in the war.

Lt Coggeshall, as he then was, wears his nickname emblazoned on both his headgear and his case.

When he was shot down on April 16, 1945, Capt Coggeshall was flying his usual P-51D Mustang, 44-15608 CY-T 'Cape Cod Express'.

Flying as Red 2 to Coggeshall's Red Leader on April 16 was 2nd Lt George A Apple. He was shot down and killed the following day.

Tudor Red Flight's Red 3 was 1st Lt Walter Strauch, who was soon after promoted to captain.

Karl Böhm, but got acting Hauptfeldwebel Ludwig Suldinger instead. Suldinger confirmed that Coggeshall was still alive and had a call placed to the nearest Luftwaffe station at Ainring four miles away – the same one Coggeshall had been shooting up less than an hour earlier.

He got four civilian recruits from inside the school house to help him carry the wounded pilot inside. They got him down from the car and Suldinger ordered them to carry him to the dispensary on the first floor of the building.

At that moment the town mayor, August Kobus, jumped in front of the stretcher bearers and blocked the entrance by stretching out his arms and legs. He told them: "In this house this man will not be carried in." Suldinger told his men to get on with it, ignoring Kobus, but the mayor repeated: "This man will not be carried in here."

Kobus, 45, joined the Germany Army when he was aged just 13 and served until 1918 when he suffered a severe head injury and lost his right hand. Now he was

the mayor of Freilassing and also the town's Nazi party leader or 'ortsgruppenleiter'. He wore a brown uniform with peaked cap and red swastika armband. He also carried a holstered .32 pistol.

Suldinger got angry with Kobus but then Lt Böhm arrived. He spoke with the mayor, then a car arrived with Böhm's superior, a captain, and Böhm reported to him. The captain told Böhm to sort out the matter of the American airman

himself and left. Kobus put his arm around Böhm's shoulder and had words with him in private.

Suldinger took the opportunity to inspect Coggeshall, who had been lying on the ground on his stretcher in the meantime. Suldinger said: "I observed that he had a wound on the left side and one on the right side. Some blood on his head. One eye was swollen and the other eye was open and looking around vividly.

I had the impression that he was not wounded dangerously."

The mayor told the soldiers that the American could not stay in the town and that he would have to go elsewhere. When asked where, he said: "Oh, some place, I will go along."

He got on his bicycle and began riding away down the street. Böhm directed his junior platoon commander, Lt Rudiger von Massow, 22, to have Coggeshall put back on the armoured car. Once the pilot was secured, von Massow and three of his men got into the armoured car and set off after Kobus. The last Suldinger saw of Coggeshall, he was reaching up and adjusting a pillow or cushion that had been put under his head by von Massow.

Preacher Markus Westenthaner saw this convoy heading down the road at about 5.45pm: "I saw a soldier in a foreign uniform on the car. He was lying flat on the vehicle. He had long black hair which was hanging down. He was a tall man. I presume he was wounded because his face showed some pain."

A Polish man working in a meadow nearby also saw them: "I was at my work. It was about 5.45 or 6 o'clock in the evening I saw the

Red 4 on April 16 was 2nd Lt Jack A Bevington. Along with Strauch, he filled out the Missing Air Crew Report for Coggeshall.

Burgomeister when he was driving down the road on a bicycle. He went into the woods and shortly after the armoured car came down."

The mayor, the soldiers and Coggeshall entered Pfarrau, a wooded area near the church and cemetery of Freilassing. Von Massow later said he felt intimidated by Kobus and followed his orders. Kobus leaned his bike up against a tree.

In a statement made a month later, Kobus said: "The American airman was removed from the vehicle. I then approached this airman, who was lying on a stretcher, and from a distance of 4m shot him twice in the

Leutnant Karl Böhm was the officer in charge of a military training unit based at the school house in Freilassing when Capt Coggeshall was shot down nearby. He was convinced by the town mayor, August Kobus, that the pilot should be taken out of the town. This mugshot was taken by American war crimes investigators after his arrest.

War crimes investigation mugshots of Leutnant Rudiger von Massow. He had only been an officer for three months on April 16, 1945, and felt intimidated by August Kobus. He put a pillow under Capt Coggeshall's head before driving him out to the woods on Kobus' instructions.

head with a pistol. The American pilot screamed after I fired the first shot at him. I silenced him with the second shot.

"Lt Von Massow and the three German soldiers from the 7th Panzer Reconnaissance Company were present during the time that I murdered this American pilot."

Less than 15 minutes later, Coggeshall's corpse was loaded on to the armoured car and driven back into town.

Kobus had the captain's still-warm body, soaked with sweat, taken to the local mortuary. When it arrived the undertaker saw that a coal sack had been placed on the head. Kobus told the man: "I bring you a dead American and we have to bury him immediately."

When he was told there was no coffin or grave immediately available, Kobus replied: "It is not necessary to have a coffin, just bury him like that."

Then a German soldier came in and said he had to remove Coggeshall's uniform, his shoes and a bandage on his head. Once he was finished, the body was only clad in underwear. The mortuary owner's wife removed Coggeshall's captain's insignia from his uniform and kept it as a souvenir.

When the coal sack was removed, it revealed a bullet wound to the airman's forehead. The soldier told the wife that "it was a shot of mercy" without bothering to explain further.

A grave was dug at 9.45am the following day in the Freilassing cemetery by undertaker Johann Mitiska. At 6.45pm, Kobus summoned Mitiska to his office and told him he suspected him of telling people that he, Kobus, had shot the American. He angrily told Mitiska: "The only choice I had was whether to shoot or hang him." Then he threatened to kill the undertaker if he talked about the body to anyone.

Nine days later, on April 25, Freilassing was hit by 44 Douglas

The front page of Capt Coggeshall's MACR.

The small area of woodland just outside Freilassing where Capt Coggeshall was shot twice in the head by town mayor August Kobus.

After his murder, the body of Chester E Coggeshall was taken to the cemetery at Freilassing and buried. The man who shot him had not wanted him placed in a coffin but as it was, his body was stripped of all military insignia.

The coffin containing the corpse of murdered pilot Captain Coggeshall is exhumed on the orders of war crimes investigators. Coggeshall's remains were taken back to the US for burial on Long Island in New York.

A-26 Invaders of the USAAF's 416th Bombardment group. Their target, from 10,000-13,000ft, was an ordnance depot north of the town.

They dropped a total of 132 100lb fragmentation bombs with "excellent results", encountering no flak. According to the official report of the mission "buildings and installations in the depot area were severely damaged, roads and railroad tracks were cut. Many fires were also kindled".

The town was devastated and there was further damage when the RAF also bombed the town that night. Whatever the truth, the towns people firmly believed they were being deliberately targeted because of what the mayor had done to the Coggeshall.

Another nine days later, on May 4, Freilassing shopkeeper Alois Denk saw Kobus on the armoured car and approached him. He asked the mayor: "Why did you shoot this American?" Kobus replied that he hadn't, it was von Massow. Denk told him: "You tell a lie, you did shoot him. Why did you do it?" Kobus answered: "I had to fulfil the order of the Kreisleiter."

Kobus later claimed he had been told "that these pilots and these crews of the enemy's bombers and enemy strafing planes are to be treated and considered not as soldiers, but as murderers". Other mayors from the area later verified they were gathered by the Kreisleiter of Berchtesgarden, Bernhard Stredele, some weeks earlier and told to "liquidate" any Allied airmen who came into their area.

The direct order to shoot Coggeshall, Kobus said, was been given to him by Stredele via telephone on the day of the incident.

A war crimes investigating team arrived in Freilassing on May 10, 1945, and Coggeshall's body was disinterred. It was positively identified by his friend, Captain Frederick E Pickens, and August Kobus was arrested.

He was tried before a general military court at Ludwigsburg, Germany, on a charge of violation of the laws of war on November 13-14, 1945, and was found guilty. He sentenced to death by firing squad but this was changed to death by hanging on February 6, 1946.

Stredele was also tried, on February 25, 1946, found guilty and sentenced to death. This was commuted to life imprisonment because the only real evidence of him giving the order to kill Coggeshall was Kobus' testimony, which the presiding military panel had found particularly compelling and convincing.

Both Rudiger von Massow and Karl Böhm were also charged with war crimes but were acquitted.

Coggeshall's body was sent back to the US, arriving in New York, where his US Navy pilot instructor brother arranged for his burial. His grave is at Long Island Cemetery, Framlingdale, New York.

14

SPITFIRES OVER BERLIN

❖

350 (Belgian) Squadron's magnificent seven in combat

Seven Spitfires were engaged in a fight to the death with
Focke-Wulf Fw 190s on April 20, 1945, on the western
fringes of Berlin. The young RAF men came out on top but
one of their number failed to return...

It was approaching sunset on April 20, 1945, as seven 350 (Belgian) Squadron Supermarine Spitfire Mk.XIVs flew northwards on a fighter sweep around the western fringes of Berlin.

The Rolls-Royce Griffon-engined single-seaters passed Nauen at gone 7.20pm and continued northwards in the direction of Neuruppin. Smoke still lingered in the air following Eighth Air Force B-17 bombing raids on rail marshalling yards at both locations earlier in the day.

Not too far away, on the opposite side of Berlin, Russian units had crossed the River Oder and were advancing on the city. The following day, April 21, the German capital would be hit by Soviet artillery fire for the first time.

Within the centre of the city itself, in the Führerbunker, beside and beneath the Reichs Chancery, Hitler was making his final decision to stay in Berlin to the last – when his staff realised that the window of opportunity to escape by air or by road was rapidly closing.

The seven

The Spitfires flew in formation in two sections. Red section, and the mission, were being led by a 25-year-old Spaniard – Flight Lieutenant Robert 'Roberto' Muls in SM825 MN-M.

Muls, from Barcelona, joined the Belgian section of the RAF on June 10, 1942, before undergoing extensive training. After converting to the Spitfire in March 1944, he was posted to 350 Squadron, his first front line unit, on May 30, 1944. At the outset of the April 20 sweep, he had just one shared aerial victory – a Fw 190 shot down 15 days earlier over Aschendorf.

Red 2 was Belgian Pilot Officer Emile Pauwels, 24, in NH697 MN-K. He had been in Belgium when it finally capitulated to the Nazis on May 28, 1940, but escaped to England on May 15, 1942. After

The leader of 350 Squadron's Red Section on April 20, 1945, and the mission leader, was Spanish Flight Lieutenant Robert 'Roberto' Muls. *via Serge Bonge*

training, he joined 350 Squadron on July 27, 1944. On March 2, 1945, he was credited with damaging a Bf 109.

The third member of Muls' section, 25-year-old Flight Lieutenant David Howorth, was from Bolton, Lancashire, and flew RM618 MN-P. He became a sergeant in the RAF Reserve on July 27, 1940, and became a flying officer exactly a year later. He had no combat victories.

Red 4 was Warrant Officer Jacques 'Pichon' Groensteen, 22, (Pichon meaning young pigeon), who fled Belgium as a refugee on May 20, 1940. He joined the Belgian Aircrew Receiving Centre in September 1941 and after training was posted to 350 Squadron on December 23, 1942. He then transferred to 349 Squadron on June 15, 1943, and more training followed until he was finally returned to 350 Squadron on January 10, 1945.

On March 2, 1945, he claimed a Bf 109 shot down in the Rheine-Munster area. On April 20 he was at the controls of NH686 MN-V.

Yellow section was led by Pilot Officer Desmond 'Des' Watkins, 23, from Llwyn-y-pia in the Rhondda Valley, south Wales, flying RB155 MN-C. Already an experienced pilot, Watkins had participated in the first Spitfire sortie over Germany with Squadron Leader Geoffrey Page and others on April 26, 1944. He had destroyed several enemy aircraft on the ground but had no air-to-air victories.

His No. 2 was Flight Sergeant Andre Kicq, 21, in RM733 MN-J. Like Pauwels, he had escaped occupied Belgium in 1942 before joining the RAF Volunteer Reserve in July that year. Fully trained as pilot by August 1943, he was posted to 350 Squadron in July 1944. On April 17, 1945, he had achieved his first aerial victory by shooting down a Fw 190 south of Hamburg.

The seventh man, Yellow 3, was 26-year-old Pilot Officer Marcel Doncq flying NH693 MN-J. Of all

Pilot Officer Emile Pauwels escaped occupied Belgium in 1942 and signed up for the RAF as soon as he was able. During the combat on April 20 he stuck with Flt Lt David Howorth. *via Serge Bonge*

A Spitfire Mk.XIV of 350 (Belgian) Squadron in 1944 – the following year noses of the unit's fighters were painted black and the tail stripes were removed.

Flight Lieutenant David Howorth, from Bolton, Lancashire, became a sergeant in the RAF Reserve on July 27, 1940. He had no previous combat victories when he set off on the fighter sweep over the western fringes of Berlin on April 20. He died on February 21, 2016, and was buried at the Polson Cemetery, Point Vernon, Queensland, Australia. *via Serge Bonge*

the men, he had perhaps had the longest journey to reach the seat of his Spitfire XIV. He was in the Belgian Army when war broke out and was captured by the Germans with his unit at Lombardsijde.

Escaping Belgium into France on April 16, 1941, he worked his way south across the whole of the occupied country, crossing into neutral Spain on April 25. Arrested near Barcelona by fascists, however, he was put in prison and languished in various cells for nearly a year.

Liberated on February 7, 1942, he reached Gibraltar on February 11, 1942. He was transferred to England on March 11, and joined the RAF Volunteer Reserve. He was next sent to Canada for training and first flew solo in a Tiger Moth on March 4, 1943.

A year later he was back in Britain and had converted to the Spitfire. He joined 350 Squadron on June 12, 1944. By April 20, however, he had achieved no victories.

The battle

The seven Spitfires had set off from Advanced Landing Ground B.118 Celle in Lower Saxony, Germany,

at 7.04pm with perhaps an hour and a half of daylight still remaining. Celle, 175 miles from Berlin and formerly home to a Luftwaffe flying school, had been captured from the Germans, largely intact, nine days earlier.

Half an hour later, the RAF aircraft had reached their target area and were flying in a north-easterly direction at 9000ft when Howorth saw something. Within seconds all hell broke loose.

According to his combat report: "When in the Nauen area I saw four Fw 190s going in the opposite direction, south, below, but owing to the R/T being in use was unable to report them for the moment."

When Howorth was finally able to report his sighting, Muls ordered Yellow section to attack.

Watkins reported: "Yellow 2 immediately went down and I was on the point of doing so when I noticed two Fw 190s coming towards me and my No. 3 slightly below us. I selected the one on the port side and made a sharp turn to port and gave a quick burst as the enemy aircraft was overshooting me.

Warrant Officer Jacques 'Pichon' Groensteen at the controls of his battered Spitfire. *via Serge Bonge*

"I observed strikes on starboard mainplane. The enemy aircraft then rolled on its back and in the process caught a long burst in its belly. The enemy aircraft turned into a tight spiral and spun towards the ground when I saw it blow up."

Yellow 3, Doncq, wrote: "Yellow 2, F/Sgt Kicq, went down and we were about to follow him when we noticed two more coming towards us on a reciprocal course and slightly below. Yellow leader and I went in to the attack – the leader taking the enemy aircraft on his port side and I selected the other one.

"As soon as the enemy aircraft which I identified as a Fw 190 saw me, it made a sharp turn to starboard and jettisoned its auxiliary tank. I turned to port and opening full throttle followed it as it started climbing very steeply. It

The leader of 350 Squadron's Yellow Section on April 20, 1945, was Pilot Officer Desmond 'Des' Watkins, from Llwyn-y-pia in the Rhondda Valley, south Wales. He was an experienced pilot despite being only 23 years old. *Greg Lance-Watkins*

then went on its back making a half roll during which time I had closed to within 200 yards. I fired twice a two second burst and the enemy aircraft blew up."

As for the diving Yellow 2, Kicq reported: "Red 1 reported enemy aircraft at 3 o'clock. I turned to starboard and caught sight of two Fw 190s some 3000ft below me proceeding on a south westerly course. I continued to turn and dived down on them.

"As soon as the enemy aircraft observed that I was chasing them, they dropped their auxiliary tanks and dived onto the deck. They were in line abreast at 30 yards interval some 300 yards from me. Every time I closed in, the one on the port side turned to port, followed three or four seconds afterwards by the other one.

Pilots of 350 Squadron at ease in the grass behind a line-up of their Spitfires. The aircraft nearest the camera, RB155, was being flown by Des Watkins when he shot down a Focke-Wulf Fw 190 over Berlin. *via Serge Bonge*

"While turning after them I fired many short bursts and observed strikes on the fuselage of the starboard enemy aircraft. I then climbed and waited until they were again in formation below me and I resumed the chase once more. That happened four times. On the fourth occasion they split up and I dived from 4000ft on one of them and fired line astern from 250 yards for a second. The enemy aircraft again turned to port but crashed into a tree."

Howorth, Red 3, wrote: "I was about to follow Yellow section when I saw a Fw 190 coming down on me from above. I pulled to one side skidding and he overshot me. I turned in and gave him a two second burst at about 100 yards closing and climbing slightly and turning starboard. I saw strikes on the engine and cockpit. I broke away to avoid the debris.

"The pilot of the Fw 190 left the cockpit but no parachute was seen to open. I was at about 8000ft. There being no more enemy aircraft I climbed above cloud (about 12,000ft) and rejoined the rest of the squadron."

The leader, Muls, reported: "Red 3 reported two enemy aircraft below flying south-west, and at the same time I saw a gaggle of eight enemy aircraft about a mile to starboard flying slightly below. Yellow section went down to attack when I saw a Fw 190 climbing towards me.

"While the enemy aircraft was turning towards me I opened fire at about 500 yards continuing to fire head on. The enemy aircraft was also firing but I was not touched. We closed to 50 yards or less when the enemy aircraft dived down. At that moment I observed an explosion followed by a trail of smoke on the enemy aircraft's starboard wing root.

"I dived to port and saw the enemy aircraft diving steeply down but did not follow on

Pilot Officer Marcel Doncq, left, with Robert Muls, right, and another pilot. Doncq, a former soldier with the Belgian Army, had escaped the Germans and fled to Spain, only to be captured by fascists. He was eventually liberated and made his way to Britain and joined the RAF to carry on the fight. *via Serge Bonge*

Jacques Groensteen was just 22 years old when his Spitfire, flying flat out at extremely low altitude as he chased a fleeing Fw 190, hit an obstacle on the ground and crashed. His remains lay undiscovered at the wooded crash site until investigators found them in 1999 and he was laid to rest in 2003 with full military honours. *via Serge Bonge*

account of other enemy aircraft being around."

Suddenly, it was all over. During the skirmishes, Pauwels had stuck with Howorth and confirmed his victory, but of 'Pichon' Groensteen there was no sign. He was last seen diving in to attack the Fw 190s but nothing had been heard from him since. After the six remaining pilots touched down back at Celle, Red section at 8.20pm and Yellow at 8.37pm, Groensteen was posted as missing.

Crash site

It would be 55 years before Groensteen was seen again. In 1999, a team of German aviation historians searching for the crash site of a B-24 bomber that went down near Berlin during the summer of 1944 were told about a promising woodland debris field comprising hundreds of metal parts.

The team investigated and immediately found aluminium wreckage that indicated the site of a plane crash. There were so many pieces that the Germans at first thought they had found the bomber. However, they soon found parts painted in colours only used in the manufacturing of British aircraft.

Part of a canopy frame was then discovered with bits of Plexiglas still stuck in it, and it became evident that this was the last resting place of a Spitfire. Further finds included a rear view mirror and pieces of the engine stamped with the Rolls-Royce logo. Guns and ammunition were found too – indicating that this was not a reconnaissance version of the Spitfire and that it therefore could not have crashed near Berlin before 1945.

An initial theory was that this was a Russian operated Lend-Lease Spitfire but this was discounted when a brass plate was found indicating this was a Griffon 61 engine – the Russians never received Griffons. It was now

clear to the team whose Spitfire they had found.

Researching the time and date of Jacques Groensteen's crash, they uncovered an account from the official records of IV./JG 51 Mölders. Oberfeldwebel Heinz Marquardt of 15./JG 51, an ace with more than 100 victories, was flying a Fw 190 D-9 south of Berlin on the evening of April 20, 1945, escorting some Fw 190 fighter-bombers on their way to attack Soviet ground units to the west of the city.

On his way back, Marquardt was radioed by a comrade to say he was being attacked by four Spitfires. Marquardt flew to the rescue but had been flying too high. As he dived down, he saw a flash on the ground and assumed his comrade had already been killed, but to his surprise he received a second communication from his comrade to say that one of the Spitfires

had "touched the wires and crashed". The battle on April 20 had taken place near two radio transmitting stations.

Bones were also found at the crash site, along with goggles and the dial of a wristwatch – the hands of which had marked it at 7.35 through the force of the impact. The investigators determined that the crash had happened at high speed, with the Spitfire flying east, and the debris field covered an area measuring 160 by 60m. Much of the debris was just bent up pieces of metal but around 200 pieces could be positively identified. Based on this evidence it was conclusively proven that the wreck was that of Jacques Groensteen's Spitfire Mk.XIVc.

In 2003, after 58 years, what remained of Jacques Groensteen was put into a small coffin, draped with the Belgian flag, and flown

Despite being the youngest of the seven Spitfire pilots from 350 Squadron flying over the edge of Berlin on April 20, 1945, Flight Sergeant Andre Kicq, 21, was the only one to have previously downed a Focke-Wulf Fw 190 single handed. *via Serge Bonge*

back to Belgium. The coffin was met by the Belgian Defence Minister Andre Flahaut and then transferred, with full military honours, to the cemetery at Evere, Brussels. A funeral was held on April 8, 2003, and Groensteen was finally laid to rest among other fallen Belgian pilots of the Second World War.

15

THE RINGMASTER'S GRAND FINALE

❖

April 26, 1945: JV 44 and Adolf Galland's last battle

One of the Luftwaffe's most influential figures from 1942 to 1944, General der Jagdflieger Adolf Galland was relieved of his post early in 1945. Shortly thereafter, he was allowed to form his own jet fighter squadron, Jagdverband 44. It was with this unit that he would fly his last mission...

The failure of Operation Baseplate had put the leadership of the Jagdwaffe, the fighter wing of the Luftwaffe, in a difficult position in January 1945. Reichsmarschall Hermann Göring was dissatisfied with what he saw as the failures of General der Jagdflieger 'General of Fighters' Adolf Galland.

The fact that Galland's rebuilt fighter force had been whittled away by Operation Watch on the Rhine was of little concern to him. Galland himself had been ground down by the constant struggle to keep his forces going in the face of overwhelming enemy opposition and the belligerence of his own High Command.

In late December 1944, Galland visited fighter units across the Western Front and was shocked by what he saw as the lack of leadership being displayed by unit commanders, the poor training being given and the general bitterness of personnel towards their leaders.

He compiled a report and sent it to Göring, who then sacked him. His dismissal was officially announced less than four weeks later on January 23, 1945, and his replacement was a former member of his staff, Oberst Gordon Gollob – a man who had apparently sworn revenge on him after a previous disagreement.

Galland requested that he be allowed to return to a front line unit flying the Messerschmitt Me 262, a type he had supported ever since first flying the Me 262 V4 prototype on May 22, 1943. Instead, Gollob set about arranging his transfer to take command of 4./JG 54 in the northern sector of the Eastern Front, flying missions against the Russians over the Courland Pocket.

Defeated and under effective house arrest in Berlin, Galland's car was seized, his telephone was wire tapped and he was placed under round-the-clock surveillance.

He then received a phone call out of the blue summoning him to the Reich Chancellery for a meeting with Adolf Hitler.

When he arrived he was surprised to be told that Hitler was unavailable but that the Führer had now put a stop to the security forces' investigation into his affairs and would allow him to establish a new unit flying the Me 262. He was told to report to Göring for the details.

The meeting began with the truculent Reichsmarschall reiterating how Galland had failed him but then Göring outlined his plan for Galland. In his autobiography, The First and the Last, Galland wrote: "I was to set up a small unit to demonstrate that the Me 262 was the superior fighter that

After his sacking as General der Jagdflieger by Reichsmarschall Hermann Göring, Adolf Galland was placed under virtual house arrest, his car was seized and his future looked bleak until his powerful connections gave him one last chance – the opportunity to lead a unit on the front line flying the new Messerschmitt Me 262 jet fighter.

I had always claimed it was. A small unit only in Staffel strength was to be organised – any more than that would not be possible.

"I would have to find the aircraft myself. He told me that Oberst Johannes Steinhoff, whom he had dismissed, and whom he had considered to be a 'sad case' could be made available to me, and that Obserst Lützow would be available immediately, if I wanted him. I was to submit my proposals.

"The unit was not to be under the command of any division, corps or air fleet – I was to be totally independent. However, there was to be no contact between the new unit and any other fighter or jet unit."

He was able to give the unit any name he chose as long as it did not include the name 'Galland', so he came up with Jagdverband 44 or JV 44. The name, loosely translated, means Fighter Association, with the '44' apparently chosen to commemorate the year of his dismissal as General der Jagdflieger.

Next, he had to decide on a base for JV 44 so he picked Brandenburg-Briest about 30 miles west of Berlin. This was close to a Me 262 aircraft acceptance park, had strong anti-aircraft defence and perhaps most importantly was already home to III./JG 7, which operated the Me 262.

JG 7 was formed by Steinhoff on January 1, 1944 and III./JG 7 had originally been Kommando Nowotny – a unit personally established by Galland under the command of Austrian ace Major Walter Nowotny to evaluate the Me 262.

Once this was approved, he set about gathering the resources and personnel. Allocation of the former – 16 Me 262s, munitions, fuel, spares, tools, flight equipment, trucks, personnel carriers, tractors, trailers, cars and bicycles – was approved by Luftwaffe Chief of General Staff, General der Flieger Karl Koller.

Mechanics and ground crew were allocated from 16./JG 54 and the first pilot Galland called was Steinhoff, who quickly agreed to sign up. After drawing up a list of the other pilots he wanted, some of the Luftwaffe's very finest, Galland attempted to recruit them. Gollob, however, stood in his way though not entirely out of malice.

He recalled later: "At exactly the moment when Galland and everyone else in the Luftwaffe knew that there was a shortage of experienced formation leaders, this gentleman in no way held back from requesting for himself – without exception – our aces. But he only got those I let him have, and a few that he 'organised' for himself by roundabout methods."

Among the new recruits were Steinhoff's former wingman and adjutant Leutnant Gottfried Fährmann, 500-mission veteran Major Karl-Heinz 'Bubi' Schnell, the similarly experienced Major Erich Hohagen, who was recovering from a serious head injury, veteran ground-attack pilot Unteroffizier

Göring and Galland examine a document together. Galland, 19 years Göring's junior, fell out of favour when it became clear that the Luftwaffe's fighter force – under Galland's direction – was engaged in a losing battle against the numerically far superior Allies.

Johann-Karl 'Jonny' Müller, twin-engined aircraft specialist and flying school instructor Feldwebel Otto Kammerdiener, Oberfeldwebel Leopold Knier, whom it was rumoured had been paid a large sum of money to deliver a Bf 109 intact to the Soviets for inspection, another

flying instructor, Oberfeldwebel Josef Dobnig, who had been about to join an 'infantry' unit using Panzerfausts against Soviet tanks, and former night flying instructor Unteroffizier Eduard Schallmoser.

Schallmoser was one of the few JV 44 pilots who had actually been

An early JV 44 Me 262 was 'Red S'. It is pictured in March 1945 at the unit's first base, Brandenburg-Briest.

Six Me 262s of JV 44 are lined up ready for takeoff at Munich-Riem. The unit's aircraft are seldom seem together in the same frame, since they were usually dispersed beyond the edges of the airfield to hide them from marauding fighter-bombers and to prevent them from being damaged if the airfield itself was bombed.

fully trained to fly the Me 262. His conversion training had just been completed when he was posted to JV 44 on March 2, 1945, arriving at Brandenburg-Briest the following day. Many of the others had never flown a twin-engine aircraft before, let alone a twin-engine jet fighter, so Galland secured a number of Siebel Si 204s for a crash course of training between March 4 and March 18.

Fighter tactics
The first Me 262s arrived on March 14 and once training had was complete, Galland set about developing his unit's tactics – setting out with a Kette, a formation of three jets, rather than the usual four-aircraft Schwarm – on March 22. The Kette had the advantage of enabling all three aircraft to take off side-by-side on a standard 60m-wide German runway, enabling them to maintain formation right from the start of the mission rather than wasting time forming up once airborne.

Combat operations began at the end of March when Steinhoff reported shooting down an Ilyushin Il-2 Sturmovik that had been attacking a German column on the ground.

With JV 44 now fully operational, Koller ordered Galland to transfer it south so its fighters could be used to defend fuel, arms and aircraft production facilities. After scouting out the area in his now returned

BMW sports car, Galland decided on the large civil airport of Munich-Riem as his unit's new home.

It had 35 off-field blast pens to protect aircraft from bombing raids, a large underground fuel store, three heavy and 12 light flak emplacements and a runway that was ample for the 1850m takeoff run required by the Me 262. By

A JV 44 jet is readied for action at Brandenburg-Briest.

Several JV 44 pilots flew Me 262 W.Nr. 111745 'White 5'. Though it is unreadable in this view, the legend on the nosewheel hatch door reads 'ACHTUNG – Nicht am Bugrad Schleppen' or 'ATTENTION – do not tow by nosewheel'. The weakness of its nosewheel was one of several Achilles heels present in the Me 262 design. In practice, the aircraft had to be towed by its mainwheels.

March 29, all of JV 44's equipment had been loaded onto a train at Berlin and ready to be transported down to Munich.

The unit had nine Me 262s at this point, all factory fresh from Messerschmitt's production lines, but six were unserviceable and

JV 44 pilot Unteroffizier Eduard Schallmoser was not a highly experienced ace like some of his fellow pilots, but he was fully trained to fly the Me 262. Even so, he still struggled to get to grips with its incredible turn of speed.

one was being repaired. The aerial transfer, with all the jets now ready to fly, took place on March 31.

More training was carried out as more pilots were recruited who had no prior experience of flying the Me 262. On April 4, at 11am, Fährmann and Schallmoser set off together to attack a formation of 12 P-38 Lightnings from the USAAF's Fifteenth Air Force near Munich.

After sighting the formation and flying in to attack, Schallmoser attempted to open fire with his quartet of 30mm MK 108 cannon, only to find that nothing happened. He looked down and realised he had failed to fully disengage the safety. When he looked up, the Me 262's incredible speed had

carried him far too close to one of the Lightnings.

He tried to turn but it was too late and he collided with it. The impact jarred him but he span away with only minor damage. Quickly finding Fährmann and preparing to return to base, he looked back and saw that the Lightning had not been so lucky – it was heading towards the ground and the pilot was bailing out.

The P-38 was 44-25761, flown by Lt William Randle of the 49th Fighter Squadron, 14th Fighter Group. One of his comrades, 2nd Lt Robert Slatter, recalled: "At 11.20am at an altitude of 15,000ft I saw the Me 262 which came past our leader and towards Randle. The jet was

'White 5' as viewed from the rear quarter at Munich-Riem.

Schallmoser, right, and another pilot at Munich-Riem with JV 44's best known aircraft Me 262 'White 5'.

Pilots had to pitch in with ground crew at Munich-Riem to dig foxholes and shallow trenches where personnel could take cover in the event of an attack. The huge airport had a great runway for jets but was also characterised, like most airfields, by huge wide open spaces with little in the way of cover.

Just two Me 262 A-1a/U4s, fitted with the enormous 50mm Mauser MK 214 cannon, were built and one of them was brought to JV 44 for active use by Major Willi Herget. W.Nr. 111899 was used on at least two occasions, its nose remaining unpainted, but without result – except for worrying American aircrew with the sheer size of its armament.

approaching very quickly and after the leader went to the left, I saw that the tail of Lt Randle's aircraft had been completely torn off. His plane fell into a flat spin and began to fall. I watched the jet and saw Lt Randle jump out. About three minutes later, I saw the parachute, floating at a height of 1000ft. I also saw a flash of fire as his plane hit the ground."

On April 5, Steinhoff, Fährmann and three others flew out to intercept B-17s of the 379th Bomb Group and shot one of them down. Fährmann, however, suffered engine trouble and was forced to bail out near the Danube after he was attacked by

the bombers' escort. He landed safely but could not return to Riem until the following day.

Priority target

By now the Allies had identified Riem as a priority target – any airfield where jet types were seen to operate was immediately pushed to the front of the queue – and on April 8 it was hit by a force of 228 B-17s.

JV 44 still only had 18 Me 262s and the attack resulted in six of them receiving damage from bomb fragments. Just seven had been serviceable to begin with. This was not the only effect on the unit, however. Riem's control tower, main hangar and administration

buildings were wrecked and six men were killed. Fifty personnel were wounded, including two members of JV 44's ground crew.

Damage to the main runway was quickly repaired, however, and that afternoon Müller took off in Me 262 W.Nr. 111745 'White 5' to go after the B-17s. He returned to base without success.

The next attack on Riem came on April 10 when P-51 Mustangs of the 353rd Fighter Group strafed the airfield. They succeeded in destroying a trio of Me 262s and causing damage to another three. Thirteen new aircraft had just

Two of the pilots who gave JV 44 its reputation as a 'squadron of aces' – Oberfeldwebel Klaus Neumann, who had previously served with IV.(Sturm)/JG 3 and had 37 victories, and Major Erich Hohagen, who had scored 55 victories but was now supposed to be recovering from a serious head injury.

Oberst Günther Lützow seated with Galland at Munich-Riem.

Four pilots of JV 44's Fw 190 D-flying Platzschutzschwarm – Leutnant Karl-Heinz Hofmann, Leutnant Heinz Sachsenberg (seated on the muddy mainwheel of Fw 190 D-9 'Red 3'), Hauptmann Waldemar Wübke and Oberleutnant Klaus Faber.

Parked alongside one of JV 44's transport aircraft, Siebel Si 204 'White 63', is Fw 190 D-9 W.Nr. 600424 'Red 1'. The pair are pictured at the unit's heavily damaged one-time base Munich-Riem airport.

been delivered to JV 44 but by the end of the day just two were left undamaged.

Again, Müller took off after them but he encountered P-47s instead, probably of the 36th Fighter Group, and this time he was able to shoot one down.

In mid-April, JV 44 was joined by Major Wilhelm Herget, who brought with him the experimental Me 262 A-1a/U4 W.Nr. 111899. This aircraft was fitted with a 50mm Mauser MK 214 cannon, the barrel of which protruded from the nose by around 2m. This is believed to have been used with JV 44 on only two occasions and it was unsuccessful on both.

April 16 saw around 14 of JV 44's Me 262s attacking a formation of 322nd Bomb Group Martin B-26 Marauders. Galland himself led the

The other side of 'Red 1', the aircraft of Platzschutzschwarm leader Leutnant Heinz Sachsenberg, bears the slogan 'Verkaaft's mei Gwand I foahr in himmel!' or 'Sell my clothes, I'm going to heaven!'.

assault and shot down two of the medium bombers. Some of the Me 262s had been equipped with the new 55mm R4M air-to-air rockets – 12 under each wing – and these were used during the attack.

Two days later, a force of six Me 262s from JV 44 was sent up

against a formation of 760 B-17s that was hitting targets across southern Germany. During takeoff, Steinhoff's Me 262 hit some debris left on the runway from a bombing raid the previous day and his port wing dipped, sending him swerving to the left.

As per Galland's 'Kette' idea, Steinhoff had been flying one of three jets taking off at the same time and his sudden change in direction almost caused him to crash into Krupinski's machine, which was rolling alongside. Krupinski just managed to pull up in time but Steinhoff wasn't so lucky. He hit an embankment at the end of the runway and, loaded with fuel, his Me 262 began to burn furiously.

In his book The Final Hours, Steinhoff wrote: "Catapulted high

JV 44's 'Red 3' pictured at Ainring.

Another of JV 44's Fw 190 D-9s, 'Red 13', had the slogan '"Rein muss er" und wenn wir beide weinen' or "He has to go" and then we both cry'.

Heavy exhaust staining is visible on the side of 'Red 13'.

into the air, the stricken bird dragged itself through several more seconds of existence. Shortly before the impact, my hands flew instinctively to the shoulder belts. I tugged so violently on the straps that my body slammed back against the seat.

"Then, all of a sudden, everything seemed to grow still. There was only the hissing of the huge flames. As if in slow motion, I saw a wheel go soaring through the air. Metal fragments and bits of undercarriage flew after it, spinning very slowly. Wherever I looked was red, deep red. Grasping the sides of the cockpit, I pulled myself up until I was standing on the parachute. I had got my feet over the cockpit rim

when the rockets started exploding under the wings.

"They skittered over the field and went off with a hellish bang. Taking great leaping strides, I ran out along the wing to escape from the inferno, and my straining lungs filled with fresh air, I sank to my knees as if under the impact of a mighty blow.

"I managed to get to my feet, and as I stumbled a few steps farther everything went black – my eyes had swollen shut. I became aware of piercing pain in my wrists where the flames shooting through the cockpit floor had burned off the skin between my gloves and the sleeves of my leather jacket."

Badly wounded, Steinhoff was taken to hospital and remained there for the rest of the war.

Warming up

That same day, III./KG (J) 54, which was being dissolved, attempted to transfer its aircraft over to JV 44 to replace its losses, only for most of them to be destroyed by American B-26 bombers after they were left at the transit field at Erding.

A trio of JV 44 fighters downed a B-26 on April 19 but perhaps the unit's greatest success of the war came on April 20 when it attacked another formation of Marauders of

A wide view of 'Red 13' as it was abandoned at Ainring, surrounded by Messerschmitt Bf 109 Gs of II./JG 52.

Another view of 'Red 13', this time with a second JV 44 Fw 190 D-9.

the 323rd Bomb Group at around 11am near Memmingen.

One Me 262 shot out the port engine of 1st Lt Dale E Sanders' B-26B-30-MA 41-31918, 'Can't Get Started aka Texas Tiff' then another fired an R4M rocket into its fuselage, blowing a huge chunk out of it.

A waist gunner in a nearby B-26, Technical Sergeant Robert M

An American GI poses with a JV 44 Fw 190 D-9 – the unevenly placed white stripes on the underside of the aircraft are clearly visible.

Radlein, later remembered: "Our top turret gunner, Staff Sergeant Edmundo Estrada, started firing. He had raised his guns straight up and was shooting at a Me 262 passing overhead. He yelled: 'I got him! I got him!' because he had seen all kinds of metal and debris come flying past our airplane. He was convinced he had hit it but

unfortunately the pieces of metal had not come from the German fighter but from our No. 3 airplane, piloted by 1st Lt Sanders.

"I looked out of my left waist window at Sanders' airplane as it started to drop away from the main formation, and I was able to see the entire radio compartment. The fighter attack had stripped away all the metal from the top of the wing, as well as the compartment for the radio man and navigator – I guess from just aft of the windows in the pilot's compartment. And, of course, one engine was also gone. As I watched the bomber falling out of formation, I reached over to snap on my chest pack parachute. Things were warming up pretty fast."

Müller, who was one of the attackers, flying 'White 15', fired an R4M rocket into B-26F-1-MA 42-96256 'Ugly Duckling', flown by 1st Lt James L Vining.

Vining himself later recalled: "In a fast glance over my shoulder, I saw a jet rapidly approaching us in a slight turn, with muzzle flashes around the four 30mm cannon in the nose. I turned my attention back to my position, tucking my wing closer to No. 4, and at that instant a terrific blast went off below my knees and the airplane rolled to the right.

"Sensing that my right leg was gone, I looked toward my co-pilot and while ordering him to take his controls, I noted that the right engine was at idle speed. So, in one swift arcing motion of my right hand, I hit the feathering button, moved to the overhead rudder trim crank and trimmed the airplane for single engine operation and – just as rapidly – pressed the intercom button to order the bombardier to jettison the two tons of bombs.

"We were losing altitude at 2000ft per minute, which slowed to 1000ft per minute with the load gone."

Incredibly, Vining managed to keep his aircraft aloft long enough, despite repeated attempts by JV 44's fighters to bring it down, to crash-land it behind Allied lines.

Schallmoser was also involved in the attack but again he struggled to get his four MK 108s to fire. He looked down again, to check the safety, but in that split second his jet took him too close to one of the B-26s. His 'White 11' was sliced open by the propeller blades of the bomber's starboard engine.

Gushing black smoke, its right wing shedding debris, Schallmoser's Me 262 rolled over and plunged through the bomber formation. The pilot managed to bail out and floated down on his parachute – only to land in the garden of his mother's home in Lenzfried-im-Allgäu. Stunned, he packed up his parachute as best he could before staggering inside.

As he sat down at the kitchen table, nursing his leg, struck by a glancing blow by the aircraft as he fell away from it, his mother set about making him pancakes.

The burned out shell of Oberst Johannes Steinhoff's Me 262 after it crashed on takeoff on April 18, 1945. Steinhoff, effectively JV 44's second in command, survived but was badly burned and spent the rest of the war in hospital.

Galland walks beside Oberst Günther Lützow at Munich-Riem.

The leg injury turned out to be more serious than he thought, however, and he ended up in the same hospital as Steinhoff for five days.

JV 44 had brought down three B-26s and seriously damaged another seven. The only German aircraft lost was Schallmoser's Me 262.

Dark humour

Around this time there was another unusual addition to JV 44 – five Fw 190 D-9s. These 'long noses' were brought in to defend the Me 262s when they were at their most vulnerable – as they landed and took off. Their pilots formed a separate unit, a Platzschutzschwarm, within JV 44 led by Leutnant Heinz Sachsenberg. Each had its underside painted bright red with unevenly spaced white stripes to provide easy recognition for flak gunners on the ground who might otherwise be tempted to open fire on them.

The Focke-Wulfs also had darkly humorous individual slogans painted on their fuselage sides. The words on Sachsenberg's own aircraft, Red 1, were 'Verkaafts mei Gwand I foahr in Himmel' or 'Sell my clothes, I'm going to heaven', Red 3's slogan read 'Im Auftrage der Reichsbahn' or 'By Order of the State Railway', Red 4's was 'Der nachste Herr, deselbe Dame!' or 'The next man, the same woman!' and Red 13's was 'Rein muss er und wenn wir beide weinen' or 'He has to go and then we both cry'.

The pilots of these aircraft were ordered to keep a watchful eye out for enemy fighters but only to defend the Me 262s, rather than to go on the offensive and pursue any attackers. They were also barred from attempting to fly their Fw 190s alongside the Me 262s for any reason. No radio contact was made between the pilots of the Fw 190s and those of the jets either.

April 24 saw 11 of JV 44's now growing number of Me 262s set off at 9.50am to combat yet another formation of B-26s, this time from the 17th Bomb Group. Most of them were equipped with R4M rockets.

As the jets approached the bomber formation, they began to launch salvos of rockets and one of the B-26s, 42-107729 'Stud Duck',

was hit in the rear. Its tailplane was torn off, a wing and the side of the fuselage were damaged and the bomb bay doors were blown open.

It peeled away to the right and plummeted to the ground. Only one crewman survived – gunner Staff Sergeant Edward F Truver, who was thrown clear by the force of the blast and able to open his parachute.

Also shot down by an R4M was B-26B 42-95991 'Skipper', flown by 1st Lt Leigh Slates.

JV 44 flew another sortie in the afternoon but this time the Americans suffered no casualties and Oberst Günther Lützow failed to return.

On April 25, the experimental Me 262 A-1a/U4 was taken into action against B-26s of the 323rd Bomb Group. It was alone and

despite making an attack run on a bomber formation it failed to fire – probably due to one of the regular mechanical failures that afflicted its massive 50mm Mauser cannon.

Brake! Brake!

The following day Galland himself led another sortie, this time against the B-26 Marauders of the 17th Bomb Group. He set off with his men at 11.30am.

In The First and The Last, he wrote: "On April 26, I set out on my last mission of the war. I led six jet fighters of the JV 44 against a formation of Marauders. Our own little directing post brought us well into contact with the enemy. The weather: varying, clouds at different altitudes, with gaps, ground visible in about only three tenths of the operational area.

Flown by 1st Lt Dale E Sanders, B-26B-30-MA 41-31918 'Can't Get Started aka Texas Tiff' was shot down by JV 44 fighters on April 20 near Memmingen.

"I sighted the enemy formation in the district of Neuburg on the Danube. Once again I noticed how difficult it was, with such great difference of speed and with clouds over the landmarks, to find the relative flying direction between one's own plane, and that of the enemy, and how difficult it was to judge the approach.

"This difficulty had already driven Lützow to despair. He had discussed it repeatedly with me, and every time he missed his run-in, this most successful fighter commodore blamed his own inefficiency as a fighter pilot. Had there been any need for more confirmation as to the hopelessness of operations with the Me 262 by bomber pilots, our experiences would have sufficed.

"But now there was no time for such considerations. We were flying in an almost opposite direction to the Marauder formation. Each second meant that we were 300 yards nearer. I will not say that I fought this action ideally, but I led my formation to a fairly favourable firing position.

"Safety catch off the gun and rocket switch. Already at a great distance we met with considerable defensive fire. As usual in a dogfight, I was tense and excited. I forgot to release the second safety catch for the rockets. They did not go off. I was in the best firing position, I had

The broken-backed wreck of B-26F-1-MA 42-96256 'Ugly Duckling', flown by 1st Lt James L Vining. Vining was badly injured when his aircraft was hit by an R4M rocket fired by one of JV 44's Me 262s but he still managed to pilot it all the way down to crash-land behind Allied lines.

aimed accurately and pressed my thumb flat on the release button – with no result. Maddening for any fighter pilot.

"Anyhow, my four 30mm cannon were working. They had much more firing power than we had been used to so far. At that moment, close below me, Schallmoser, the jet-rammer, whizzed past. In ramming he made no distinction between friend or foe."

Schallmoser, flying 'White 14', fired off his R4M rockets and blew up one of the B-26s.

Galland wrote: "This engagement had lasted only a fraction of a second – a very important second

The nose art of Martin B-26 Marauder 42-107729 'Stud Duck'. The aircraft was shot down by JV 44 jets on April 24, 1945, with only one crew member surviving.

Seated atop his Republic P-47 Thunderbolt 'The Irish Shillalah' is 1st Lt James J Finnegan, left. The 10th Fighter Squadron, 50th Fighter Group, pilot shot up Adolf Galland's Me 262 and forced him to make a hasty landing. The German general met Finnegan after the war and the pair became friends.

to be sure. One Marauder of the last string was on fire and exploded. Now I attacked another bomber in the van of the formation. It was heavily hit as I passed very close above it.

"During this breakthrough I got a few minor hits from the defensive fire. But now I wanted to know definitely what was happening to the second bomber I had hit. I was not quite clear if it had crashed. So far I had not noticed any fighter escort. Above the formation I had attacked last, I banked steeply to the left, and at this moment it happened: a hail of fire enveloped me. A Mustang had caught me napping."

In fact, Galland had been hit by defensive fire from one of the B-26s – Technical Sergeant Henry Dietz, a former weapons instructor, had targeted him as he tried to assess the damage he had caused to his most recent victim.

Dietz remembered: "Probably the most important thing I remembered from gunnery school was to fire short bursts and forget about the tracer bullets – just use your sights.

"That day, we were flying as flight leader, and we were about 10 minutes from the target. I flew in the waist position from where I could see all the mechanical parts of the aircraft. I had never seen a jet

before. Galland slowed down to the speed of the B-26 so that he could observe and take score. I thought 'dummy'. He was flying low, right into the sights of my machine gun. I shot a burst. Nothing happened. A little higher, a little lower, I just kept shooting."

As Dietz poured fire into Galland's machine, the pilot of a Republic P-47 Thunderbolt escort fighter, 1st Lt James Finnegan of the 10th Fighter Squadron, 50th Fighter Group, had also spotted him.

Finnegan later recalled: "I was leading the top-cover of P-47s that was escorting the B-26s to their target. As I gazed down I saw two objects come zipping through the formation, and two bombers blew up immediately.

"I watched the two objects go through the bomber formation, and thought 'That can't be a prop job, it's got to be one of the 262 jets'. I was at about 13,000ft and estimated them to be at about 9000-10,000. They were climbing, and I pulled a split-S toward the one that turned left, and almost ended up right on top of him – about 75 yards away.

"I gave a three second burst and saw strikes on the right hand engine and wing root. I was going so fast, I went right through everything, and guessed my speed at about

500mph. I recorded it as a probable. I was flying a D model Thunderbolt with a bubble canopy, a natural metal finish and a black nose. The 262 had green and brown mottled camouflage with some specks of yellow. That turned out to be my last flight in a P-47."

Galland wrote: "A sharp rap hit my right knee. The instrument panel with its indispensable instruments was shattered. The right engine was also hit. Its metal covering worked loose in the wind and was partly carried away. Now the left engine was hit too. I could hardly hold her in the air.

"In this embarrassing situation I had only one wish: to get out of this crate, which now apparently was only good for dying in. But then I was paralysed with terror of being shot while parachuting down. Experience had taught us that we jet fighter pilots had to reckon on this. I soon discovered that my battered Me 262 could be steered again after some adjustments.

"After a dive through the layer of cloud I saw the Autobahn below me. Ahead of me lay Munich and to the left Riem. In a few seconds I was over the airfield. It was remarkably quiet and dead below. Having regained my self-confidence, I gave the customary wing wobble and started banking to come in.

Another postwar shot of a JV 44 Me 262, this time W.Nr. 500490, which was captured relatively intact.

At the end of the war there was no paint available for new aircraft and this one, Me 262 W.Nr. 111712, entered service with JV 44 in bare metal finish with lines of panel gap filler paste, giving it a very distinctive look.

"One engine did not react at all to the throttle. I could not reduce it. Just before the edge of the airfield I therefore had to cut out both engines. A long trail of smoke drifted behind me. Only at this moment I noticed that Thunderbolts in a low-level attack were giving our airfield the works.

"Now I had no choice. I had not heard the warnings of our ground post because my wireless had faded out when I was hit. There remained only one thing to do: straight down into the fireworks. Touching down, I realised that the tyre of my nosewheel was flat. It rattled horribly as the earth again received me at a speed of 150mph on the small landing strip.

"Brake! Brake! The kite would not stop. But at last I was out of the kite and into the nearest bomb crater. There were plenty of them on our runways. Bombs and rockets exploded all around; bursts of shells from the Thunderbolts whistled and banged.

"A new low-level attack. Out of the fastest fighter in the world and into a bomb crater, that was an unutterably wretched feeling. Through all the fireworks an armoured tractor came rushing across to me. It pulled up sharply close by. One of our mechanics. Quickly I got in behind him. He turned and raced off on the shortest route away from the airfield. In silence I slapped him on the shoulder.

"He understood better what I wanted to say than any words about the unity between flying and ground personnel could have expressed.

"The other pilots who took part in this operation were directed to neighbouring airfields or came; into Riem after the attack. We reported five certain kills without loss to ourselves. I had to go to Munich to a hospital for treatment of my scratched knee. The X-ray showed two splinters in the kneecap. It was put in plaster. A fine business."

With Galland now out of action and Steinhoff still in hospital, Oberstleutnant Heinz Bär assumed operational command of JV 44. On April 28, the unit received orders to relocate to Salzburg-Maxglan, where it was to operate from woodland positions along the sides of the Munich-Salzburg Autobahn. This proved to be JV 44's final move.

On May 4, with the Americans closing in, the unit destroyed its Me 262s by placing grenades in their engine intakes. The surviving pilots were captured and taken in for interrogation. Galland surrendered to American forces the following day and JV 44 was no more.

16

VOLKSJÄGER VICTORY

❖

May 4, 1945: Heinkel He 162 pilot Leutnant Rudolf Schmitt claims a Typhoon

The last German fighter to enter service during the war was Heinkel's He 162. It went from drawing board to front line combat in just six months but at a terrible cost – from the slave labourers who died building it to the pilots who died trying to fly it. But did it achieve any success at all?

The Heinkel He 162 was an aircraft born out of urgent requirements, innovative design under pressure and pure desperation.

Efforts to produce a single-jet fighter aircraft began in Germany as early as 1938 when Messerschmitt, Heinkel and Junkers all came up with designs but these were soon dropped in favour of a twin-engine layout when it became clear that a single turbojet at that time would be insufficiently powerful for a fighter.

By the summer of 1943 the Jumo 004-powered Me 262 was well established as the Luftwaffe's jet fighter in waiting and Heinkel's plans to develop the much more powerful HeS 011 turbojet were, the company said, well advanced. Therefore, both Messerschmitt and Focke-Wulf were asked to begin designing single-jet fighters.

While Messerschmitt worked on various designs under the designation P 1092 before largely abandoning the idea, Focke-Wulf launched a series of projects aimed at refining the design of a single jet fighter. By the spring of 1944 the company felt it had come up with the best possible configuration – a twin-boom design known internally as the 'Flitzer'.

Finally, in July 1944 a specification was issued for the design of a new single-jet fighter in a competition known as 1-TL-Jäger. The first conference to compare designs was scheduled for September 8-10, with Heinkel, Focke-Wulf and Messerschmitt participating.

When the conference began, with Blohm & Voss also attending but not offering a design, it was quickly discovered that the three designs tendered could not be properly compared because each company had used a different set of equations to work out their projected performance figures.

Then on the third day, the offices of each company and those of Arado, Fieseler, Junkers and Siebel were sent a second specification for a single jet fighter – differing from the July spec in several key areas.

It called for a fighter of "the cheapest construction" with "extensive use of wood and steel" where the 1-TL-Jäger could be made using an agreed percentage of light alloys. In addition, the new fighter would be propelled by a single BMW 003, a unit less powerful than even the Jumo 004. The 003 E-1 had a thrust of 1760lb-ft, the 004 B had 1984lb-ft and the Hes 011 was calculated to have 2866lb-ft in production form.

The sorry remains of Flying Officer Tom Austin's Hawker Tempest JN877 SA-Y being recovered on the back of a lorry. Was this the only aircraft ever shot down in combat by a Heinkel He 162?

Where the 1-TL-Jäger spec called for a top speed of 1000kph (621mph), the new design needed only a more modest 750kph (466mph). And where the former needed to be capable of flying at full throttle for a whole hour, the latter only needed 30 minutes.

The catch was that the participating companies had to present their designs in time for a comparison conference in just four days' time, on September 14.

This new design was very quickly given the name 'Volksjäger' or 'People's Fighter', perhaps to differentiate it from the other single jet fighter competition since it was sent to the companies under the name '1-TL-Jäger' even though it was a different competition to the one already in progress under that title.

Just three of the companies had something ready to present in time – Arado, Blohm & Voss and Heinkel. The meeting took place in Berlin and was chaired by Heinkel technical director Carl

Francke – who was also presenting the Heinkel design, a downgraded version of the company's original submission for 1-TL-Jäger. He gave the delegates a detailed lecture which emphasized that Heinkel had worked on its design longer than the others (Messerschmitt having refused to participate in Volksjäger, Focke-Wulf being too slow to respond, and neither Arado nor Blohm & Voss having been long-time participants in the first single jet competition) and that the spec for armament, flight time and take-off distance could not be met so his

company had decided only to meet a more modest brief, including just 20 minutes' flight time.

This was a downgraded version of the company's 1-TL-Jäger design, the P 1073. Richard Vogt, representing Blohm & Voss, was deeply unimpressed with what he saw – citing difficulties that would be caused by the design's dorsal engine position and the fact it would be difficult to get the wings off for transportation by rail. Not only that, the P 1073 only used wood for its wing – the rest was of light alloy.

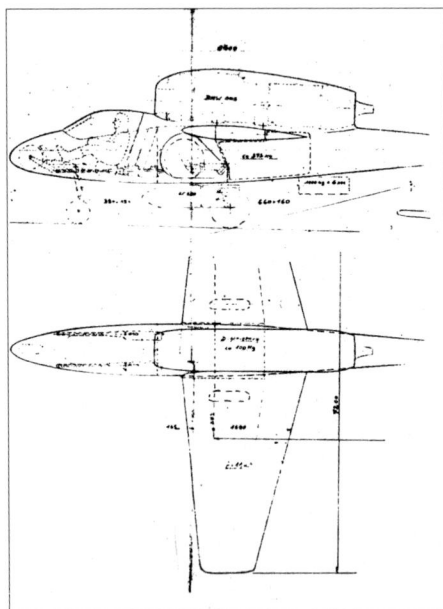

A drawing of the Heinkel P 1073 design from a report dated September 23, 1944. Work on the project had begun two months earlier for the 1-TL-Jäger competition, envisioning a larger aircraft. This drawing shows the P 1073 close to its final form as the He 162.

A large wind tunnel model of the He 162 being tested in early 1945 at Berlin-Adlershof.

A row of rear fuselages awaiting components. Manufacturing delays were commonplace as essential parts took days to arrive to where they were needed and regular powercuts caused blackouts underground.

In a report entitled Aktenvermerk über Projektarbeiten für den Volksjäger und die geführten Besprechungen, or 'File notes on project work for the People's Fighter and the related meetings' dated October 12, 1944, Vogt notes that when he pointed this out and said he had a design with none of these problems, Francke "took the clock in his hand and called a time span of five minutes, which was all he could spend looking at my documents!" Blohm & Voss's design was the P 211 – an impressive-looking swept-wing design based on a simple steel structure.

Arado's design was the E 580 – a small fighter with the turbojet mounted on its back like that of the P 1073 and the rear part of the cockpit canopy slightly within the engine's intake.

The Arado design attracted negative comments but no firm decision was immediately made. The next Volksjäger meeting was on September 19, at which projects drawn up by Arado, Blohm & Voss, Focke-Wulf, Fieseler, Junkers and Siebel were presented. Today, the design of the Fieseler and Siebel projects is lost – though Vogt's account confirms that they were presented at the meeting – while the Junkers design is known only from photographs of a model rather than drawings.

Workers fit the wiring connections inside a He 162 fuselage at 'Languste'.

Precisely which Focke-Wulf design was presented is uncertain since the only known Focke-Wulf Volksjäger presentation document is dated September 20 – the day after the meeting – and features a Volksflugzeug, which is somewhat similar to the P 211, a downgraded version of the company's 1-TL-Jäger 'Flitzer' design and another 'option'

Fuselages under construction at the underground 'Languste' facility near Hinterbrühl. This was one of five sites involved in He 162 production.

in the form of a turboprop version of the 1-TL-Jäger design – known in other company documents as 'Peterle'.

Again, no decision was made. But on September 30, Knemeyer announced a decision had been

The sixth He 162 prototype, M6, rolls down the runway at the beginning of a test flight in early 1945.

The first He 162 A-1 off the production line, W.Nr. 120001, is readied for its first flight on January 14, 1945.

One of the pilots who flew the He 162 with JG 1 – Oberleutnant Wolfgang Wollenweber. He came close to shooting down an RAF Typhoon in the aircraft but his guns jammed at the critical moment.

made and that Heinkel's He 162 would be built.

In his autobiography The First And The Last, Adolf Galland wrote: "From the beginning I had strongly opposed the Volksjäger project. In contrast to the creators of this idea, my objections were based on factual reasons such as insufficient performance, range, armament, bad conditions of sight, and dubious airworthiness.

"Furthermore I was convinced that this aircraft could not be brought into worthwhile operation before the end of the war. The terrific expenditure of labour and material was bound to be at the expense of the Me 262.

"To my mind all forces ought to be concentrated on this well-tested jet fighter in order to make the best of the possibilities remaining to us.

A row of He 162s lined up at Leck and ready to be surrendered to the British. In the foreground is 'White 1' W.Nr. 120013 – the aircraft flown by Leutnant Rudolf Schmitt on May 4, 1945, when he claimed to have shot at an RAF Typhoon 'with effect'.

If we scattered our strength once more in this last phase of the war, then all efforts would be in vain."

He went on: "My suggestion was to increase mass production of the Me 262 by having it built under licence by all aircraft factories that were not working to capacity, and further to use all these planes only for the air defence of the Reich. This earned me a sharp rebuke from Göring which ran something like this: 'This is unheard of! Now the general of the fighter arm refuses a jet fighter plane which the armament production is offering him by the thousands within a few months.'

"The Volksjäger was to represent a sort of levee en masse in the air. Incredibly schedules were fixed, astronomical production figures were planned. Göring himself became a victim of the national frenzy with which the planning of the Volksjäger had infested almost everyone connected with air defence.

'Hundreds! Thousands! Umpteen thousands!' he cried. 'Until the enemy has been chased back beyond the borders of Germany.'

Building the people's fighter

Work on building the first prototypes began on October 25, 1944 – 10 days before the last of the detailed construction drawings had even been completed. The He 162 was to be tested with both 30mm MK 108 and MG 151/20 cannon, designated the A-1 and A-2 versions respectively.

It was also to be fitted with a BMW 003 jet engine, an undercarriage derived from that of the Bf 109 to cut production time and cost, and a Heinkel device first seen on the He 219 night fighter – the world's first operational military ejection seat.

The He 162 M1 (V1) was finished and ready to fly on December 1, 1944. Its maiden flight came on December 6. Four days later, during another test, it was destroyed when instability combined with poor glue bonding led to the leading edge of the starboard wing coming off mid-flight. Test pilot Gotthold Peter was killed.

The second prototype, He 162 M2 W.Nr. 200002, first flew on December 22. Another eight prototype and pre-production machines followed

in quick succession and were soon used to test everything from landing gear and armament to vibration and directional snaking. Meanwhile, Heinkel's factories were gearing up for full production – a quota of 30 He 162 A-1s was expected by the end of January 1945.

There were five facilities involved: EHAG (Ernst Heinkel AG) Nord Rostock-Marienehe, EHAG Süd Wien-Schwechat, Junkers' Bernburg factory and the underground facilities at Hinterbrühl, codenamed 'Languste', and Mittelwerk Nordhausen.

All of them employed slave labourers – some 22,500 in total, including 8000 at Rostock alone, accounting for 55% of the work force.

During an inspection of the production lines on January 27 it was determined that so far, two production machines had been flown, 12 had had engine tests completed, 58 fuselages were complete and another 71 were nearing completion.

A second test pilot was killed on February 4, 1945. Oberleutnant Georg Weydemeyer crashed the

The He 162s of JG 1 at Leck. They were lined up in two neat rows ready to greet the arrival of British forces. After they were 'captured' in this way, the jets were divided up between the victors.

One of the He 162s at Leck as seen from the rear.

After Germany's capitulation, the Allies were amazed to discover the extent of facilities dedicated to production of the Luftwaffe's single-jet fighter. This is the Junkers facility in a former salt mine at Tarthun, near Egeln.

sixth prototype during its 11th test flight. It was found later that there appeared to have been insufficient glue used on the plywood skin covering the ribs of the tail unit.

The first five production machines were ready to go by February 9 – work at Heinkel's factories having been slowed by blackouts resulting from the damage caused to Germany's electrical power infrastructure during heavy bombing.

It was decided in January that rather than form a new Luftwaffe unit to operate the He 162, an established unit should be converted to it, and JG 1 was chosen. I./JG 1 was pulled back from the front line on February 6 for this purpose and its 23 surviving Fw 190 A-8s and A-9s given to II./JG 1 to replace losses it had suffered.

The Gruppe, now minus its aircraft, transferred to Parchim, 50 miles south of Rostock, on February 9. No He 162s were immediately available, so I./JG 1's pilots and crew began familiarisation training with EHAG personnel on February 12.

An Auffangsstaffel or 'collection squadron' from 2./JG 1 was sent to Heidfeld – the airfield at Heinkel's Rostock headquarters – on February 27 to pick up a single aircraft brought over from Junkers at Bernburg. This was He 162 M19 W.Nr. 220002.

A second group of pilots, from I./JG 1, arrived at Rostock on March 4 to collect more aircraft but none were available and were told they too would have to make do with M19.

A third pilot was killed in a He 162 on March 14, when Unteroffizier Tautz of 2./JG 1 hit a stack of barrels while attempting to land M19. The aircraft span into the ground and Tautz, thrown clear of the cockpit, suffered fatal injuries.

Now there were no He 162s available for conversion training. On March 26, it was announced that JG 1 would relocate in readiness to receive completed aircraft leaving the Junkers production line. A group of 15 pilots from 3./JG 1 moved to Lechfeld but there was still nothing available to fly.

On the 27th, Hermann Steckham attempted to take off on a test flight at Bernburg in production He 162 W.Nr. 310001 but suffered engine failure which resulted in the aircraft coming down hard. It was a total write-off and Steckham was badly injured.

I./JG 1 was told on March 31 that it would have to move to Leck at the northernmost extreme of Germany. On the same day, with JG 1 personnel now scattered across Germany, He 162 deliveries finally began.

Simultaneously, as the enemy advanced from east and west, evacuation of He 162 production facilities began. EHAG Süd at Wien began shutting down on April 1.

He 162 'White 1' was flown by 2./JG 1's Leutnant Rudolf

Heinkel He 162 A-2 W.Nr. 120230 'White 23' is believed to have been the personal aircraft of JG 1's commander, Oberst Herbert Ihlefeld. It was captured at Leck by the British but then turned over to the Americans.

ABOVE and BELOW: After its transfer to the US, 'White 23' was given Foreign Equipment number FE-504 and an erroneous new tail number, 120222, and after undergoing a few tests was shown as a static display at air shows across America. It is now in storage at the National Air and Space Museum in Washington DC.

Schmitt for 20 minutes at Parchim on April 3. Having joined the Luftwaffe as an 18-year-old in August 1943, he initially trained at Luftkriegschule 2 in Berlin before moving to Flugzeugführerschule C6 in Kolberg. In May 1944 he was transferred to 2./JG 107, which was stationed in Hungary, and then 5. and 6./JG 108, based at Wiener-Neustadt. Finally, on February 16, 1945, he joined 1./JG 1, switching to 2./JG 2 shortly thereafter.

Unteroffizier Helmut Rechenbach of 2./JG 1 crashed and was killed while ferrying a He 162 from the factory on April 6, bringing the aircraft's death toll to four.

By April 12, 1945, I./JG 1 had 16 He 162s at Parchim, of which 10-12 were serviceable. Two days later, one of the unit's most experienced pilots, Feldwebel Friedrich Enderle, was killed when his He 162 came down shortly after take-off at Ludwigslust and exploded.

The following day, April 15, I./JG 1 began its delayed move to Leck. Flying He 162 'White 7' from Ludwigslust to Husum, a fuel stop along the way, Leutnant Schmitt encountered a Spitfire at 3.40pm but used his aircraft's speed to avoid an engagement, as he had been ordered.

On April 17, Unteroffizier Josef Rieder had a problem with his He 162's flaps on take-off and crashed, suffering serious spinal injuries. The following day Unteroffizier Wolfgang Hartung of 2./JG 1 came down during another transfer flight and was killed in the crash – the sixth He 162 fatality.

Last stand at Leck

With I./JG 1 now settling in at Leck, it wasn't long before they were called into action. A report of enemy aircraft in the vicinity at 12.20pm resulted in a pair of He 162s, piloted by Feldwebel Günther Kirchner and Leutnant Gerhard Stiemer, being sent up.

Stiemer reported that just as they left the runway, two enemy fighters flew right over them. Within seconds, Kirchner had activated his ejection seat – but he was still barely off the ground and although the device performed correctly, there wasn't enough time for his parachute to open and he fell to his death.

All Stiemer could do was evade the fighters, which he believed to be American P-47 Thunderbolts. When he came in to land, his undercarriage failed to deploy and he was forced to make a belly landing.

These enemies were, in fact, Hawker Tempests of 222 (Natal) Squadron.

Flying Officer Geoffrey Walkington later reported: "I was flying as Blue 1 strafing Husum airfield when I sighted an aircraft flying in a northerly direction away from the aerodrome. I immediately broke off my attack on the airfield and chased this aircraft which was camouflaged mottled green with a yellow underside and appeared to have twin fins and rudders and one engine.

"The nose of the aircraft had a drooping appearance and the wings (plan view) resembled those of an Me 109. Due to my loss of speed on turning the enemy aircraft pulled away to about 1500 yards. Having recognised this aircraft as hostile by its camouflage, I gave chase, but was unable to close, my IAS being 360mph.

"The enemy aircraft did a 360° turn to starboard which I followed, turning inside. During my turn I managed to close to 1000 yards. Being unable to gain further I trimmed my aircraft carefully and, allowing about three quarters of a ring above the enemy aircraft, I fired short bursts.

"The enemy aircraft then pulled up through cloud which was eight tenths at 3000ft. I followed through a gap and passed the enemy aircraft spinning down out of control from about 3500ft. I then watched the enemy aircraft explode on the ground near Husum aerodrome."

The accounts of the action differ significantly, but the date, time and location matches. It was the first combat loss of a He 162. It would not be the last.

April 20 saw four He 162s dispatched to intercept RAF Typhoons strafing targets in the Leck area. 'Yellow 7' and 'Yellow 11' took off first, followed by 'Yellow 1'. 'Yellow 3', piloted by Oberleutnant Wolfgang Wollenweber, was delayed by 10 minutes due to engine problems.

Once he was in the air, he heard that the other three had been unable to locate the Typhoons but when he spotted a burning bus below he realised he must be on their trail. Pressing on, he found the British attacking Husum.

Having already released the safety switch on his cannon, Wollenweber lined up the last Typhoon and pressed the trigger but nothing happened. He lined up the second machine and tried again but still nothing. In frustration, he shot over the Typhoon barely 5m from its canopy and climbed steeply away.

Spotting him at last, the Typhoons broke off their attack and tried to follow but were rapidly outpaced. Wollenweber flew home.

That afternoon, Leutnant Schmitt had cause to use his machine's ejection seat after suffering a malfunction during a familiarisation flight and yet another pilot, Unteroffizier Gerhard Fendler, was killed during a ferry flight. This brought the total number of non-combat related He 162 deaths to seven.

Another pilot, Feldwebel Erwin Steeb, was forced to eject due to a mechanical failure on April 21. Feldwebel Rolf Ackermann of 3./JG 1 was killed while attempting to land another new He 162 after a ferry flight on April 23 and the following day, the commander of II./JG 1, Hauptmann Paul-Heinrich Dähne, was also killed.

Dähne, new to the He 162, encountered a common problem – when accelerating into a turn, the jet wash from the engine forced the rudder to jam. This made the aircraft uncontrollable and at low level the only thing to do was eject.

It is believed that Dähne did attempt to eject but neglected to jettison the canopy of his machine first – not an automatic process. This resulted in him smashing his head against the inside of the canopy, probably killing him before his He 162 hit the ground.

On April 25, Leutnant Schmitt took off in 'White 5' to intercept a low-flying British de Havilland Mosquito at 11.20am but there was no engagement. Two pilots, Unteroffizier Helmut Rechenbach and Fähnrich Emil Halmel, were injured when their He 162s both crashed during ferry flights on April 26. Three more pilots crashed their He 162s during ferry flights on April 30. One of these, flown by Leutnant Hans Rechenberg of II./JG 1, was shot at by a Spitfire before it went down near Wismar.

On May 1, Oberleutnant Wollenweber and his men had to detach the final two He 162s from their construction jigs at Rostock before they could be ferried to Leck. After attempting and failing to get them to work, Wollenweber, two other pilots and an engineer were forced to escape the airfield in a Fieseler Storch as the advancing Russians threatened to overrun the facility.

JG 1 now had around 45 He 162s stationed at Leck but since the airfield was one of the few places left in Germany where aircraft could operate relatively freely, it was now becoming crowded with a variety of other units and aircraft.

On May 4, the war diary of JG 4 recorded: "Orders arrive at 0200 – the serviceable aircraft must fly on, either to Norward or the Protectorate, to avoid being captured by British troops. Take-offs should be completed by 0600. The three Bf 109s of the former III./JG 4 are to remain at Leck. German forces in north Germany have signed a surrender, capitulating to Montgomery.

"It is forbidden to fire at any low-flying aircraft. At the same time no further take-offs are authorised. A lone Spitfire circled the airfield. The war is over! The Helferinnen Dobner and Augsen arrived on the airfield after an incredible journey. They are the only two service-women from their convoy that have been able to reach us here at Leck."

Seemingly undaunted by all this, Leutnant Rudolf Schmitt took off in He 162 A-2 'White 1' at 11.38am and flew south. He was attempting to intercept RAF Typhoons that had been reported in the area and it wasn't long before, at 11.45am, he found an Allied aircraft south-east of the airfield at Husum.

During a brief encounter, Schmitt opened fire and later recorded in his logbook: "Typhoon wirksam besschossen" or 'Typhoon fired on with effect'. This would seem to indicate that Schmitt believed he had fatally damaged a Typhoon fighter-bomber, though had not necessarily witnessed its final destruction.

The only corresponding Allied loss in about the right area and at anything like the right time was that of Flying Officer Tom M Austin's Hawker Tempest JN877 SA-Y. Austin, of 486 Squadron, crash-landed after suffering what he described as engine trouble in the Satrup area – though the 'trouble' did cause it to blow up.

Satrup was a good 20 miles east from Husum and perhaps seven or eight miles north of it. In addition, Austin is believed to have gone down at around 7.10am. Nevertheless, in the confusion of those final days of the war, the possibility remains that Austin was indeed the one and only combat victim of a He 162.

It is believed that, in the end, some 171 He 162s were built, with 116 actually being delivered. The Luftwaffe received 56 of these before production finally collapsed at the end of April. At least nine men had been killed in flying accidents involving the He 162 – whether due

A rare view of the He 162 in flight – in this case the captured He 162 A-2 W.Nr. 120098, which was given the serial VH513 in British service. It is pictured here at RAF Farnborough in mid to late 1945.

to a failed airframe, a failed engine, inherent design flaws or simply the sheer trickiness of piloting the delicate little aircraft.

Whether Rudolf Schmitt actually managed to shoot down an Allied aircraft with a He 162 may never be known for certain.

17

FINAL DOGFIGHT

❖

May 8, 1945: Who scored the last aerial victory of the air war in Europe?

While most of the Luftwaffe facing the western Allies had officially surrendered by May 8, some units, particularly those on the Eastern Front, continued a desperate resistance right until the end of the day. But who fired the final shots in aerial combat?

With Adolf Hitler having committed suicide on April 30, 1945, the Third Reich staggered on for another week with Reichspräsident Karl Dönitz, formerly Grand Admiral of the Naval High Command, at the helm as his chosen successor.

From May 1, his first day in office, until the end of the war, Dönitz did everything he could to ensure as many German servicemen as possible could surrender to the British and Americans while simultaneously continuing the war against the Soviets by whatever means remained available.

He first surrendered his forces in the Netherlands, Denmark and north-western Germany to Field Marshal Bernard Law Montgomery on May 4 – the terms including a complete ban on flights by Luftwaffe aircraft. With Luftwaffe opposition ended, this effectively brought hostilities to a close for the RAF.

The only known exception was at around 6.30am on May 5 when a patrol of three 130 Squadron Spitfire XIVs came across a Siebel Si 204 twin-engined transport/trainer flying over the sea west of Hamburg. After it began evasive manoeuvres, it was shot down and jointly claimed by Flight Lieutenant Dudley Guy Gibbins and Warrant Officer Vic J Seymour – the last British victory of the air war.

The fighting carried on elsewhere however. Dönitz had Admiral Hans-Georg von Friedeburg begin negotiations with US commander General Dwight D Eisenhower at Reims in France on May 5 and the German Chief of Staff Generaloberst Alfred Jodl arrived on May 6. Dönitz had told him to hold off on agreeing to a full surrender for as long as possible so that more German forces could escape the Soviets.

He managed less than 24 hours, signing the instrument of unconditional surrender at 2.30am on May 7 with Dönitz's permission. The critical phrase in the instrument was "all forces under German control to cease offensive operations at 23.01 hours, central European time, on May 8, 1945".

In the west, May 8 began with American airmen stationed in England preparing for two very different missions. Mission 986 was the Eighth Air Force's last operational mission over Europe during the war and it involved 12 B-17s of the 306th Bomb Group dropping leaflets over key locations.

Aircraft of the 369th Bomb Squadron set off at 7.45am to fly over Dunkirk. The fortified town was still in German hands, having been surrounded and then bypassed by the British during the drive into occupied Europe. The leaflets told the garrison that they had been ordered to surrender – which they eventually did the following day.

The day before, the 369th had been dropping leaflets over Buchenwald concentration camp, telling inmates in six different languages to stay put and that help was on the way.

The Americans' other major air operation of May 8 was Trolley Mission 2. The Eighth Air Force had actually ceased combat operations on April 25 but its mission planners had not been idle. They came up with Operation Trolley to "provide all ground (non-rated) personnel with an opportunity of seeing the results of their contribution in the strategic air war against Germany".

The last Luftwaffe aircraft to be shot down by an RAF fighter during the war was a Siebel Si 204. Three days later, another Si 204 became the last German victim of a USAAF fighter.

Effectively, ground crews would be flown over areas bombed by the Eighth to show them what they had helped to achieve.

Both B-17s and B-24s were used, but with crews pared back to five – pilot, co-pilot, navigator, engineer and radio operator – plus 10 passengers. The passengers each got a parachute and a life jacket plus candy and a pack of sandwiches for the six to seven hour trip.

Every effort was made to avoid accidents with pilots being instructed on "the deplorability of needless loss of life to carelessness, particularly now that hostilities in Europe are at an end". They were required to maintain an altitude of at least 1000ft over terrain for the whole flight with no buzzing or circling.

An escort aircraft, known less than affectionately as the 'Gestapo a/c', accompanied each group to make sure the rules were followed. Even so, the day before, during Trolley Mission 1, a 389th BG B-24 had crashed into the remains of a railway bridge over the Rhine, killing 19 men.

On the opposite side of Europe however, combat was still raging. The highest scoring fighter ace of all time, 23-year-old Major Erich Hartmann of I./JG 52, took off with his wingman in their Bf 109s from his unit's base in Czechoslovakia at 8am to intercept Soviet fighters over Brno.

Recalling the events later in life, he said: "My wingman and I saw eight Yaks below us. I shot one down and that was my last victory.

I decided not to attack the others once I saw that there were 12 Mustangs on the scene above me.

"My wingman and I headed for the deck where the smoke of the bombing could hide us. We pulled through the smoke and saw once again the two allies fighting each other above us. Incredible! Well, we landed at the field and were told that the war was over."

Hartmann, who ended the war with 352 victories, and his men fired off all their remaining munitions into the woods, destroyed their 25 remaining aircraft and set off in search of some British or American forces to surrender to. He succeeded in finding Americans but was then turned over to the Soviets anyway.

Also stationed in Czechoslovakia was Fw 190-equipped ground attack unit III./SG 77. Pilot Unteroffizier Bernhard Ellwanger recalled: "On May 8 all aircraft, with the exception of four, were drained of fuel. Why my crate was one of those four, I don't know to this day.

"Led by Hauptmann Günther Ludigkeit, Kapitän of 7. Staffel, we took off in the direction of Prague. Our mission was to destroy Prague radio station which was in the hands of Czech partisans. When we were at 4000m Prague came in sight.

"Then I saw something I couldn't take my eyes off: hundreds of American fighters filled the sky like some gigantic flypast at an air show. The whole mass flashed silver in the sun. The sight almost made me miss our attack. Our Schwarm dived away to port with me following.

"With the target centred in my Revi, I released my bomb at 1500m. A direct hit. Then we got out of there, eastward back to base. So ended my last sortie on the very day of the capitulation, and with it my last chance of landing in the American zone."

Leutnant Gerhard Thyben of JG 54 and his wingman Fritze

Just days after joining 130 Squadron on the front line, Flight Lieutenant Dudley Guy Gibbins, flying a Spitfire XIV, shot down a Si 204 – a victory shared with Warrant Officer Vic Seymour – as the final RAF 'kill' of the war.

The last known wartime photo of the highest scoring fighter ace of all time, Major Erich Hartmann of I./JG 52, was taken shortly after his 350th kill on April 17, 1945, beside his Bf 109 G-10. On May 8, he shot down a Yak-9 for his 352nd.

Hangebrauck, escaping from the Courland pocket in Fw 190s, shot down a Pe-2 together at 7.54am on May 8 but Oberleutnant Fritz Stehle, Staffelkapitän of 2./JG 7, is believed to have scored the final Luftwaffe victory of the Second World War over Czechoslovakia at 4pm that day. He had taken off in Me 262 A-1a W.Nr. 111690 'White 5' at 3.20pm to intercept Soviet Yak-9 fighters and succeeded in destroying one of them.

He then flew 'White 5' to Fassberg, where it was captured by the British.

The final American victory, and possibly the last Luftwaffe aircraft to be shot down during the war, was another Siebel Si 204. At 8pm, just three hours before the official cessation of hostilities, 2nd Lieutenant Kenneth L Swift, of the 429th Fighter Squadron, 474th Fighter Group, USAAF Ninth Air Force, was flying his Lockheed P-38 Lightning 'Beauty Juny' three miles southeast of Bad Rodach, Bavaria, when he encountered the German aircraft.

He fired warning shots, which were enough to prompt its pilot to crash land it. While most other USAAF units were stood down by this point, the 474th continued to provide tactical air support for the US First Army until May 9 from its base, R-2 at Bad Langensalza. It was the only group in Northern Europe flying the P-38 by the end of the war.

The Siebel was Swift's first and only victory of the war – although he would go on to fly North American F-86 Sabres during the Korean War, adding a further 'kill'. Promoted to major, he later became an instructor in the German Air Force.

Overall, it is believed that nine German aircraft were shot down on May 8, 1945. How many Allied aircraft were shot down by Luftwaffe machines is unknown.

The last RAF pilot to die before the war's official end was killed on May 8. Flight

One of 474th Fighter Group's used and abused P-38 Lightnings, pictured in Belgium in February 1945. The final aerial victory of the Second World War, three hours before the official capitulation of all German forces on May 8, 1945, was achieved by 2nd Lieutenant Kenneth L Swift of the 474th's 429th Fighter Squadron, flying his Lightning 'Beauty Juny'.

Lieutenant Donald James Hunter, 22, of Upminster, Essex, a member of 322 (Dutch) Squadron, was killed after his Spitfire, LF XVI, TB383 3W-A, suffered engine failure during a victory flypast near the unit's base at Varrelbusch, Germany, and he made an unsuccessful emergency landing.

Finally, there are numerous reports of American and Soviet aircraft engaged in combat with one another on May 8 and afterwards. In one case, on May 8, Captain Malcolm L. Nash of the 39th Photographic Reconnaissance Squadron, 10th Photographic Group, Ninth Air Force was flying a PoW camp pinpointing mission in the vicinity of Dresden when his unarmed F-5E Lightning was attacked by Second Lieutenant Lazuta of the Soviet 106th Guards Fighter Air Regiment, based at what had been Focke-Wulf's Cottbus factory airfield. Lazuta fatally damaged the Lightning and it crashed about 40km west of Dresden. Nash survived without serious injury.

In another instance on the same day, a pair of F-5s piloted by First Lieutenant Thomas P. Petrus and Second Lieutenant Thomas Jackson were attacked by Soviet P-39s from the 100th Guards Fighter Air Regiment near Prague. Major Pschenitchnikov shot down Petrus, who parachuted to safety despite suffering severe burns, and claimed it as a Focke-Wulf Fw 189 for his 13th and final 'kill' of the war.

As late as May 11, Avro Anson Mk.XI PH539 of the Desert Air Force Communication Flight was attacked by a trio of Soviet Yaks while off course near Graz in Austria. It force-landed in a field before crashing into some trees.

18

AFTERMATH

❖

May 9, 1945, and beyond

With Germany defeated the remaining world powers
focused their attention on the war still ongoing elsewhere
and on dismantling the German war machine.

The process of German weapons and equipment being handed over to the victorious Allies began long before May 9 but from this point on it took place in earnest.

Britain had built up quite a collection of German aircraft by now. Some fell into Allied hands when their pilots accidentally landed in Britain due to a navigational error or were forced to land there due to mechanical failure.

A unit had even been set up in 1941 to operate these – 1426 (Enemy Aircraft) Flight, otherwise known as the 'RAFwaffe' – though this was disbanded on January 31, 1945 and its surviving machines handed over to the Central Flying Establishment.

The first German jet to be captured intact had fallen into American hands, however. An Arado Ar 234 suffered engine failure west of Cologne in February 1945 and made a belly landing. Having been seized by the US Army, it was taken back to the Royal Aircraft Establishment (RAE) at Farnborough for examination.

As the end of the war drew near, Air Technical Intelligence teams were given the task of locating and securing the most advanced German aircraft while a team led by test pilot Captain Eric 'Winkle' Brown, who could speak German, was given the job of getting them back to the RAE.

The Americans combined their numerous efforts to gather German technology under the heading of Operation Lusty. Leading the effort to find and extract completed aircraft was test pilot Colonel Harold 'Hal' E Watson.

The first fruits of the British effort were the two-seater Messerschmitt Me 262 B-1a/U1 night fighter 'Red 8' and an Arado Ar 234 B, captured at Schleswig in April.

Later, at Farnborough, the former was given the Air Ministry number AM 50 while the latter became AM 54.

A single Me 163 B Komet was also captured during April, though the circumstances are unknown. It was given the RAF serial VF241. Also in April, the Americans found an intact Me 262 at Giebelstadt airfield, dismantled it, and had it flown to Bovington in England by Curtiss C-46 Commando for examination.

Focke-Wulf's Bremen works was overrun by the British on April 8, which effectively ended any further development of the Ta 152 and also put an end to efforts directed towards building the next generation German single jet fighter – the Ta 183.

When the Gotha facilities near Leipzig were captured in mid-April, the US Third Army found the almost complete, but outer-

The Americans found a number of complete examples of the Dornier Do 335 when they captured the company's Dornier's München-Oberpfaffenhofen factory on April 29. The aircraft pictured here is parked beside the burned-out remnants of a Heinkel He 162, left, and a Messerschmitt Me 262 on the right.

One of the most sought-after German jets at the beginning of 1945 was the Arado Ar 234. However, soon after the first example was captured and examined in February, the Allies managed to acquire many more in various states of repair ranging from factory fresh to worn and damaged, and finally to absolute wrecks.

and needed substantial work to make it airworthy.

Also on April 29, the Americans discovered the Messerschmitt facility at Oberammergau, and captured the only prototype of a new single jet engine design, the P 1101.

British forces occupied the Blohm & Voss aircraft factory at Hamburg on May 3 and captured a single incomplete prototype for the BV 155 B high-altitude fighter – the only flying example having been crash-landed by a German pilot several weeks earlier. An extreme development of the Bf 109, the project was handed to Blohm & Voss due to Messerschmitt's preoccupation with other projects in September 1943. The BV 155 B V1 having been wrecked, the V2 was crated up and taken back to Britain. This aircraft, W.Nr. 360052, was eventually handed over to the Americans.

That same day, the Americans took over the Prien am Chiemsee airfield in the south east of Germany and found a highly unusual aircraft still under construction there – the Darmstadt Munich DM-1, a glider designed by Alexander Lippisch to test the aerodynamics of his planned Lippisch P 13a ramjet-propelled rammer aircraft.

wingless Horten 8-229 V3 flying wing jet fighter prototype, plus the skinless centre sections of the V4 and the steel frame centre section of the V5. Elsewhere they found a set of completed wings which were later attached to the V3.

Advancing French forces captured the first Dornier Do 335s at the company's Friedrichshafen-Löwenthal airfield on April 27 but these had been blown up by retreating German forces and were little more than wrecks. The Americans found a number of complete examples when they captured Dornier's München-Oberpfaffenhofen factory on April 29. Since this was to have been the main Do 335 assembly plant, they found a large number of partially completed ones too.

Two examples, including a two-seat Do 335 A-10 trainer (W.Nr. 240112 – later AM 223) and a single-

seater (later AM 225) were gifted to the British. The French captured the prototype single-seat Do 335 M14 at Mengen and the two-seat M17, which had not yet flown

When the 54th Air Disarmament Squadron got their hands on 50mm cannon test-bed Me 262 A-1a/U4 W.Nr. 170083, they painted their own unit number on one side and 'Wilma Jeanne' on the other. The Me 262 held a particular fascination for the Americans and they tried to acquire as many working examples as they could.

W.Nr. 170083 with the 54th ADS's artwork as seen from the other side.

On May 4, the USAAF's 54th Air Disarmament Squadron (54th ADS), the 'Feudin' 54th' took over the Messerschmitt company's main headquarters airfield at Lager-Lechfeld, near Augsburg. There they found some 50 Me 262s, most of them shot up and ruined by "rampaging GIs" who had reportedly driven tanks into some of them or crushed them with bulldozers.

Also found at Lechfeld were several Heinkel He 219 Uhu night fighters, Focke-Wulf Fw 190s and Heinkel He 177s. Over the next few days, more aircraft arrived from all

The name given to W.Nr. 170083 by Watson's Whizzer-in-chief Colonel Hal Watson himself was 'Happy Hunter II', the second aircraft he had named after his son, Hunter. The captured aircraft was ferried from Lager-Lechfeld to Melun near Paris on June 10. Then, on June 30, ex-Messerschmitt test pilot Ludwig Hofmann was flying it to Cherbourg when it suffered engine failure, crashed and was destroyed.

over the region as German forces attempted to surrender to the Americans rather than risk capture by the advancing Soviets.

Lechfeld became the base of Colonel Watson as he attempted to gather 15 flyable Me 262s for delivery back to the United States – his unit eventually becoming known as 'Watson's Whizzers'.

Five intact Me 262s were captured by the British at Fassberg on May 5: Me 262 A-2a fighter-bomber 'Yellow 7', from Fassberg, became AM 51 and a second example, 'Yellow 17', was AM 52. Me 262 A-1a 'White 5' was AM 80 and Me 262 A-2a 'Black

WATSON'S WHIZZERS

Most of Colonel Watson's Me 262s were first named by the 54th ADS but then renamed by their pilots.

000 Wilma Jeanne/Happy Hunter II (Me 262 A-1a/U4 W.Nr. 170083. Renamed by Col Watson after his son, Hunter. Hunter I had been a P-47 Watson used as a runabout)

111 Beverly Anne/Screamin' Meemie (Possibly 'White 5' JG 54. Renamed by Bill Strobell as in something that gives you the jitters, although his original choice was The Blowtorch)

222 Marge/Lady Jess IV (Me 262 A-1a/U3. Renamed by Ken Dahlstrom)

333 Pauline/Delovely (Me 262 A-1a. Renamed by Bob Anspach after the lyrics to Cole Porter's 1936 hit It's Delovely)

444 Connie the Sharp Article/Pick II (Me 262 A-1a/U3 W.Nr. 500453, later FE-4012. Renamed by P-47 pilot Roy Brown, his first aircraft having been Pick)

555 Vera/Willie (Me 262 B-1a W.Nr. 110639 'White 35'. Renamed in honour of Messerschmitt test pilot Ludwig Hoffmann, who worked with the Americans and earned their trust)

666 Joanne/Cookie VII (Me 262 A-1a/U3 W.Nr. 500098. Renamed by P-47 pilot Fred Hillis. Cookie was his daughter's nickname and it was his seventh aircraft)

777 Doris/Jabo Bait (Me 262 A-1a 'L', later FE-110. Renamed by Messerschmitt test pilot Karl Baur)

888 Dennis/Ginny H (Me 262 A-1a W.Nr. 500491 'Yellow 7' of 11./JG 7, later FE-111, then T2-111. Renamed after Jim Holt's then-girlfriend)

999 Ole Fruit Cake (Me 262 B-1a/U1 W.Nr. 110305 'Red 6' of IV./NJG 11. USA 2, later FE-610)

X' was AM 81. The number and fate of the fifth is unknown.

On the same day, at Stravanger in Norway, four more Arado Ar 234s were captured by Allied forces. While this was going on, the Allies were also in the process of capturing scores of conventional Luftwaffe machines, accepting the surrender of Luftwaffe personnel across the Western Front, disarming them and sending them to holding camps or home to their families.

Perhaps the greatest coup of the British mission came on May 6-8

when the airfield at Leck was captured along with between 22 and 26 of JG 1's Heinkel He 162s. At least 10 of these were shipped, rather than flown, back to Britain and kept by the RAE while at least three more were handed over to the Americans.

On May 8, the British captured the nearby aerodrome at Husum where II./JG 400 had ended up and captured at least 23 Me 163 Komets. Again, some were given to the Americans.

The next day, General George S Patton arrived at Prien am Chiemsee

Captured by British forces from IV./NJG 11, Messerschmitt Me 262 B-1a/U1 W.Nr. 110306 'Red 6' was earmarked for the Americans, who took possession of it and allocated it the serial FE-610.

Also from NJG 11 was Messerschmitt Me 262 B-1a/U1 W.Nr. 110305 'Red 8', given the serial AM 50 by the British.

airfield to view the DM-1 glider, on which work was now to continue under American supervision.

At Lechfeld, meanwhile, Watson had managed to assemble 10 airworthy Me 262s and a selection of other types. The jets had initially been 'named' by the 54th ADS but Watson and his pilots decided to give them colourful new names such as 'Happy Hunter II', 'Jabo Bait' and 'Screamin' Meemie'.

While the British continued to ferry their prizes the relatively short distance home, during early to mid-July, the Americans' selected test aircraft were gathered at Cherbourg in France and loaded onto a Royal Navy aircraft carrier, the HMS Reaper, for transfer to the United States. The Reaper had actually been built in the US as the USS Winjah but was allocated to the UK under the Lend-Lease programme before seeing service with the US Navy.

The Reaper set off on July 20, bound for New York. On board were 41 airframes – 10 Me 262s, four Ar 234s, two Do 335s, one Ta 152 H, four Fw 190 Ds, five Fw 190 Fs, three He 219s, three Bf 109s, two Bücker Bü 181s, one WNF 342 helicopter, two Fl 282 helicopters, one Ju 88 G, one Ju 388, one Bf 108 and a single American P-51.

Numerous other types were transferred individually on other vessels – the Horten 8-229 was loaded onto the SS Richard J Gatling before loading of the Reaper had been completed and was dispatched for the US on July 12.

The DM-1, meanwhile, was not packed into its crate for the journey to the US until November 9, 1945. It finally arrived at Boston on January 19, 1946.

It is interesting to note that for all the fanfare and acknowledgement given to the American effort in capturing German war gear, the British managed to capture more than three times as many machines and ended up giving many of them to the Americans to make up for gaps in the US 'collection' of types.

There was no British 'Watson's Whizzers' yet the British undoubtedly captured more German jets intact and Watson needed machines from America's ally to make up his numbers.

A selection of the British held machines were displayed to the public in Hyde Park from September 16-22, 1945, including a Heinkel He 162 and Messerschmitt Me 163. A larger and longer-lasting exhibition was staged at RAE Farnborough from October 29 to November 9 that same year. In addition to the other jets, this one featured a pair of Arado Ar 234s and a Messerschmitt Me 262.

Also on show were a Ta 152, Dornier Do 335, Fw 190/Ju 88 Mistel, Fi 103 V-1, Fa 330, Horten Ho IV glider and the Fw 190 D-9 of Leutnant Theo Nibel, 'Black 12'. Conventional types abounded too, including a Bü 181, Bf 108, Bf 109 G, Bf 110, Me 410, Do 217, Fi 156, Fw 189, Fw 190 A, Ju 52, Ju 352, Ju 88 G-6, Ju 188, Ju 290 A and Si 204 D. There was even a flying display

The full history of Messerschmitt Me 163 B W.Nr. 191190, later FE-500 and then T-2-500, is unknown but it was most likely given to the Americans by the British.

involving 10 of the captured types on Sunday, November 4.

Advanced technology
Meanwhile, the Allies also sought out technical data and information both on the aircraft they had captured and on design projects still in progress when the war ended. This work began in 1944 under CIOS – the Combined Intelligence Objectives Subcommittee.

Headquartered at the seemingly innocuous London address of 32 Bryanston Square, CIOS teams travelled all over Germany in the wake of the Allied advance during 1945, visiting a series of key 'targets' and 'black list' locations drawn up before the D-Day invasion.

These were primarily sites deemed to be of scientific, technical and engineering importance. High on the list were the offices, design

Lend-lease American-built Royal Navy aircraft carrier HMS Reaper was used to ferry a 'treasure trove' of captured Luftwaffe aircraft to the US two and a half months after the war's end. Some survive, many were scrapped.

studios and factory facilities of Germany's aircraft manufacturers and their vast armies of sub-contractors.

When CIOS personnel arrived at their target sites they sometimes found them untouched with all the most top secret material still where the Germans had left it. On other occasions they found the sites already looted or sabotaged, with many important documents burned or missing. Nevertheless, even in these instances they were usually able to track down the people who worked at these facilities and encourage them to revisit or reconstruct their most recent work.

For example, the investigation of airborne gun sights involved visits to Zeiss in Jena, Leitz in Wetzler, Steinheil in Munich, Görtz in Vienna and the Berlin-based facilities of Siemens, Blaupunkt, Telefunken,

Lorenz and Askania. Key personnel were interviewed, made to write monologues about their work and, if necessary, taken back to Britain for further interrogation.

It is stated time and again that German technology at this time was far in advance of anything the British or Americans were working on but this proved not to be the case in many instances. The report on airborne gun sights concludes: "As regards technical development it appears that the Germans were in general behind us." Though it concedes: "The main projects of interest being the stabilised fighter armament scheme, the automatic triggering project, the television scanning and the work on infrared radiation, all of which seem worth following up."

Much valuable information was also gleaned from sites such as

the Luftfahrtforschungsanstalt Hermann Göring weapons institute at Volkenrode, Brunswick – which worked on stabilisation to aid fighter gun aiming, research on automatic guns, theoretical ballistic work and fire control systems.

Interrogation of Telefunken staff in Hamburg and Berlin gave an insight into work on coaxial ceramic radio valves – the British and Americans used more problematic glass ones.

A visit to the Focke-Wulf structural research facility at Bad Eilsen yielded valuable information about stressed-skin structures for aircraft, methods of bonding metal with wood and the use of high tensile steel.

The list was long and interrogations of hundreds of German engineers, scientists and designers went on throughout the remainder of 1945. Some ended up working for the British, some for the Americans, but in time many – but by no means all – who chose to work for the British ended up in America due to the availability of much larger research budgets.

As thoughts turned towards the development of new technology, particularly the development of rockets and missiles, the captured German aircraft were left to rot and most were scrapped during the two or three years that followed.

In July 1945, CIOS was split up into BIOS, the British Intelligence Objectives Subcommittee, and FIAT, the American Field Information Agency, Technical. BIOS teams usually included personnel from the Ministry of Aircraft Production as well as experts from individual British aircraft manufacturers such as Shorts and de Havilland, and the work continued.

As peace settled across Europe, many German military aviators started new lives as civilians and some, including Johannes Steinhoff, formerly of JV 44,

Typical of the 'Watson's Whizzer' aircraft, this Me 262 A-1a, its only known German marking being the letter 'L', went through a series of paint jobs after being captured. Starting out in its original markings it was then painted up as 'Doris' by the 54th ADS, before being renamed 'Jabo Bait' by Messerschmitt test pilot Karl Baur. In the US, it was repainted again in plain black with its serial, FE-110, more prominently displayed.

The sole Henschel Hs 129 B ground-attack aircraft captured by the Americans and brought back to the USA. It was probably the only Henschel type to be taken intact by the Allies and today none of the 865 built remain.

and Erich Hartmann eventually joined the postwar Luftwaffe in West Germany. Heinz Bär became a test pilot for sports aircraft, Hajo Herrmann became a lawyer, Galland went to Argentina and flew with the Argentine Air Force before returning to Germany to set up an aviation consultancy firm.

Similarly, Allied airmen found themselves beginning new lives beyond those dark days at the beginning of 1945 when it seemed as though the air war in Europe could only end in a welter of death and destruction.

One of the more unusual German aircraft captured by the Allies was the Flettner Fl 282 V23. The Fl 282 Kolibri or 'Hummingbird' was the world's first series production helicopter. After the war, its creator, Anton Flettner, went to work in the US. After his own company failed he then joined Kaman Aircraft as its chief designer.

CAPTURED AIRCRAFT LISTS

Large numbers of German aircraft were either flown or shipped out of Europe by the British and Americans. This index is intended to serve as a guide to what was captured, rather than what ultimately became of these war prizes, since that is documented, where known, elsewhere.

GERMAN AIRCRAFT GIVEN BRITISH AIR MINISTRY NUMBERS:

AM 1 – Junkers Ju 88 G-6 W.Nr. 622983 4R+RB of NJG 2
AM 2 – Junkers Ju 88 G-6 W.Nr. 620560 4R+CB of NJG 2
AM 3 – Junkers Ju 88 G-6 W.Nr. 622838 3C+AN of II./NJG 4
AM 4 – Siebel Si 204 D-1 W.Nr. 322127 BU+PP
AM 5 – Siebel Si 204 D-1 W.Nr. 321523
AM 6 – Junkers Ju 290 A-1 W.Nr. 110186 A3+OB of III./KG 200
AM 7 – Dornier Do 217 M-9 W.Nr. 0040 KF+JN
AM 8 – Junkers Ju 352 A-0 W.Nr. 100010 KT+VJ also VP550
AM 9 – Junkers Ju 88 G-6 W.Nr. 621965 4R+DR of III./NJG 2
AM 10 – Focke-Wulf Fw190 A-6/R6 W.Nr. 550214 PN+LU of III./NJG 11
AM 11 – Focke-Wulf Ta 152 H-1 W.Nr. 150004 6+ of JG 301
Second AM 11 – Focke-Wulf Ta 152 H-1 W.Nr. 150168 9+ of Stab/JG 301
AM 12 – Siebel Si 204 D-3 W.Nr. 351547
AM 13 – Siebel Si 204 D-1 W.Nr. 251922
AM 14 – Junkers Ju 88 G-6 W.Nr. 620788 C9+AA of NJG 5
AM 15 – Messerschmitt Bf 110 G-4/R8 W.Nr. 180560 3C+BA of NJG 4
AM 16 – Junkers Ju 88 G-6 W.Nr. 622311 3C+DA of NJG 4
AM 17 – Arado Ar 232 B-0 W.Nr. 305002 A3+RB of III./KG 200
AM 18 – Junkers Ju 352 A-1 W.Nr. 100015 G6+WX of V./TG 4
AM 19 – Junkers Ju 252 A W.Nr. unknown G6+YX of V./TG 4
AM 20 – Heinkel He 219 A-3 W.Nr. 290126 D5+BL of I./NJG 3
AM 21 – Heinkel He 219 A-2 W.Nr. 310109
AM 22 – Heinkel He 219 A-5/R2 W.Nr. 310108 D5+CL of I./NJG 3
AM 23 – Heinkel He 219 A W.Nr. 310200 D5+DL of I./NJG 3
AM 24 – Arado Ar 234 B-2 W.Nr. 140466 8H+HH of AufklGr.33
AM 25 – Arado Ar 234 B W.Nr. 140608 T9+GL of 3./Versuchsverband.d.OKL – also coded VK880
AM 26 – Arado Ar 234 B-1 W.Nr. 140476 8H+DH of AufklGr.33
AM 27 – Focke-Wulf Fw 189 A-3 W.Nr. 0173 3X+AA

AM 28 – Siebel Si 204 D-1 W.Nr. 221558 BJ+90
AM 29 – Focke-Wulf Fw 190 F-8/U1 W.Nr. 584219 'Black 38'
AM 30 – Messerschmitt Bf 110 G-4/R3 W.Nr. 730037 D5+DK of I./NJG 3
AM 31 – Junkers Ju 88 G-6 W.Nr. 623193 C9+HB of NJG 5
AM 32 – Junkers Ju 88 G-6 W.Nr. 622960 +VH
AM 33 – Junkers Ju 88 G-6 W.Nr. 622186
AM 34 – Messerschmitt Bf 110 G-4/R6 W.Nr. 730301 D5+RL of I./NJG 3
AM 35 – Junkers Ju 188 D-2 W.Nr. 150245 shipped to the US and became FE-1597/T2-1597
AM 36 – Focke-Wulf Fw 190 F-8/U1 W.Nr. 580058 '55'
AM 37 – Focke-Wulf Fw 190 S-1 W.Nr. 582044 '54'
AM 38 – Messerschmitt Bf 110 G-4/R8 W.Nr. 180551 D5+DM of II./NJG 3
AM 39 – Messerschmitt Me 410 A-1/U2 W.Nr. 420439
AM 40 – Focke-Wulf Fw 190 F-8/U1 W.Nr. 580392 '51'
AM 41 – Junkers Ju 88 G-6 W.Nr. 622054 7J+OV of NJG 102
Second AM 41 – Junkers Ju 88 G-6 W.Nr. 622461 7J+CV of NJG 102
AM 42 – Siebel Si 204 D-1 W.Nr. 251147 7J+XL of NJG 102
AM 43 – Heinkel He 219 A-2 W.Nr. unknown
AM 44 – Heinkel He 219 A-2 W.Nr. 310106
AM 45 – Junkers Ju 188 A-2 W.Nr. 180485
AM 46 – Siebel Si 204 D-1 W.Nr. unknown
AM 47 – Junkers Ju 88 G-6 W.Nr. 620968
AM 48 – Junkers Ju 88 G-6 W.Nr. 622811 3C+MN of II./NJG 4
AM 49 – Siebel Si 204 D-1 W.Nr. 251104 D5+OM of II./NJG 3
AM 50 – Messerschmitt Me 262 B-1a/U1 W.Nr. 110305 'Red 8' of IV./NJG 11
AM 51 – Messerschmitt Me 262 A-2a W.Nr. 112372 'Yellow 7' of I./JG 7
AM 52 – Messerschmitt Me 262 A-2a W.Nr. 500210 'Yellow 17' of I./JG 7
AM 53 – Bücker Bü 180 W.Nr. unknown
AM 54 – Arado Ar 234 B W.Nr. 140113 F1+AA of KG 76

AM 55 – Siebel Si 204 D-1 W.Nr. 321288

AM 56 – Siebel Si 204 D W.Nr. 251190

AM 57 – Junkers Ju 290 A-2 W.Nr. 110157 9V+BK of 2./***r.5

AM 58 – Heinkel He 162 A-2 W.Nr. 120221 of JG 1

AM 59 – Heinkel He 162 A-2 W.Nr. 120076 'Yellow 4' of JG 1

AM 60 – Heinkel He 162 A-2 W.Nr. 120074 'White 11' of JG 1

AM 61 – Heinkel He 162 A-2 W.Nr. 120072 of JG 1

AM 62 – Heinkel He 162 A-2 W.Nr. 120086 of JG 1

AM 63 – Heinkel He 162 A-2 W.Nr. 120095 of JG 1

AM 64 – Heinkel He 162 A-2 W.Nr. 120097 of JG 1

AM 65 – Heinkel He 162 A-2 W.Nr. 120227 of JG 1

AM 66 – Heinkel He 162 A-2 W.Nr. 120091 of JG 1

AM 67 – Heinkel He 162 A-2 W.Nr. 120098 of JG 1

AM 68 – Heinkel He 162 A-2 W.Nr. unknown of JG 1

AM 69 – Blohm & Voss Bv 138 W.Nr. unknown

AM 70 – Blohm & Voss Bv 138 C-1 W.Nr. 0310081 of FA 125

AM S-2 – Blohm & Voss Bv 138 B-1 W.Nr. unknown

AM 71 – Blohm & Voss Bv 138 W.Nr. unknown

AM 72 – Messerschmitt Me 410 A-1/U2 W.Nr. 420430

AM 73 – Messerschmitt Me 410 A-1 W.Nr. 130360

AM 74 – Messerschmitt Me 410 B-6 W.Nr. 410208

AM 75 – Junkers Ju 88 H-1 W.Nr. unknown/Focke-Wulf Fw 190 A-8/R6 W.Nr. 733682 Mistel S 3B of IV./KG 200

AM 76 – Junkers Ju 88 H-1/Focke-Wulf Fw 190 A-8 Mistel S 3B of IV./KG 200

AM 77 – Junkers Ju 88 W.Nr. 2492/Focke-Wulf Fw 190 A W.Nr. 733759 Mistel S 3A of IV./KG 200

AM 78 – Unknown

AM 79 – Messerschmitt Me 262 A W.Nr. unknown

AM 80 – Messerschmitt Me 262 A-1 W.Nr. 111690 'White 5' of I./JG 7

AM 81 – Messerschmitt Me 262 A-2a W.Nr. 500200 9K+XK 'Black X' of II./KG 51

AM 82 – Junkers Ju 86 P W.Nr. 5132 T5+PM of Aufkl.Gr.100

AM 83 – Junkers Ju 388 L-1/V6 W.Nr. 500006 PE+IF

AM 84 – Messerschmitt Bf 108 B W.Nr. 1547 GJ+AU

AM 85 – Messerschmitt Bf 110 G-5/R1 W.Nr. 420031

AM 86 – Messerschmitt Bf 110 G W.Nr. unknown

AM 87 – Messerschmitt Bf 108 D-1 W.Nr. 3059 VE+LI

AM 88 – Messerschmitt Bf 110 W.Nr. unknown

AM 89 – Messerschmitt Bf 108 B-1 W.Nr. unknown

AM 90 – Arado Ar 196 A W.Nr. unknown

AM 91 – Arado Ar 196 A-5 W.Nr. 127

AM 92 – Arado Ar 196 A-5 W.Nr. 514

AM 93 – Arado Ar 199 W.Nr. unknown

AM 94 – Focke-Wulf Fw 200 C-4/U1 W.Nr. 176 GC+AE Himmler's personal aircraft

AM 95 – Focke-Wulf Fw 200 C W.Nr. unknown possibly Fw 200 C-4/U1, W.Nr. 0240 TK+CV Hitler's personal aircraft

AM 96 – Focke-Wulf Fw 200 C W.Nr. 0111

AM 97 – Focke-Wulf Fw 200 C W.Nr. 0181 GC+SJ

AM 98 – Unknown

AM 99 – Fieseler Fi 156 C-7 W.Nr. 475099 VD+TD

AM 100 – Fieseler Fi 156 C W.Nr. 2008 CV+KB

AM 101 – Fieseler Fi 156 C-7 W.Nr. 475081 RR+KE

AM 102 – Junkers Ju 52/3m W.Nr. 6840

AM 103 – Junkers Ju 52/3m W.Nr. 6567

AM 104 – Junkers Ju 52/3m W.Nr. 641038

AM 105 – Dornier Do 217 M W.Nr. unknown

AM 106 – Dornier Do 217 M-1 W.Nr. 56527 U5+HK of I./KG 2

AM 107 – Dornier Do 217 M-1 W.Nr. 56158 U5+?? of KG 2

AM 108 – Junkers Ju 188 A-1 W.Nr. 230776

AM 109 – Junkers Ju 352 A W.Nr. unknown G6+RX of V./TG4

AM 110 – Junkers Ju 352 A W.Nr. unknown G6+SX of V./TG4

AM 111 – Focke-Wulf Fw 190 F-8/R15 W.Nr. unknown

AM 112 – Junkers Ju 88 A-6/U W.Nr. 0660 1H+MN of II./KG 26

AM 113 – Junkers Ju 188 A-2 W.Nr. 190327 1H+GT of III./KG 26

AM 114 – Dornier Do 24 T W.Nr. 1135 of SNG 81

AM 115 – Dornier Do 24 T-3 W.Nr. unknown of KG 200

AM 116 – Dornier Do 24 T W.Nr. 3435 VH+JM of SNG 81

AM 117 – Focke-Wulf Fw 58 C-2/U6 W.Nr. 2093 TE+BK of Ekdo.40

AM 118 – Unknown

AM 119 – Siebel Si 104 A W.Nr. unknown

AM 120 – Arado Ar 96 B W.Nr. unknown

AM 121 – Bücker Bü 181 W.Nr. unknown

AM 122 – Bücker Bü 181 C-3 W.Nr. 120417

AM 123 – Arado Ar 96 B W.Nr. unknown

AM 124 – Messerschmitt Bf 108 W.Nr. unknown

AM GD1 – Junkers Ju 52/3m W.Nr. 5375

AM GD – Siebel Si 204 D W.Nr. unknown

AM 200 – Messerschmitt Me 163 B W.Nr. 191329of JG 400

AM 201 – Messerschmitt Me 163 B W.Nr. 191330 of JG 400

AM 202 – Messerschmitt Me 163 B W.Nr. 191915 of JG 400

AM 203 – Messerschmitt Me 163 B W.Nr. 310061 'Yellow 13' of JG 400

AM 204 – Messerschmitt Me 163 B W.Nr. 191454 'Yellow 11' of JG 400

AM 205 – Messerschmitt Me 163 B W.Nr. 191905 of JG 400

AM 206 – Messerschmitt Me 163 B W.Nr. 191902 of JG 400

AM 207 – Messerschmitt Me 163 B W.Nr. 191461 of JG 400

AM 208 – Messerschmitt Me 163 B W.Nr. 191912 of JG 400

AM 209 – Messerschmitt Me 163 B W.Nr. 191315 of JG 400

AM 210 – Messerschmitt Me 163 B W.Nr. 191316 'Yellow 6' of JG 400

AM 211 – Messerschmitt Me 163 B W.Nr. 191095 of JG 400

AM 212 – Messerschmitt Me 163 B W.Nr. 191965 of JG 400

AM 213 – Messerschmitt Me 163 B W.Nr. 191954 of JG 400

AM 214 – Messerschmitt Me 163 B W.Nr. 191660 of JG 400

AM 215 – Messerschmitt Me 163 B W.Nr. 191659 'Yellow 15' of JG 400

AM 216 – Messerschmitt Me 163 B W.Nr. 191309 of JG400

AM 217 – Messerschmitt Me 163 B W.Nr. 191917 of JG400

AM 218 – Messerschmitt Me 163 B W.Nr. 191654

AM 219 – Messerschmitt Me 163 B W.Nr. 191904 '25' of JG 400

AM 220 – Messerschmitt Me 163 B W.Nr. 191914? of JG 400

AM 221 – Messerschmitt Me 163 B W.Nr. 191961 of JG 400

AM 222 – Messerschmitt Me 163 B W.Nr. 191907 of JG 400

AM 223 – Dornier Do 335 A-12 W.Nr. 240112

AM 225 – Dornier Do 335 A-1 W.Nr. unknown

AM 226 – Arado Ar 234 B W.Nr. 140336 of II./KG 76

AM 227 to AM 229 – Arado Ar 234s but AM numbers to W.Nr. unknown

AM ??? – Arado Ar 234 B W.Nr. 140141 of 1(F)/Aufkl.Gr.123
AM ??? – Arado Ar 234 B W.Nr. 140493
AM ??? – Arado Ar 234 B W.Nr. 140581 of 1(F)/Aufkl.Gr.123
AM 229 – Messerschmitt Bf 109 G-14 W.Nr. 413601 'Black 7'
AM 230 – Focke-Wulf Fw 190 A-8 W.Nr. 171747 '13'
AM 231 – Junkers Ju 88 G-1 W.Nr. 712273 4R+UR of III./NJG 2
AM 232 – Unknown
AM 233 – Focke-Achgelis Fa 223 E W.Nr. V14 DM+SR

GERMAN AIRCRAFT CAPTURED BY THE BRITISH BUT SET ASIDE FOR THE AMERICANS

USA 1 – Messerschmitt Me 262 A W.Nr. 500443 'Yellow 5'
USA 2 – Messerschmitt Me 262 B-1a/U1 W.Nr. 110306 'Red 6' of IV./NJG 11 allocated FE-610
USA 3 – Messerschmitt Me 262 B-1b W.Nr. 110165 allocated BuNo. 121441
USA 4 – Messerschmitt Me 262 B-1/U1 W.Nr. 110635 'Red 10' of IV./NJG 11
USA 5 – Arado Ar 234 B W.Nr. 140489 allocated either FE-202 or FE-303
USA 6 – Arado Ar 234 B W.Nr. unknown
USA 7 – Arado Ar 234 B W.Nr. unknown
USA 8 – Heinkel He 219 A-0 W.Nr. 210903 SP+CR allocated FE-612
USA 9 – Heinkel He 219 A-2 W.Nr. 290060 CS+QG allocated FE-613
USA 10 – Heinkel He 219 A W.Nr. 290202 allocated FE-614
USA 11 – Focke-Wulf Ta 152 H-0 W.Nr. 150003 allocated FE-112
USA 12 – Focke-Wulf Fw 190 D-9 W.Nr. unknown allocated either FE-119 or FE-120
USA 13 – Focke-Wulf Fw 190 D-9 W.Nr. 401392 'Black 5' of JG 26 allocated FE-121
USA 14 – Focke-Wulf Fw 190 D-13 W.Nr. 836017 'Yellow 10' of JG 26 allocated FE-118
USA 15 – Focke-Wulf Fw 190 D-9 W.Nr. 500618 allocated either FE-119 or FE-120
USA 16, USA 17, USA 18, USA 19 – possibly allocated to Me 410s
USA 20 – Unknown
USA 21 – Junkers Ju 88 G-6 W.Nr. unknown allocated FE-611
USA 022 – Junkers Ju 290 A-4 W.Nr. 110196 PI+PS allocated FE-3400
USA 23 to USA 39 – untraced
USA 40 – Arado Ar 234 B-2 W.Nr. 140311 of II./KG 76 allocated FE-1011
USA 41 to USA 49 – Unknown
USA 50 – Arado Ar 234 B-2 W.Nr. 140312 of II./KG 76 allocated FE-1010

AIRCRAFT GIVEN FOREIGN EQUIPMENT NUMBERS BY THE AMERICANS

FE-107 – see FE 711
FE-110 – Messerschmitt Me 262 A-1a 'L' W.Nr. unknown
FE-111 – Messerschmitt Me 262 A-1a W.Nr. 500491 'Yellow 7' of 11./JG 7
FE-112 – Focke-Wulf Ta 152 H W.Nr. 110003 of JG 301
FE-113, FE-114, FE-115 – All apparently Fw 190 As
FE-116 – Focke-Wulf Fw 190 F-8 W.Nr. unknown
FE-117 – Focke-Wulf Fw 190 F-8/R1 W.Nr. 931884 'Yellow 10'
FE-118 – Focke-Wulf Fw 190 D-13 W.Nr. 836017 'Yellow 10' of 3./JG 26
FE-119 – Focke-Wulf Fw 190 D-9 W.Nr. 210010 'White 14' 5./JG 26

FE-120 – Focke-Wulf Fw 190 D-9 W.Nr. 601088 of IV./JG 3
FE-121 – Focke-Wulf Fw 190 D-9 W.Nr. 401392 'White 5+-' of JG 26
FE-122 – Messerschmitt Me 109 G-10/U4 W.Nr. 611943 'Yellow 13'
FE-123 – Messerschmitt Me 109 G-10 '7' W.Nr. unknown
FE-124 – Messerschmitt Me 109 G-10/U4 W.Nr. unknown
FE-489 – Heinkel He 162 A W.Nr. 120077, 'Red 1' of 2./JG 1
FE-490 – Horten Ho 229 V3 W.Nr. unknown
FE-494 – Heinkel He 162 A W.Nr. 120017, 'Yellow 6' of 3./JG 1
FE-495 – Messerschmitt Me 163 B W.Nr. unknown
FE-496 – Messerschmitt Me 109 G-6 W.Nr. unknown
FE-499 – Messerschmitt Me 410 A-3 W.Nr. 018 F6+WK of 2.(F)/FAG 122
FE-500 – Messerschmitt Me 163 B W.Nr. 191190
FE-501, -502, -503 – Messerschmitt Me 163 Bs
FE-504 Heinkel He 162 A W.Nr. 120230 'White 23' of 1./JG 1
FE-505 Blohm & Voss BV 155 B V2 W.Nr. unknown
FE-610 Messerschmitt Me 262 B-1a/U1 W.Nr. 110306 'Red 6' of 10./NJG 11
FE-611 Junkers Ju 88 G possibly W7+IH of 1./NJG 100
FE-612 Heinkel He 219 A-2 W.Nr. unknown
FE-613 Heinkel He 219 A-7 W.Nr. 290060
FE-614 Heinkel He 219 A W.Nr. unknown
FE-711 Messerschmitt Me 262 A W.Nr. 111711
FE-1010 Arado Ar 234 B W.Nr. 140312 of KG 76
FE-1011 Bachem Ba 349 B-1 W.Nr. unknown
FE-1012 Dornier Do 335 W.Nr. unknown
FE-1597 Junkers Ju 188 possibly W.Nr. 150245, British serial AM 35
FE-1598 Junkers Ju 88 D-1/Trop W.Nr. 430650 British serial HK959
FE-1599 Junkers Ju 88 A W.Nr. unknown
FE-1600 Heinkel He 111 H-16 W.Nr. 8433 +DC
FE-2000 Dornier Do 217 W.Nr. unknown
FE-2100 Heinkel He 177 A-7 W.Nr. unknown of KG 40
FE-2600 Schneider Grunau Baby LZNC
FE-2700 Gotha Go 242 B-1 W.Nr. unknown
FE-3400 Junkers Ju 290 A-7 W.Nr. 196, PJ+PS
FE-4010 Junkers Ju 388 L-1 W.Nr. 560049
FE-4012 Messerschmitt Me 262 A-1a/U3 'White 25' W.Nr. unknown
FE-4600 Henschel Hs 129 B W.Nr. unknown
FE-4610 Messerschmitt Me 108 B W.Nr. 8378
FE-4611 Bücker Bü 181 W.Nr. unknown
FE-4612 Bücker Bü 131 W.Nr. unknown
FE-4613 Flettner Fl 282 V23 Possibly CI+TW W.Nr. unknown
FE-4614 Flettner Fl 282 W.Nr. 28368
FE-4615 Doblhoff/WNF 342 V4 W.Nr. unknown
FE-4617 Focke-Achgelis Fa 330 W.Nr. unknown
FE-4618 Focke-Achgelis Fa 330 W.Nr. unknown
FE-? He 162 A W.Nr. 120067 'White 7' 1./JG 1
FE-? Me 163 B W.Nr. 191301
FE-? Messerschmitt P 1101 V1 W.Nr. unknown
FE-? Lippisch DM-1 W.Nr. unknown

Index

Bibliography

Battle of the Airfields – Operation Bodenplatte 1 January 1945 by Norman Franks, Grub Street 1995
Bodenplatte: The Luftwaffe's Last Hope by John Manrho and Ron Putz, Hikoki 2004
Design for Flight – The Kurt Tank Story by Heinz Conradis, MacDonald 1960
Eagle's Wings by Hajo Herrmann, Guild 1991
Focke-Wulf Fw 190 Vol. 1, 2 and 3 by J Richard Smith and Eddie J Creek, Classic 2014
French Eagles Soviet Heroes by John D Clark, Sutton 2005
Heinkel He 162 Spatz by Robert Forsyth and Eddie J Creek, Classic 2008
Jagdgeschwader 301/302 "Wilde Sau" by Willi Reschke, Schiffer 2012
JV 44: The Galland Circus by Robert Forsyth, Classic 1996
Me 163 Vol. 1 and 2 by Stephen Ransom and Hans-Hermann Cammann, Midland 2006
Mistel – German Composite Aircraft and Operations 1942-1945 by Robert Forsyth, Midland 2001
Mistel – The Piggy-Back Aircraft of the Luftwaffe by Hans-Peter Dabrowski, Schiffer 2004
Projekt Natter – Last of the Wonder Weapons by Brett Gooden, Midland 2005
The First and The Last by Adolf Galland, Meuthen 1955
The Last Days of the Luftwaffe by Manfred Griehl, Frontline 2009
The Last Flight of the Luftwaffe by Adrian Weir, Cassell 2000
War Prizes by Phil Butler, Midland 1994

Websites

At the time of writing there were several websites offering scans of primary source material and databases which were invaluable in researching and writing the stories presented in this volume.

8th Air Force Historical Society – includes a detailed database of groups, targets and missions
https://www.8thafhs.org/

Fold3 – featuring scans of thousands of historical documents including Missing Air Crew Reports
https://www.fold3.com/

American Air Museum in Britain – excellent source of information about individual airmen and units
http://www.americanairmuseum.com/

WW2 Aircraft Performance – scans of wartime documents giving performance stats for fighters
http://www.wwiiaircraftperformance.org/